WILLEM ZEYLMANS VAN EMMICHOVEN

Willem Zeylmans van Emmichoven, 1955

WILLEM ZEYLMANS VAN EMMICHOVEN

An Inspiration for Anthroposophy

A Biography by Emanuel Zeylmans

TEMPLE LODGE

Translated from German by Matthew Barton

Temple Lodge Publishing
Hillside House, The Square
Forest Row, East Sussex
RH18 5ES

www.templelodge.com

Published by Temple Lodge 2002

Originally published in German under the title *Willem Zeylmans van Emmichoven, Ein Pionier der Anthroposophie, Sein Leben erzählt von Emanuel Zeylmans* by Natura Verlag, Arlesheim, 1979

The Publishers would like to thank Josiana Arippol for her active support of this volume

A catalogue record for this book is available from the British Library

ISBN 1 902636 35 X

Cover by Andrew Morgan
Typeset by DP Photosetting, Aylesbury, Bucks.
Printed and bound by Cromwell Press Limited, Trowbridge, Wilts.

CONTENTS

Introduction

This book tells of someone who intended to write his own life-story. We can be sorry he did not do so, for he was very good at telling stories, and his life was full and eventful. He undertook great journeys and met many different people. He had profound, far-reaching ideas which he shared, the whole world over, in numerous lectures. His books are treasure-troves which people read gladly. He had high ideals that were important for the world, only a few of which he was able to realize; and he helped many people with his advice.

He did however tell of his own childhood and youth, and the present biography begins with excerpts entitled 'From Bender Bole's Life Story', which document the early path of an individual human soul.

When he was young he wanted to become a writer and travel the world; and since he knew the meaning of poverty he sought a profession that would keep the wolf from the door—and chose to study medicine. 'I'll become a ship's doctor,' he thought, 'and then I'll always have plenty of time for writing.' At the time he was able to pay for his studies by signing up for medical service in the Tropics. But on his life's path he soon met people who saw what was needed better than he, and who intervened in his life, giving him great gifts. Thus his plans changed, he developed real love for his doctor's profession and specialized in psychiatry, researching the effects of colours on human feelings. His first book tells how he applied this in his clinic.

As a child he already had a rich inner life, full of dreams and ideals, and a great longing. He knew that his life on earth would not be complete without the woman of his dreams—he waited and sought patiently, and did indeed find the ideal that lived in him. He himself described how he met the woman who was later to be his wife, and it sounds like a fairy tale. There was much in his soul, however, of which he never or hardly ever spoke—trials he had to endure in his youth, about which he remained silent. As a student he had to fight real inner battles. And he underwent more pain and suffering than one could have suspected—privations of the soul, years of burning pain, temptations that matured him and made him wiser. One could sense that this was someone who knew from experience what he was talking about.

He first met his great teacher before his inmost being had awoken. He was twenty-seven years old, and later gave a striking account of the nature of this meeting—which set the course of the rest of his life, up to his death, although he was unaware of it at the time. But his teacher knew it, and guided him in the right direction. In this way Willem Zeylmans was able to find and realize the goal of his life on earth.

Then there were new trials to survive—of the kind faced by anyone who has decided to serve what is true and good in the world rather than himself, for that is where the real life-and-death battle is waged. He endured the crises which his life confronted him with, and 'died' inwardly to overcome them and be transformed. This perhaps was why he exerted such healing force.

He knew that a secret is bound up with the human soul, one that each person bears within him, and of which only few are aware. The whole world, with all that manifests in it, with all its wisdom, lives in each person. The world itself has a soul, and the highest attainment of the human soul is to marry itself with this world-soul. Willem Zeylmans spoke of this on hundreds of occasions, and the book which was most important to him dwells on this soul riddle.

Later he researched and studied the folk-souls of nations and peoples, and tried to portray them to others in comprehensible terms, so as to evoke insight and understanding between nations instead of antipathy and war. In the same way that he understood foreign cultures and people of the most diverse race, he also nurtured contact with the most wonderful, colourful characters. It was astonishing what unusual people there were among his regular visitors—he could converse for hours on end in the liveliest fashion with drunkards, burglars and beggars. And on his travels he made the most varied acquaintances. His biography could have been called a 'book of encounters'.

Together with others he wanted to write a book for people born at the end of the twentieth century, about the heavenly hierarchies—a 'welcome and way-marker' to show how the heavenly hierarchies are at work in all areas of life—so that a future generation would be able to find comfort and certainty that man has not been forgotten and left to fend for himself in the cosmos, but is guided, helped and loved by high, divine powers, even if he does not know it!

Willem Zeylmans' life was rich; and already as a child he brought great riches with him, though outwardly he chose poverty. Although he was a highly respected doctor and researcher, lecturer and traveller, at his death he left little more than a student might own. He rarely spoke of all he perceived in supersensible realms—usually only in cheerful, joyful moments, to avoid a sense of earnest, self-concerned mysticism. It was often only later that one realized what he had really been talking about.

The very finest thing of all was his humanity among other human beings—he was a true contemporary! There is much material available about his life, and one can fill in the details of his biography with hardly a gap . . . So now, eighteen years after his death, how does his true being unfold from this fullness?*

Novalis said: 'The life of a truly exemplary person must be symbolic through and through.' In saying this he grasped the significance of a human biography, and at the same time highlighted biographical method. A person is truly exemplary who lives according to the laws of his destiny and so realizes the deeper intentions of his life. 'Symbol' means that idea and reality merge in one and become visible. A life that is symbolic 'through and through' is at the same time one that becomes the visible expression of the idea underlying it—that is, of the individuality concerned. In other words, if the idea becomes deed one must be able to perceive it. This is what I will now try to show in the life of Willem Zeylmans van Emmichoven.

* The German edition of this book was first published in 1979.

I. CHILDHOOD

Willem Zeylmans was born in a place called Helmond: a small town in southern Holland in the Noord-Brabant region, lying on an old bed of the river Meuse in flat, peat moorland. The name Helmond is said to come from 'hell-mouth', because the Teutons had a burial site here; and Hel, the goddess of cloud-land (the same figure as Mother Holle), guarded the souls of the dead.

Around 1879 Helmond was a factory town. Several dynamic business men had moved to Helmond from the Protestant West, such as Piet Fentener van Vlissingen from Amsterdam, along with one of the largest cotton printing enterprises in the country. The proletariat was still very poor—people dwelt in bothies on the moor, and many factory workers lived in misery and degradation. At the same time, in contrast, the first wealthy business families were appearing.

It was at this time that the 'red-dyer' Friedrich Wilhelm Malsch, Willem Zeylmans' grandfather, moved here from nearby Barmen in the Ruhr region with his seven children, and began work as a chemist in a well-known cotton-dying works. In a red-dying works such as this, thread, yarn and also material were dyed in Turkey or Adrianople red, a colour which in those days was easy to sell in the Far East. His wife related that he sometimes woke up suddenly in the night. As the factory's technical director he lived on site and could therefore easily go into the laboratory and do colour experiments in the middle of the night, to improve on 'the colour, which did not please him'.

His imposing figure, with long white beard, made a deep impression on his grandchildren. When he sat with his family at the end of the day, a factory boy was sometimes sent to ask him whether the cotton, which was spread out to dry on long racks in the factory grounds, should be left out overnight or brought inside. Old grandfather Malsch would stand up, look the sky all over and consider whether it was going to rain in the night or not. He was able to forecast the weather for the coming night.

Willem's father, Pieter Cornelis Zeylmans van Emmichoven, was born in 1861. He had to stand on his own feet from an early age because of the death of his own father (who as a civil servant had been transferred to Helmond in 1857). In 1889 he married Emma Malsch. The first child, Peter, was born in 1890; and on 23 November 1893 Frederik Willem was born, the second and last child of the family. He was born on a Thursday, at two in the morning.

Willem's mother was a beautiful woman. He described her as having a figure like the Venus de Milo. In old photographs she sometimes looks a little severe or perhaps unhappy. The Malsch family introduced the

At the seaside, aged 7

Zeylmans family to elements of Central European culture. In his childhood Willem often heard German folk songs being sung; and Christmas was celebrated in the German manner, with a tree and a crib.

At the time of Willem's birth, his young father was working as bookkeeper in one of the businesses, and also running an insurance agency. To begin with the family lived in very modest circumstances. In 1895 his father-in-law Hugo Malsch formed the idea of starting a cocoa and confectionery factory. Pieter Zeylmans became the sub-director. By the turn of the century this business had achieved financial success, and later, when it came to supply the Dutch royal family, was allowed to call itself the Koninklijke Helm-Cacao Fabriek or Royal Crest Cocoa Factory, and have a grand knight's helmet as its insignia. In 1895 the family moved to a larger house with a small garden, where the two boys spent most of their childhood.

In his younger years, Zeylmans' father is described to us as a fiery idealist, interested in social and political issues. The cocoa factory was at that time one of the first businesses to introduce social security for its workers.

The fine-sounding, double-barrelled name had arisen in 1790 when a certain Petrus Zeylmans married a Sophia van Emmichoven. 'Emmichoven' was a small family estate near Almkerk, between the two great rivers of Meuse and Waal, south of Gorcum. Its coat of arms contained two silver fishes, as one can still see today on the gable of the local public house. The word 'Zeylmans' sounds to Dutch ears like 'zeil' or 'sail', which would suggest a 'sailor'. In fact it probably derives from 'zijl', a sort of sluice-gate.

In later years Willem Zeylmans looked back on the intimate experiences of his young soul and noted them down in poetic, romantic form. By doing so he came to an objective view of his younger self, which led him to choose the title 'From Bender Bole's Life Story'. All three chapters of this 'Life Story' have survived intact, and it represents the point of departure upon which Dr Zeylmans founded his whole life's work as a psychiatrist. Again and again we see how all his activity was based on a deepened and subtle portrayal of the human soul as an autonomous entity mediating in us between spirit and nature. The fine, discreet way in which he sensed and described the soul of the child and youth bears witness to the profundity of Zeylmans as doctor and psychiatrist, and to his power of spiritual perception and understanding.

From Bender Bole's Life Story
*1. Paradise Lost**

Bender's first clear memory leads him back to his second year of life. It is the summer of 1895. He sits on a stool beneath the kitchen table and looks out through the open door to the sun-flooded garden. A broad strip of sunlight falls upon the red floor-tiles beside him. Blossoming bean-flowers on their poles stand out against the blue sky like white butterflies between the spiralling green leaves. Then comes a dark figure between him and the light—the neighbour's small girl: she appears like a giant to him.

His earliest memory is of flooding light, into which his smarting eyes stare unceasingly. The first years of his childhood are full of such pictures. Radiant or shimmering light falling upon everything, in which the most beautiful colours appear; then again, trembling, quivering light, so powerful that all colours pale. There are dark objects and figures within this light: a pile of black earth, then a large bird against the bright blue sky; a horse on the sunny street, someone at a window.

He always has the feeling—or did it only seem so to him later?—that the dark gives him a sense of pain, or frightens him, but that the light fills him with quiet joy, or with almost alarming rapture. He has countless memories of giving himself up entirely to the light. Lying on the grass in full sunshine, he looks up to the sky's radiant blue, and sees a cloud as mighty as a mountain, shining white, but some parts of it even whiter than the rest. It seems to him as though he were running around in this cloud. The cloud is soft, even softer than cotton wool, and all around him everything is blindingly white, like glittering snow. He stretches his arms and reaches out on all sides, then overcome by happiness and light he closes his eyes.

Returning to earth everything seems to him blacker than before: the garden fence painted with brown tar, the swing's tall poles, the small shed—all has become dark and even threatening.

Although it was not very large, the garden of his childhood became the whole world for him. Down at the bottom grew five mighty poplars, mysterious beings for the boy, for he believed that their swaying created the wind. If they swayed gently, the wind was soft; if they swung back and forth a strong wind blew.

Along the fence were flowerbeds. Spring brought crocuses, tulips and hyacinths; then the yellow and red primroses appeared, later golden wallflowers, stock and heliotrope. There were also many pansies, large violet ones, yellow, and dappled ones. Above all he loved the many varieties of roses, their different colours, on high thin stems or on small, low bushes. In summer butterflies fluttered about the colourful flowers, birds sang and the sun shone upon everything, the roses' perfume

---

* Original texts by Willem Zeylmans are distinguished in this volume by italic script.

filled the air and all was bathed in golden light. Then the world appeared to the boy to be as it ought. He tried to look at, smell, and touch the flowers all at the same time. The best way of doing this was by creeping inside them. It was easy to sit inside a tulip by making yourself very small, though you had to do it very carefully so as not to touch the filaments—otherwise the black pollen would cover you. He most liked creeping into one of the red tulips, whose petals flamed yellow lower down. Their perfume was not as good as that of the roses or heliotropes, but almost more mysterious: a perfume that belonged to the juicy green of their long, pointed leaves, indeed to the green of all plants.

The house in which Bender grew up bordered on a lane where three low workers' dwellings stood. He sometimes spoke through the open window overlooking the lane with the children who lived there. He was embarrassed to see how poor they were, and now and again gave them some of his toys. He was a little appalled to see how dirty they were, with black hands and naked feet, as they ran in summer through the muck. And why were people so ugly? When the workers returned home from near-by factories at the end of the day, passing his house in long files, he saw their pale, dirty, unkempt figures—women and children too. He saw that their hands and arms bore the signs of hard toil: thin, bowed figures with hollow cheeks and deep-set eyes. A seemingly endless train of exhausted, care-worn people, who evoked in him an uncertain feeling of sympathy mixed with aversion.

Why were people so ugly? In the garden everything was beautiful: the grass, the flowers, butterflies, birds. But people were ugly: their clothes, faces and limbs. They mostly belonged to the dark things, to the dark places that stole the light. Not always though. The eyes of his mother were beautiful, especially when she smiled at him. And there were other things like that—but in general what he perceived of people was their ugliness.

It was a world that was foreign to him, which he could not inwardly accept, and which, in order to live, he must turn away from. He defended himself against it by imagining a world in which lived lovely young people with shining eyes, curly hair, fine limbs, lightly clothed in bright, colourful clothes. The models for his fantasy were people in his neighbourhood whom he liked—above all children and people who were young and beautiful. This was a world in which the sun always shone, the flowers always blossomed, the birds sang, in which there stood splendid palaces of white marble where only young, lovely, radiant people lived. He was the king of this world and rode around on a white horse in a magnificent golden robe, a silver helmet on his head with a feather crest. Everything there was perfect, except that he did not yet have a queen. He would set about finding her directly.

When he was five he played one afternoon with a little girl whom he had only known a short while. Suddenly, as he stood before her, he saw her grey-blue eyes that were larger than those of other children, and her thick blond hair falling in two bunches either side of her face. He immediately felt the same as before, when dizzy from looking at the light-flooded summer sky. He took her by the hand: 'Come,' he said quickly, 'you will be my wife.' She agreed immediately, and hand in hand they went into his garden, where he showed her all his treasures, the sword he had made himself and his soldiers' caps. All the secret places, too, and the hut in the bushes beneath the poplars.

From that moment on there was a queen in his fantasy world. What joy now to return home from a great war! Thousands of enemies had fled before his small, brave army, and now he came home. People lined the streets everywhere and shouted: 'Hurray, long live our king!' But the king hardly has eyes for them, for his gaze is turned only on the great white palace at the far end of the square. High doors lead on to a balcony—they open . . . she appears. Her clothes shine like her golden hair. She wears golden sandals on her feet, a belt adorned with precious stones around her waist. He hurries up the stairway and calls out: 'For you, it was all for you!'

The child, in his earliest memories, takes refuge from the painful contrast of light and dark, and later from the oppressive question of the ugliness of his fellow human beings, by creating an imaginary world of pure beauty. As he grows older, his youth too is filled with more such contrasts.

From roughly the same time, when he was about six, he remembers lying on a thick carpet on the floor of the living room on a winter evening, looking at an old book with pictures. He has only just learned to decipher the letters, and reads the title: *Faust*; then asks his father, who has just entered the room, what that means. His father replies with a special tone of voice (his 'Sunday voice', which he also used for reading fairy tales): 'That is about the tragedy of human beings!' The child is fully satisfied with this answer. As small as he is, he knows there is such a thing.

It must have been about his fifth year that the first demons appeared. They waited until it was evening and the boy lay alone in his little room. It was twilight and a yellow oil-lamp shone on top of the cupboard, casting dark places and shadows everywhere. The moment everything was quiet they emerged from these shadows. They appeared from all the dark places, from under the cupboard, under the bed. It was no use shutting his eyes—they still came. There were tiny ones, that looked like animals but were not: rats on two legs with bird-heads, and flat, broad beaks, birds with frightful human faces, dogs with their heads on their backsides, their snouts turned upwards, gaudy-coloured beasts of prey, with wide-open mouths and rows of sharp, pointed teeth, great beasts with four eyes, four nostrils and forked tongues. He lay there without moving. They were all as frightful as each other, and he could feel himself going rigid with fear. He could only wait for it all to end. Later other figures appeared too, like the small, fat ugly man with the boar's head and two long tusks. He wore a red cap with ribbons, from which two long, pointy, hairy ears stuck out.

There was also a threatening being that stayed motionless a long time. It wore a white coat and a head-scarf around its sun-burned face. Its eyes were like green rays, strange and evil. Unnoticeably it stepped nearer, its eyes became large as green-glowing spheres, and larger still. When that happened the boy felt he must cry out in fear, but he did not cry because his voice failed him.

Worst of all was the black man with the covered face. He looked like a knight in black armour, with closed visor. One day the visor would open and the boy would see a face so appalling that no one could bear the sight. He lay there in deathly fear and waited.

Many years later, on an evening when all this was happening as bad as ever, an inner voice told him: 'Look them in the eye and they will vanish.' He did this. Then it seemed that the demons gathered all their forces together for a single onslaught. The whole room was full of them, led by the man with the scarf around his head. His eyes glittered, more evil than ever, and came towards him like green-glowing spheres. The boy went cold as ice, but he stood his ground. His breath stopped, his heart was in his mouth, but he did not turn away his gaze, and gradually the whole army of them faded, the figures dissolved.

From that moment onwards he knew what to do. The demons still came, for years after, especially if he was tired or inwardly ill at ease, as often happened later. But from then on he could conquer the whole lot of them when he wanted, and this knowledge calmed his fears.

These experiences resurfaced later on in his life, when he recorded them in tales he wrote as a student at the age of 23. It is as if, in the summer of 1916, he once more gets to grip with this theme. In later years he suggested that candles set up at vigils for the dead should not be allowed to cast shadows on a dead person's face and body. 'The shadow realm,' he said, 'has a great power of attraction for certain demons.'

When Bender first went to school he was not quite six. The school building was friendly and sunny, and classroom windows were decorated with vases of flowers. But for the boy it was a prison.

It is true that he could still see the sky and white clouds through the large windows. Birds flew by and the clouds kept changing shape. A bee buzzed about the flowers, or a caterpillar had lost its way and climbed a twig outside the window. But he was not really meant to see all this. He was meant to look at the board or at his book, or listen to the teacher who stood at the front of the class and explained everything: letters, words, numbers and so forth. The teacher was tall and gaunt. She had reddish hair and usually wore a green blouse with a high white collar. Her hair was beautiful, it is true, especially when the sun shone on it, but the boy detested the sight of her pale skin covered in small freckles.

In his recollections he cannot find enough words to describe his revulsion, hatred, anger and the years of boredom he had to endure. He took refuge in a 'fantasy world' the teacher neither knew nor was able to know anything about, 'for a tall, gaunt teacher with freckles had no way of entering such a world'.

His inner kingdom was a refuge from the poisoning influence of an intellectualism which penetrated the whole school curriculum. His resistance was probably what enabled him to escape the completely rigid mentality of an education system that, at the end of the nineteenth century, had fallen prey to the power of materialism.

But he could not talk about it with anyone. Nor did his parents understand. They were both serious, caring people, but now and again they made it clear that they did not think much of his dreaminess. His father often said that it was high time he became a 'hard-working' boy and applied himself to learning. But he himself could not imagine that there was anything more important than a king on a white horse with a plume in his helmet. So he kept quiet, secretly thinking to himself that everything would sort itself out in time.

Sometimes he felt the need to test how far a king's power might extend. For instance, when it started to rain one fine summer's day, and would not stop, the boy, alone in his room, went to the window. He stretched his arm out and commanded: 'Rain, stop falling!' He repeated this order three times, but it kept raining. So that was no good.

It went better at school. If the teacher forbade them to do something, he told the other children they could go right ahead and do it. Some of them looked at him doubtfully, but were reassured when he repeated it. Naturally this led to much unpleasantness and punishments, but once this was past he felt deeply satisfied.

He could make his dreams reality in his games. As a knight he roamed through the garden. For days he had been working at making a great sword with a cross-handle. It was hard to make a helmet, but a triangular paper hat with ribbons did the job. Unfortunately his mother insisted on him wearing a cotton apron with sleeves that was done up at the back. But if one put it on back to front it was like a coat. A belt around his middle completed his outfit.

This knight had great adventures. There were dragons to slay and virgins to rescue from the hands of frightful robbers. Fortunately things always ended well, even if the knight first had to languish in a dungeon for years on end. Through cunning he managed to make his escape, and the highest rewards awaited him on his return to his castle, where his loved one watched and waited for him.

On another occasion he was a hunter, hunting lions, tigers, deer and wild boar with bow and arrows. One day the hunter was passing so silently through the bushes that he came face to face with a great fat crow. He was afraid for he had never before seen a bird from so close at hand. The crow appeared much larger but also very different from what he had imagined. This encounter was of great significance for him. From then on he observed all animals with the greatest interest. He began to see what they were really like. Every animal had something mysterious about it. You couldn't quite say what it was, but once you had seen it, you never forgot it again. And it was really only then that you knew what kind of animal it was. You could tell this from its head, or whole shape, or the way it looked. The sparrow had this 'something', so did the dove and the crow; and the robin redbreast had it particularly.

This 'something' could be friendly, gentle, delicate—but also eerie and frightening. A mouse, a squirrel, a foal in the meadow or a large horse—all of them occupied his attention equally strongly.

He was actually always a little afraid of this: it was as if one suddenly saw the animal for the first time. A being observed you, wanted to tell you something, and you couldn't understand it. It was touching, and funny, but above all mysterious.

As he grew older, his life brought other experiences too, which sometimes occupied him deeply. Near the house where he lived, was the Zuid-Willemsvaart, a canal for freight-transport, which gave Helmond an important link with other industrial towns. In winter one could skate on it, and in summer sometimes swim there (although the local policeman was always on the look-out to prevent this). Now and then someone would fall in and drown. Once a farm-girl fell in and was only just pulled to the bank in time by people who lived near-by. Everyone stood around her unconscious figure, and the boy, small as he was, pushed his way through between people's legs and saw the woman just as she regained consciousness. The first words she uttered, and which he heard, were: 'I saw my whole life before me!' And so the lad learned at first hand of a fact that has only gradually become known to modern science: that people close to death see the whole panorama of their life unfurl before them.

Drunkards were a familiar site in Helmond, and Zeylmans was later able to distinguish drunkenness caused by wine, beer or spirits with absolute precision. No alcohol was drunk in his house, and other people he knew were also teetotal. No doubt this was true of the small gentleman whom he and his friends saw pass by daily in the street, and whom they called 'the dandy'. The small, slim man was always perfectly attired and lightly perfumed. He also wore a wig. The lads had always looked on him mockingly and sometimes perhaps called rather rude things after him as he passed by. But they saw another side of him one day when one of the workers got drunk again—a giant of a fellow who now grew extremely aggressive. He was walking along beside the factory with bloody hands, punching in the window-panes as he went. He raged and bellowed and no one dared approach him. Suddenly they see the 'dandy', who walks up to him undeterred and takes him by the wrist. Then they hear his high voice saying calmly to the great chap: 'Now come along with me! That's dreadful, you've hurt yourself. Let's go and get you bandaged up quickly!' The drunkard looks at the little man with bloodshot eyes and lets himself be led away as quiet as a lamb! After this, quite understandably, the lads formed a different opinion of the 'dandy'. From then on they greeted him respectfully, and Zeylmans later told how this incident had taught him how variously and unexpectedly *courage* manifests in different people.

After the age of seven, we gradually see a different picture emerging—the soul of the boy begins to turn outwards. He finds a new girl friend, with whom he goes on long walks and ice-skates in winter. He also mentions the dancing classes at which, whenever possible, the two of them danced together. She was a beautiful girl whom he loved very much for years: delicate, with translucent skin and long, dark plaits. The whites of her eyes around the dark pupils had a pale bluish tinge, which gave her whole face an unearthly look. Her voice had a lovely, bright sound, like a birdcall or a distant bell. Her movements also had a bird-like quality. When she laughed suddenly, she drew one foot up in the air.

He could not bear people to speak dismissively of this love. When older friends called it childishness or puppy-love, a feeling of impotent rage rose up in him. How could they fail to see that this was the highest, noblest, greatest thing of all?

He was most deeply indignant when adults used such expressions. He had already seen too much to be unaware that love between man and woman was not always a fine thing. In these years love for him was something which belonged completely to the world of light. Nothing bad or common, ugly or dark was able to obscure it.

This was the shining light of paradise, which he had brought with him as a memory and now sought everywhere in the world. He rediscovered it anew each spring and summer in blossoming nature—in the radiant colours, the play of light, the sweet, intoxicating perfumes. And above all he found it in his delicate, still blossoming love. But nowhere else otherwise.

The boy found it harder and harder to cope with ugly things. The older he became, the more he encountered them. There were, for instance, schoolboys who said coarse, common things, and did them too. He was also one of the lads, and certainly no angel, and sometimes such things tempted him strongly. He took part now and then when bad things were done, but afterwards he always felt revulsion.

Worst of all were the factory workers' children, who said dreadful things, especially about girls and what you could do with them. In those years he found it harder and harder to hear ugly, dirty things.

One boy was his particular enemy. He had a shrill, ugly voice and the coarsest expressions, which he had picked up, no doubt, from hanging around taverns in the evening. They hated each other. Now and then they fought, and laid into one another without mercy.

Willem was known as a fighter, who also picked quarrels with lads older than himself. His brother, who was four years older than him, sometimes had to protect him when he let himself in for more than he could cope with.

There were two goats in the factory grounds with whom he often held bull-fights—a rather risky undertaking—and this impressed his friends greatly. He could also tell his companions the finest stories. Some of them listened spellbound as he related romantic stories about beautiful girls.

The things he had experienced inwardly as a five-year-old he now took out into the world. But from the daily world in which he had to live, paradise increasingly faded. The darkness which people and things spread around them became more opaque through the years—darker, more sombre, more threatening. A mood of sadness, mixed with longing for a return to paradise, increasingly took root in his soul.

Mourning for lost paradise, unquenchable longing to live there.

The year that his brother Peter turned eighteen and went to Amsterdam to attend commercial high-school, the cocoa factory's circumstances took a turn for the worse. The price of raw materials rose steeply, sales plummeted. Their father had often travelled far afield—there were branches of the business in Germany and Vienna—had also often visited Moscow where advertisements for Crest Cocoa appeared in the Russian newspapers; and there were good trade links with England as well. But fate hit hard and the factory had to choose between complete liquidation or new management. Thus the two sons-in-law were dismissed.

In 1909 the Zeylmans family moved to Amsterdam, where the father began a confectionery business.

Times of financial hardship now began, which Willem took deeply to heart. He often saw his father sitting in the living room in the evening, spending hours on calculations under the light of the lamp. 'He's counting himself back to wealth,' said the son to himself...

II. YOUTH

From Bender Bole's Life Story
2. Soul's awakening

Although the family's move to Amsterdam came fairly suddenly, the boy was not surprised. For a long time already he had had the sense that something would change in his life. Everything old had run dry, nothing of all that had occupied him until then could satisfy him any longer, but had become dreary. He was overtaken by a vague restlessness and a longing for something as yet unknown, which meant that he often wandered around for hours on end without seeing or even dreaming much.

His encounter with the town of Amsterdam in 1909 brought him a wealth of powerful new experiences. He had just turned fifteen.

The great city, which had remained with him as a gloomy memory from a previous visit, now seemed quite different. There was life and activity everywhere. The streets were constantly full of people, until late at night, and everyone seemed to be busily pursuing their affairs. He enjoyed watching all the hustle and bustle. The boys and girls he got to know at school were also quite different. He was in the second year of a secondary school near his home, and his fellow pupils were full of plans, knew a lot about things. One intended to become a helmsman for an overseas export company, and told him about the steamers that travel to distant parts of the globe. Another wanted to become an actor, and was already playing the main part in a school production of a real theatrical drama. Bender looked on in amazement. Another played the violin and secretly told him that he had composed music himself. Later, he said, he would become this or that . . . everything was equally fascinating.

To begin with the others laughed at Bender's funny country dialect, but they soon took him into their circle. He was very attracted to the old town: each Sunday he roamed along the quiet old canals and looked at the great and splendid houses. They were all different but all equally beautiful, and seemed to suit one another, the glittering water of the canals, and the old trees hanging down over the water. Some looked like palaces, had mock-columns on their gables and wide stairways leading up to grand entrances.

He spent hours hanging around the harbour, where the great steamers lay. He read the names of the ships and tried to find out where they were going. In his thoughts he went with them.

It was as if he had been continually going hungry in recent years, and now suddenly had plenty to eat. A sense of fullness streamed through him. Sometimes Bender suddenly felt a great longing for his former surroundings, for the moor above all and the woods. He felt this especially when, after a few months at school, he was asked to write a free composition: he wrote a detailed account of a long ramble he and his friend had once taken together:

'One holiday day they started out early in the morning, each with a strong stick, with sandwiches and an apple. Beyond the great park with the old oak trees they soon came to the brook that was straddled by a rotten old bridge. From there you could already see the moor. Beside a broad sandy path, between flowering gorse and low pine trees stood Jenneke's small hut—she was a bent, old woman with a white bonnet on her head, and a special friend to the two lads. It was hard to tell how old she was. Her whole face was lined and wrinkled and her eyes were grey and friendly. Leaning on her small stick she hobbled about in her garden and beckoned to the two boys. They bought potatoes from her which she brought out from a box under her bed. For a penny they got as much as they wanted, and could also pick plums from the crooked tree behind her hut.

'Then they went on their way and visited the miller, a wizened little fellow whose cap and clothes were dusted white with flour. He lived in the great mill at the edge of the moor. Through a small round window one could see the whole plain for miles around, with its shimmering lakes, the low, dark copses, and far in the distance a church tower lifting its spire. The mill's wooden wheel clattered round peacefully but busily. The little miller was a man of few words. Usually he just smiled at the boys; but when he spoke they listened with great respect, considering him to be a wise man.

'On they went again, until they came to the white hills, where they looked for a place to dig a deep fireplace with a tall, smooth chimney for the smoke to rise through. Dry heather and brushwood soon produced a crackling blaze and much glowing ash, into which they laid the potatoes and covered them in sand. Now they had to wait for the potatoes to cook in the ash. They roamed about, climbed a high pine-tree to see what they could see, came to the shore of a peat-lake where the ground became marshy, and crept carefully on through the cotton grass. For a while they lay in a shady hollow between sand-dunes, where great blue gentians bloomed between thick and flourishing heather. Insects buzzed by, little blue butterflies fluttered around them. Far in the distance they heard a wheelbarrow squeaking . . .'

Bender had written all this in his story.

The next day the teacher came into the classroom, with their essays in his hand. 'Children,' he said, 'I want to read you one of these. We have a poet in the class.'

Bender did not know what a poet looked like, and looked around inquisitively wondering who this might be. All he knew of poets was that they wrote verse.

The teacher began to read. Suddenly he recognized his own story. He went pale, then blushed. His heart was thumping. Was he a poet?

From that day on he often wrote long essays, that were usually read out to the class. He began to read books: stories, poems, novels, anything he came upon. A new world, of which he had known nothing until now, opened before him, a rich inner world full of beautiful ideas, wonderful images, heartfelt words.

This teacher later gathered around him those youngsters who loved literature. And while the other pupils did other school-work, he told these ones about the great literary works. In Zeylmans there awoke, in the space of a few years, a burning love of world literature, about which he developed a wide knowledge early on.

It was a time of wonders, discoveries. Each new discovery was more surprising than the last. He did not quite know how to take everything in, and there was never enough time for all he wanted to do. He found it hard to begin with to keep up at school, for his soul was full of all these new experiences.

One free afternoon he went to the near-by museum. At first he felt put off by the large exhibition rooms with all the paintings hanging there; but suddenly, like a flash of lightning, he saw what was around him: deep shimmering colours, radiant bright colours, fiery blazing colours, colours that quietly drew him into the distance. Slowly he began to see the paintings themselves, to distinguish one from another and at last to know them.

Here too he discovered something that felt, at first, like a hand round his throat—but then gave him deep satisfaction: the demons again, which had tormented him as a child! This lifted a great weight from him, for he had often thought that someone who saw such things could not be quite normal. He had once asked his friend very cautiously whether he too had ever seen such things, but the friend had not understood what he meant. Was it a kind of madness he suffered from? But here were these demons in the gallery, so painters had seen them too, and had carefully portrayed them—so painstakingly that he recognized most of them. He was completely reassured.

Towards the end of his sixteenth year he fell ill with typhoid. His mother watched by his bedside for nights on end, for he had high fever with hallucinations. Once he had got over the worst, he was so weakened that he could hardly even raise his hand.

During a long convalescence he lay on the divan beside the window and just watched the world outside. The old family doctor used to come and sit with him: a friendly man with clear, grey eyes and a quiet, calm voice. He talked to Bender as to a grown-up—about the benefits which people gain from suffering a severe illness, and how one only really knows the meaning of life when one has almost lost it, and then feels it gradually returning. How all that one formally took for granted now becomes miraculous . . . Bender listened reverently. He did not have much to say in response, but there was no need for him to. And when he did say something, the doctor listened and took it seriously.

This became a rich time. Spring had come by now and Bender saw the buds swelling on the trees in the park opposite, and here or there a green leaf unfurling. On sunny days he was allowed to have the window open, and then the spring air streamed into his room.

From what one can gather this doctor must have been Dr Samuel de Lange, who had a large practice in that part of town. He was much loved, and was responsible for the municipal old people's home, the orphanage, and for adolescents who fell into bad ways. Later he became director of the Boerhaaven Clinic for eye complaints, where he also gave courses for the nurses. He also lectured at Amsterdam university, on visual defects among other things.

For a short while an element of church-religion surfaced in Willem's life:

When I was seventeen I suddenly felt the need to be part of a Christian community, and was baptised and confirmed. Yet this did not satisfy my need and I did not pursue a closer connection with the church.

The family apartment stood in a crescent behind the famous Concertgebouw, the Amsterdam concert hall. There were as yet no houses between the crescent and the back of the concert building, but only a small park. At the time the city's musical life was greatly influenced by the energetic young conductor Willem Mengelberg, a man of genius and ambition who grew to world-fame before the Second World War. Within a few years he hauled Amsterdam's musical life onto the international stage by performing all the great works of Beethoven, Brahms, Bruckner, Mahler etc. in a great series of concerts. The Zeylmans' apartment was on the ground floor, and on sunny days Willem lay beside his open window listening to the rehearsals for these concerts, played by the Concertgebouw orchestra and directed by Mengelberg.

Several times a day, pupils from his school came past his house, among them a girl who lived in the same part of town and always went to school with a friend of hers.

Bender knew her—she was one class below him, in the second year, and the older lads said she was the most beautiful girl in the school. She was average height, strong rather than slim, and moved with a swift, springing gait. The thick locks of her ash-blond hair, tied with a bow, fell upon her shoulders, and danced up and down as she moved. Her face was very bright: she had a fine, straight nose and clear blue eyes that always seemed to have laughter in them. Her name was Christie.

Bender loved seeing her walk to and from school every day; and soon he found he was spending most of the time waiting for her to appear.

The weeks went by in quiet happiness, until the day came for him to return to school. To start with he found it hard to get back into the old busy schedule of the day again, but before long his interest in all that was going on around him came back. Yet something had happened that had altered everything: Christie had entered his life. Never mind that she hardly knew him—the very fact that she was there shone through his life, and every day became special because he could see her.

For a long time he felt no need to speak to her; it was quite enough to go to the same school, to see her and to live in her neighbourhood.

In the summer, shortly before the holidays began, he met her one day in the corridor—she was looking for something where the coats hung. She couldn't find her drawing pencils. Bender offered her his. They spoke a few words to one another. He said something or other rather disjointedly, and she looked at him a bit astonished, but smiling. And that was all. It wasn't until winter came round again that anything else happened. There was a school festival followed by a dance. Bender, who had liked dancing in the past, did not give it much thought, but he stayed for Christie's sake. She was more beautiful than ever in her pale green ball-gown with its white, pointed collar, and the white silk bow in her thick blond hair. She danced every dance, her cheeks red with joy.

Bender watched her for a long time, in wonder at her radiant beauty, and also somewhat dismayed.

Then he asked her to dance. At first the conversation did not flow, but suddenly it began to. They spoke about music, for Bender knew that she had piano lessons with a well-known musician.

'Are you going to train as a pianist?' he asked. He thought it a wonderful thing that she would one day be a famous pianist.

'Yes,' she said, 'this is probably my last month of school. I'm going to study music in Germany. I'm very pleased!'

Bender stopped in consternation. 'You're pleased to leave here?' he asked. For a moment it seemed that he would have to call out: 'And what about me? Am I to remain here alone?' But he said nothing.

'Yes,' she said, 'I'll be glad to see another country, other people.'

'I'll miss you,' said Bender quietly. She looked at him astonished. 'Why?' she

asked. 'Because I like seeing you so much,' he replied simply. She went red and said nothing more. At this moment Bender felt deeply unhappy. He wanted to say more but the music started for the next dance, and Christie was asked to dance by another boy.

Bender went home. Only one thought lived in his soul, which he kept repeating over and over again to himself: 'She's going away, she's going away!' At home he took a sheet of paper and wrote a poem, a farewell poem to her. He decided to write it in French. On the following day he wrote out a fair copy, on a Christmas card—a snowy moorland scene by a well-known painter—and sent it to her.

The Christmas holidays began. A few times he went towards her house, but he did not see her, either then or in the following days. But then, one day, her friend came up to him and said:

'Christie is very unhappy, she's been crying all day long.'

Bender felt his heart stop. 'Why?' he asked.

'She's crying about your poem. She thinks it's very beautiful. Much too beautiful for her,' she said.

'Nothing would be too beautiful for her,' said Bender with feeling.

'And she's also crying because it is so sad for you.'

'For me?' asked Bender astonished.

The friend glanced down at her feet, embarrassed. An awful suspicion rose up in Bender. He wanted to speak it quickly, for otherwise he couldn't have said it at all.

'She loves someone else?' he stuttered out hastily.

The friend nodded and said: 'The music teacher. You know him.' Yes, Bender knew him. He lived in the same neighbourhood. Quite a young, likeable, dark-haired man, whom he had often seen passing in his elegant black fur-coat, a soft black hat on his head.

Yes, well, if that was who it was. He was a well-known pianist who gave concerts, was often mentioned in the newspapers and would certainly be very famous one day. Yes, he could understand it. There was no room for him in that case.

He turned round, even forgetting to say good-bye to her friend, and ran off. He did not know where. He ran through the streets. Suddenly he found himself standing before her house, and looked up. 'No point any more,' he said to himself, and ran on. He felt nothing. No pain, or jealousy. Nothing. He was just full of a great emptiness. He was empty and cold.

It grew dark and still he went on. The streets were wet and dirty with melted snow. Where was he? He looked around and saw he was in front of her house again. Again he went on. He suddenly realized he was continually shaking his head: No, no, no—on and on. What else could he do?

She would go away, to Germany. He would not see her anymore. And while she was away she would write letters to the other one. He had nothing to do with it.

Everything around him was empty, cold, black. Everything grew weaker. He suddenly felt how cold and tired he was. His feet were hurting as though they would fall off.

He wanted to sleep. A warm room, where there was light, and then sleep. Forget everything. Slowly he stumbled home.

She didn't go to Germany. After the Christmas holidays she came back to school, and Bender saw her every day.

After the first while, in which he felt nothing but a gaping emptiness, the great sorrow entered his soul and took complete possession of it. Like a burning pain it sat there day in, day out, month after month without pause, like an all-consuming, almost unbearable suffering. This lasted for more than three years.

During this time he read a great deal: the great idealists and romantics. He found particular comfort in Heine's Book of Songs, *for there he recognized the suffering he himself had to endure. Goethe's* Werther *impressed him too, though it was more alien to him, he did not recognize himself in it. He wrote a lot himself, as well: love stories full of melancholy and longing, and poems in the style of Heine. Sometimes he wondered if he should send some of them to her, but he never did.*

In difficult moments he had help from a friend of his, who witnessed all this and gave the gift of his friendship without saying much. Sometimes they went walking together, and this gave Bender a sense of warmth and security, but it did not make the pain grow any less.

The spring of 1911 came, and then the summer. Autumn came, then winter. Bender still felt overwhelmed by the pain, almost every day and in every season. Instead of growing less it grew worse that first year. Once he spoke with her, on the way home from school. She showed a kind of quiet awe of him, for she knew of his great love. She was careful not to say anything that could wound him. He was happy in a way to tell her what he was doing, reading and writing. After that they sometimes went to an exhibition together, for he went to all the exhibitions: whether classical or modern art, he was interested in everything.

During this time he experienced much more than he could express in words. The Old Masters of the Renaissance were his favourites: the rich splendour of their colours, the almost heathen beauty of Michelangelo's figures, the wonderful, heavenly harmony of Raphael's Madonnas, Leonardo's mysteriously smiling women. He was also deeply moved by the Flemish naive painters: He sensed that they no longer painted external beauty, but the soul in all its suffering, humility and piety.

He vaguely began to discern two different paths that he saw in these paintings: one which led upwards to the shining glory of heaven, the other leading downwards to earthly pain, to the suffering of human existence that awaited redemption through the child. In Raphael the child is enthroned like a small god on the arm of the heavenly, cloud-born mother. In Memlinc he rests like a small, still saint in the delicate hands of a surprisingly gaunt virgin, in whose eyes one can already see the suffering that is to come.

He only later recognized Rembrandt's greatness, when he discovered that in his paintings an inner light is born from earthly figures, filling their surroundings with radiance.

He also came into deeper contact with music in those years. He often went to the symphony concerts that took place in winter in the near-by Concertgebouw. His first impression there had been so overpowering that he felt himself dissolving into tones and sounds. He hadn't been able to discern things clearly—it was as though he had floated away from the earth in heavenly ecstasy.

Gradually, though, he distinguished the various instruments, melodies, themes and variations, and experienced a recurring rapture from all this. He loved all the composers: Bach's clear revelations; the mighty symphonies of Beethoven, born of will and pain; Brahms' inward, feeling music, which sometimes made his breath fly out of him in tears and laughter. It was all equally overwhelming and intoxicating. There were parts of Mahler's songs and symphonies that he could barely endure because they took such powerful hold of him. He had the sense of being transported to a threshold where, if sorrow increased any further, one would have to die. When he later got to know Bruckner, it seemed to him that he was led into the world of the all-creating gods themselves, surrounded by the stillness of eternity.

Sometimes, after a concert, he went home together with Christie. She felt the music very deeply, and so they usually did not speak much as they walked back through the quiet streets. But in such moments something still and beautiful wove between them, which they both tended with care. He never asked himself whether she might after all come to love him. He regarded the fact that it was not so as a matter of destiny, and accepted it together with the pain it brought.

One time, when everything again seemed unbearable to him, a friend brought him a little book. It was a novel of little literary merit, but it contained a thought which moved Bender deeply: 'Suffering,' it said, 'is a privilege of life.'

Like a flash of lightning suddenly illuminating everything, this thought struck deep into his soul. The suffering he had been living with for more than two years, that tormented him, that woke him up at night and made him toss and turn in his bed, that led him close to madness, to states in which he was even afraid of himself—this was a privilege?

The thought did not leave him. He saw before him the great artists whom he honoured: the painters and composers. Had not most of what they created come from suffering? Certainly their greatest achievements had, which were destined for immortality.

And the reformers in history, the pioneers, those who were alone and misjudged? And the saints, the founders of religions? And Christ?

His relationship to life began to change. It was as if he saw much that he had been incapable of seeing before.

Now he looked at people with particular attention, and read on every face signs of the suffering they bore. The children in the narrow streets, old and young from all walks of life: all bore suffering in themselves. Where was there none? This gave him a sense of connection with people, with all people—a feeling he had not known before.

And at the same time he felt a healing process begin in his hurt soul.

It still took a year to get his inner cheerfulness back. He had already left school and become a student. He met Christie seldom; but when he did by chance, he was quite calm and just took quiet pleasure in her beauty.

And then the strange, incomprehensible thing happened.

One spring evening, as he was peacefully studying, a letter from Christie arrived. He had never received a letter from her before, and he began to read with great curiosity. It was a long and slightly confused letter, which he had to read several times to understand what she was actually saying.

For years, it appeared, she had always thought she loved the other, the musician; but it had come as a great disappointment to her to find that he did not appreciate the real person in her, but only the cheerful, pleasant child—and this had increasingly given her a sense of emptiness. Gradually she had started to feel a different image surfacing in her, the image of Bender. Their conversations, his interest in all that was good and beautiful . . . she had come to love him more and more; and now that she hardly ever saw him any longer, she felt she could not live without him.

The letter ended by asking whether Bender would like to come and collect her for a walk, so that they could speak to each other fully about all this.

After their long evening walk together, Bender once more sat alone in his room, staring out through his open window into the dark night.

Was this the joy at last that he had longed for? He felt strangely calm. As he had held her in his arms and kissed her lips, a terrible certainty had come over him: his love for her no longer existed. She had become someone for whom he felt a delicate, inward affection, but it was more a feeling of compassion and pity.

For more than three years he had suffered the deepest pain because of her. He had not avoided this pain, had not fled it. He had tried to drink the cup to the last bitter drop. But by doing so, all that had bound him to her had passed away. It had dissolved and been consumed in his suffering, and all that was left was a quiet, heartfelt feeling of friendship. Compassion rose up in him, for he knew that she must now suffer because of him.

On the following evening they went walking together once more. They took the same path to the meadows outside the town. Tactfully he tried to tell her what was going on inside him. She was in such despair that Bender grew alarmed, and asked himself whether he had done the right thing by being so honest.

It was late at night before he managed to bring her home.

This was a profound mystery which Bender pondered long and hard. How could something like this happen? How was it possible that two people could suffer, one after another, from the same hurt? Was he wrong? Had pain dulled him? Or was she living in illusion? Or were they both meant for one another, and another phase would come in which they could both devote themselves wholly to their love? It did not seem likely to him, but it filled him with unease.

After a whole year he heard that she had got engaged and would soon marry.

Only then did this unease fade from his soul.

These events in Willem Zeylmans' own account bear the archetypal signs of a trial of the soul, a burning soul-pain lasting from the age of 17 to 20 (1910–1912), that lives in him as a mystery. Later he writes:

I had experienced something which, from that time on, I could carry within me as a treasure. The power of suffering endured . . .

Joy is like a great light that streams in from without. Suffering, in contrast, awakens an inner light that begins to shine in the soul: small to start with, but stronger than the other light. And it was with this inner light that I wanted to meet my future wife, and become one with her, as the human spirit strives to become one with the world-soul itself. . .

III. STUDENT YEARS

Let us briefly look back over the Amsterdam years and draw the threads together. In January 1909 Zeylmans, only just fifteen, arrived in this city. In the summer of 1914 his parents move to The Hague, and Zeylmans, who has now started his medical studies and is nearly twenty-one, transfers to the University of Leiden.

His interest in modern art has awoken, and with great attention he follows contemporary painters' efforts to develop a new approach to art. In these very years, artists such as Kandinsky, Kokoschka, Mondrian, Franz Marc and Paul Klee are struggling to form a new view of the world. In the near-by Stedelijk Museum and the 'Galleries' he sees exhibitions which show new, turbulent developments in art. The book *The Blue Rider* also appears during this period.

Among such artists, and in literature too, there develops an aversion to 'civilized culture', and a search for new paths. The extraordinary progress of technology at this time, which spreads through the world like a kind of cultural intoxication, is brought up short by the shock of the Titanic catastrophe: the largest, most modern passenger ship in the world runs into an iceberg at Easter 1912, and 1,500 people go to a watery grave.

But close at hand too, in Amsterdam, Zeylmans experiences a new epoch breaking through. In September 1910, beside the broad Amstel river, he holds his breath as he watches the Belgian aviator Jan Olieslagers rise into the air in a shaky flying contraption and stay up for seven minutes! The 'Antwerp Air-Devil' evokes great hopes (and illusions) in people, for they think that this newly invented monstrosity is so terrifying, and might fly so freely across all national borders, that wars would in future be impossible!

In the Concertgebouw, where he goes to concerts as often as he can, his attention is one day drawn to a young music critic in the dress circle with fine, chiselled features, wrapped up in an old coat, who, looking around him scornfully at the whole Amsterdam audience, provocatively puts his fingers in his mouth at the end of the concert and whistles in derision! This is Matthijs Vermeulen (1888–1967), only a few years older than Zeylmans, who like him grew up in Helmond. The figure of the young musician, who was himself already composing music at the time, and later made a name for himself with a series of symphonies, impresses itself deeply on his imagination—and he immediately writes a short novella about the incident:

. . . He, the dreamer, who always wandered through the woods . . . the great idealist . . . he moved, without a penny, to Amsterdam, where I saw him: haggard, tall, pale. Deathly pale his countenance, with its sparkling black eyes . . . In the old days he walked proud as a prince through the streets . . . Now he stood there in the dress circle, in stark contrast to the magnificent concert hall around him, the only one who dared oppose the wealthy audience's taste . . .

In later years Zeylmans found it a stirring experience to read the feared critic Vermeulen's articles, and to see him enter into conflict with Willem Mengelberg. Matthijs Vermeulen was a man of high intelligence and a great prose-writer, who exerted an influence on Zeylmans for years. In some of his early writings he composed aphorisms that highlight his view of life, for instance: 'Every direction has its particular conditions, and is therefore limited. Thus whoever pursues a certain direction also limits himself and the scope of his mind.'—'Whoever follows one direction, directs his soul to perdition. Not much attention is usually taken of this.'—'In everyone there is a tendency to judge. The sum of these tendencies makes up the public.'—'Whoever says he loves the public says, at the same time, that he would like to be shown his mistakes. But people rarely say this, even though it is the only means of improving.'

From Bender Bole's Life Story
3. Stella Maris

Only a short time after Bender's last meeting with Christie, the First World War broke out. For a long time he could not form any inner relationship to this.

In his early youth he had fantasized a good deal about leading great armies to victory. Later, when the Boer war broke out, he ardently took sides. Dressed up as a Boer from the Transvaal, a loaded gun on his shoulder, he lurked behind bushes waiting doggedly for English soldiers to appear.

At school he had become acquainted with the world's great generals: Alexander, Julius Caesar, Napoleon. He looked up their trails of conquest on the map, and fought by their side in his imagination. He marvelled, spellbound at great, heroic deeds.

But this war was not like any other. At first it seemed as though it might be, but the Marne slaughter soon changed his mind. It turned into the obstinate, mechanical annihilation of thousands, hundreds of thousands, millions of people, an annihilation that was unleashed by all possible means and machines that modern technology could devise.

There was no lack of heroism, but it had assumed a different form. It was expressed in hard and bitter endurance, in the endless sufferings of surviving mud and swamp, filthy, louse-ridden trenches, and the continual threat of missiles, grenades, poisonous gas, sickness and death.

Now and then, it is true, heroism surfaced in the old, personal-type, romantic style. A cruiser that sailed far from its base and went battling like an old pirate vessel was food for the imagination—and there were other such incidents, but they were exceptions. In the trenches lay millions of unknown soldiers, waiting for an unsung death.

All this affected him deeply. Is that what the world was like? Was the inner protest of these millions so weak that they could do nothing against it? Or was it not rather that in each one of these millions, in every human being ultimately, there was something that somehow wished for this war, this annihilation. He could not grasp the idea that a few politicians without conscience, a handful of capitalists and arms manufacturers were responsible for it all. It seemed to him that everyone was responsible, as long as people still had failings—and who didn't? During this period he had long conversations with a friend who was a conscientious objector and believed that everyone should adhere literally to the commandment 'Thou shalt not kill'. Then there would no longer be any war. He valued the nobility of this view, but regarded killing not as the place to start from, but the end-result of something else. These people in the trenches did not want to kill, certainly not the innumerable young, gifted idealists of all nations, from all walks of life. The fact that they did kill was the final consequence, an impersonally suffered consequence, the unavoidable final result of a series of factors and events, that had their roots elsewhere. All of life, both material and spiritual, had produced a particular configuration of circumstances. And into this was drawn each individual with his own egotism and imperfections, and so shared responsibility for it.

Someone who gets angry, he said to his friend, when his neighbour's chickens get into his field, has no right to draw back from this war, for he has had a share in bringing it about. The friend smiled, rather embarrassed, for in his daily life he had rather a fierce, unruly temper.

Willem's older brother Peter Zeylmans had emigrated to England some time before, where his father still had business connections from the cocoa factory period. War broke out only a short time after he had begun his commercial career in London. Peter signed up as a volunteer soldier straight away (which meant that he lost his Dutch nationality) and fought against Germany in the French trenches for more than four years. Thus Willem Zeylmans was more personally involved than most Dutch people in the progress of the war. And his mother, who was herself German by birth, could often hardly bear the worry she felt for her son on the Western Front. She suffered from increasing anxiety, and in later years was prone to attacks of emotional instability. Peter Zeylmans survived the war—twice being the only one of his company to come through alive. He later became a successful businessman, and died in 1959.

In these years Bender was tugged strongly to and fro: sometimes he fell into a cynical, bitter mood and then liked to speak in paradoxes. He felt himself completely at odds with the world, even above it all, like an observer who gazes down from a high, bare cliff—interested in what he sees but without any real involvement. Then, in contrast, he was filled with a mood similar to the one he had felt in his childhood years, when he discovered that paradise had vanished and only darkness and ugliness remained on the earth. A deep melancholy held sway in his soul.

At the same time, though, he could be gripped by deep compassion when touched by human suffering. Newspaper reports about the war could rob him of his sleep for hours: he pictured to himself the misery that the soldiers had to endure, and put himself in their place.

Lesser suffering too, such as poverty and illness, moved him deeply. He talked to an unhappy child in the road and helped him sort out his problems. Children had a big place in his life. Already as a child he had liked playing with younger children, and felt inwardly connected even with newborn babies. He felt friendship for all children, for in their being he found something of the world in which he himself still lived or at least wanted to. Little children's eyes, their laughter, their voices transported him back to that paradise to which they were still so close.

Thus his inner life was complicated and divided in these war years. There was much that made him melancholy, brooding and cynical. But the child within him stayed alive and, mostly unconsciously, sought the warm glow and light-filled beauty of paradise.

On arriving in Leiden he was at first asked to work in the editorial department of *Minerva*—an established and well-regarded weekly Dutch student paper, in which his novella 'The golden girl' was immediately published.

But he took little further part in public student life after joining a small literary circle, INA, which was of enormous importance for his life at the time. A group of friends formed here, outside the usual student associations. These were young people of the most varied talents and interests. More important for him even than the literary and philosophical exchanges that regularly took place in this circle were the social relationships that developed. There were students here from every faculty, and among them were some highly intelligent, gifted individuals and artistic types.

Though he had read widely, he had until now rarely looked critically at what he read. In this circle he not only learned to discuss and form judgements, but also write critical essays himself.

A letter to him from a female student gives us an idea of the kind of impression Zeylmans may have made on his friends in those days:

> You—you have friends and ideals, and belief in human beings . . . You are one of those who, in a terrible storm, asks the others if they saw the beauty of the lightning! . . . Someone for whom dream is more real than ugly reality. You are a sun-child. At a young age you were overwhelmed by great pain, but it did not cripple you inside. Your laughter is real . . . you told me about yourself, and the summing up of what you said could have been a finale by Bach: always love, love and more love!—Whatever may have gone before, we come to higher understanding in the end!

In this circle of friends Zeylmans could feel free to unfold fully. In meeting with others, who were often highly talented, he experienced himself as 'a grateful pupil of life, at the same time elevated into the sphere of true friendship'.

In those years Willem Zeylmans wrote a great deal (an overview of his writings is given in the appendix). 1916, when he was twenty-three, was a particularly productive year. From the wealth of his writings at that time we will only reproduce one short text, so that the reader can gain an impression of his style. It is a piece of prose in rather mysterious vein, and concerns an encounter with a sort of 'double', who, like an embodiment of vanity itself, of gaping emptiness, intoxicated self-obsession or ice-cold, deadly hate, tempts and cajoles in a voice driven both by self-destructive urges and undisguised hatred for humanity. This piece only becomes fully comprehensible when we consider something that Zeylmans said to a friend thirty years later:

You spoke of an encounter with yourself, or rather with a double . . . yes, that is the precise term . . . yes, my dear friend, you did see your double. You are one of those who have had the good fortune to meet their double . . . and I am perfectly serious when I speak of good fortune!

Here and there in literature you can find descriptions of the double. In every single case such an encounter has special significance. In your case it means that you were able to perceive the forces active in hatred, embodied in a form that resembles you closely, but which you have distanced yourself from, put outside yourself. By doing so you have, at least to some extent, liberated yourself from hatred, which is a great gift of grace. What is important now is to take the next step.

'And what is the next step?' asked the friend.

'To try to free your double from diabolical rigidity that chains him, so that you can once more take up your true being into yourself.'

'But how should I do that?'

'The way is shown us in the words: knowledge and love. Know the nature of hatred, and love people and humanity. It is a hard, difficult path, but one that must be followed . . . You have survived an appalling shock, so you will also find the strength to follow this path further. Once we have encountered the double, he accompanies us until we redeem him.'

These sentences sound like a commentary to his youthful composition 'The Mirror', which the poet Albert Verwey published in his magazine *Die Bewegung* (The movement) in December 1916.

The Mirror
by Willem van Emmichoven

In the twilight he sat opposite me and spoke: 'Why do lonely people love the night? When it is dark people are far away, and therefore life too. And a lonely person hates life, because it tears him away from himself and so shows him the endless emptiness of his being. That is why a lonely person loves the night, which leaves him alone with his delusion. But I . . . I hate the night! When it grows dark, people are far away, and when they are far away, they do not see me. And when they do not see me, how can they think and speak of me? And if they don't think and speak of me, how can I know I exist?'

I saw his face vaguely before me in the twilight. It resembled mine, but there was an alien, alluring light in his eyes. He went on: 'When it is dark, everything flies away from me. Great black birds fly away up into the gloomy sky and vanish. They are near still, mysteriously close—but no one sees them any longer. That is how I experience life around me when night falls. I hate sleep! Then I am alone for hours and hours. Is that life—existing without anyone knowing, without knowing it myself? When I feel sleep approaching, it is like a ship that slowly slips from the shore without rudder or sail. The night wind catches it and plays with it, moving it this way and that.

Horrifying things happen in the night and I do not see them. They happen to me but I do not know it. Cries ring out, mad cries; and in a low, dark cellar hangs the lukewarm steam of blood. A grey, lonely house stands there. Heavy, low voices sing a corpse-song. Organ-notes accompany it. No one is there to hear it . . . Alien birds fly before the windows, not singing, just quietly beating their wings. No one is there to see them . . . The night is full of horror and fright! Sometimes in the morning I have a confused and vague memory of it, the remembrance of a dream.

I hate dreams! For dreams are cruel—crueller than people can be. Life already knows what my soul demands, and gives it me. Dreams also know what my soul demands, and give me the opposite! Dreams destroy what life gives me. And when I wake up I am poorer than before . . . The nights are for lonely people, but the day is for me!'

I looked at him: his face was pale and haggard like death, but his eyes shone deep and enticing.

He went on: 'Who knows the beauty of losing yourself in life? Who knows the ecstasy of going under in pleasure? A glow deeper than pearls! A shivering sparkle, in which a sob can faintly be heard. A crystal laugh, that fades like a sigh. A wide, waving cloak of the most delicate silk, wrapping itself warm round our vanity! Is there anything sweeter? . . . But the nights remain with their cruelty.'

Gloomily he looked down. His consumed features twitched, and into his eyes came a mad fire.

He said: 'But the nights are not always cruel, sometimes they are gentle and beguiling. Strange melodies rustle through the darkness. The delicate contours of the soul are bright and shining as silver. Perfumes float, heavy as incense, but they bewitch more sweetly, more deeply. Seraphim sing through the night with crystal voices . . . then everything softly floats away from us. Like great, pale butterflies thoughts flutter around us, butterflies that rise ever higher and then vanish. And nothing remains.' He had brought his thin hand up to his forehead, and clasped his fingers, cramp-like, together, as though trying to grasp hold of something. Then he covered both eyes with his hand and I saw only the nervous movements of his skinny fingers. He looked up! A devilish sparkle had entered his eyes! He went on: 'They do not know! They do not know what I steal from them day after day, hour by hour: all that they struggle so hard to gain, that they make such sacrifices to achieve, that they shed so many tears over—all of it I steal from them! It is an alien, sweet-smelling food for my perverse soul. Flowers of gold thread sewn on the silk cloak of my vanity. And people are even happy for me to steal it from them, for they think that the pleasure I suck from life is like their dreams of joy. And to this joy they so gladly sacrifice all! And the generous smiles I give them in return for their souls' tears they see as the gentle laughter of life. In my mocking, wily laughter they think they see the all-encompassing bliss of universal spirit!'

I saw him get up. His long, skinny figure stood tall and threatening before me. His face was ghostly pale and his eyes full of mockery and hatred. He went on: 'Slaves they are! Slaves to pleasure, and all the time they think they are serving life. My slaves! For my greatness wholly encompasses their smallness!'

He took one step forwards and fixed me with his gaze:

'With every fibre of their being they are riveted to my iron desires! And no liberation is possible. Centuries upon centuries have glorified this slavery, like a beautiful battle!'

Now he looked gravely before him, all light gone from his eyes. They were hollow and empty, but unfathomably deep.

He said: 'What is life to you now, now that you know this? Isn't the monotonous peace of death more to you now than this miserable, slavish existence? Is the dark stillness of the grave not better than the screaming folly of life?'

A cutting coldness almost froze my heart. Breathless, wide-eyed, I listened. He went on: 'All that you call life is a short, pointless delusion! The feeble twitching of a dying body, the feverish laughter of a lost spirit! Nothing is more ridiculous than the short-sightedness of human beings, who think they play a king's role in life, and are really nothing but drunken clowns!'

A great rush of blood flooded my head. All of a sudden I knew how to free myself from the witchcraft of his dead eyes. I leapt up from my chair and went to meet him with raised fists. And hit home! Hard!

A shrill cry sliced the air, then there was a loud shattering, as of glass breaking. He had gone! Before me lay countless sharp, silver-bright splinters. It was dark in the room. I felt warm blood dripping from my wrists . . .

The night came on—peaceful, quiet night! Night with its dreams!

During the holidays he often walked along the North Sea coast, and through the dunes at Scheveningen. The sea had a particular attraction for him. It was here that he experienced the endlessness of the cosmos spreading over all creation, and the surf-roar of eternity encompassing all time. The heavens arched high over the immeasurable surface of the water, and between water and sky wove light, conjuring ever new colours on the surfaces of the waves. Over long periods he went to the shore each evening to watch the sun setting. No sunset was like another. Sometimes the sun was a great, ominous red disc that slowly vanished into the blue-grey waves. Or sometimes there was an indescribable play of colours, constantly changing, beginning with orange-red flames that merged gradually into crimson-violet sheen. It was always wondrous, even on cloudy days when there was only a dull-red glint reflected in the iron-grey waves.

By the shore he could spend a long time watching the waves gathering, breaking then flowing back. They rolled in from the distance, splintered upon the sand, crept rustling up to his feet, then slid back. A sublime rhythm, a solemn, celebratory song sung by the elements, monotonous yet fascinating—a song of eternity.

And then the sea-gulls! In great numbers, sometimes hundreds, they flew over the shore. Was there any weight in them? Were they not born entirely of light and sea-foam? The way they swept over the water, swooped down and rose up, sailed in great circles, or suddenly turned with an angular movement: they had slipped earth's leash. Gravity had no hold on them, they belonged to the world of light. No darkness had yet brushed their white wings.

In summer he often roamed through the dunes. There were deep hollows, in which all kinds of rare flowers grew. At the edge of such a hollow stood a hawthorn, or a flowering elder. Small, pale blue violets grew between the tough salt-grass. Once he found a dog-rose. Honeysuckle wound itself round buckthorn. In the low pine-scrub reigned absolute quiet, the sea rustling in the far distance.

Here he sensed a mood that reminded him of childhood, when he used to roam over the moor. But now his soul no longer dwelt in fantasy. There was much to ponder. Nature was a rich, beautiful background and source of inspiration.

But inwardly he continually sought for something. When, after roaming far afield, he climbed the high crest of a dune and saw the sea before him, it sometimes seemed to him as though he had found what he was searching for. There, beneath the broad, blue sky, lay the endless expanse of waves like an image of eternity. This was the world. Full of light and colours, sounds and rhythms and melody. Plants slumbered softly, blossoming in colours, exhaling their fragrance. The birds sang, floated and fluttered about. In this world lived the human soul, in space and time, in light, tone and colour, as though embedded in an all-encompassing world-soul. Was his quiet longing for love not also a longing to become one at last with this world-soul? Surely longing for love was itself the same as the deep, inner urge to return to this world of light, sound and colour, from which the human soul had been banished? To return to a place where the human soul was still wholly penetrated, woven through with world-soul, which poured love into the soul at the same time as beauty.

As a child he had grown up in a Catholic area, and there learned to honour Mary as the holy virgin. Most of what he had seen of this had meant little to him: it had all been rather ugly, course and inartistic. Occasionally a long train of pilgrims had passed his house: men and women, making their arduous way, murmuring their prayers. Some had put hard peas in their shoes, and looked exhausted, and their prayers sounded weary and monotonous. It gave him an anxious, suffocating feeling. Sometimes they sang a song: 'O, beautiful, pure virgin, full of blessings.' He had never forgotten this song: the virgin, beautiful and radiant, the heavenly queen full of love and grace!

There had also been church festivals, with colourful processions. Carts would pass by with young girls dressed in white, wearing long veils, their hair decorated with flowers, while the queen of heaven spread her wings protectively over them.

Once he was summoned to one of the small neighbouring houses: the smith's daughter had died. She lay in a small coffin of dark wood in her white communion dress, white, a veil on her head, and a wreath of white flowers in her hair. Entwined in her folded hands was a rosary of blue beads. 'Now she has gone to be a little bride of heaven,' said the smith's wife, looking at Bender with her tear-stained, friendly eyes. He stood there motionless and gazed on the little waxen face. He had sometimes played with her—and now she was a little bride, a bride of heaven. For a long time this stayed with him . . .

The human soul seeks the queen of heaven. Each man seeks his heavenly queen, each woman her heavenly bridegroom.

Was love not a reuniting of human soul and world soul? Did every man not seek in every woman he met the virgin who could reveal something of the glory of the heavenly queen? Human soul and world soul, both lived in the human being. In the man the earth spirit was stronger, and made his soul lonely. In the woman the world soul still lived, vague and unformed. So they sought one another. The restless, continually striving spirit seeks the world soul, the soul of the woman that is still connected with heavenly powers, to rest in her, and in her to find his boundaries, ultimately also to experience his real being through her.

The woman, born from the wide realms of the cosmos, finds her deeper meaning in encompassing and protecting the restless spirit.

So they protect one another. On earth the man is protector of the woman, who is more delicate, less earthly, more heavenly. In the soul world the woman protects the man, who, without her, remains banished from the heavenly realm.

Only in their union is the real human being born: the human being who is both man and woman, who contains both heaven and earth, uniting earth spirit and world soul.

In these years this seemed to him to be the deepest meaning of life. Had love not always ruled all existence? Was history not full of tales, poems and hymns that praised love? Had the names of Romeo and Juliet, Abelard and Heloise, and Tristan and Isolde not become symbols of this unique mystery?

Tristan and Isolde—separated by everything, again and again: by misfortune, sickness, betrayal; and continually reunited through the love that overcame all, that spared life and death no second thought. 'The eternal feminine draws us onward!' For him this had become an ultimate truth.*

The time would one day come when he too would meet his Isolde, his Juliet. The heavenly bride with whom he would unite, reunite, for ever.

★

One summer's day in 1915 he had been walking through the dunes. It was a warm, summery day. The elder gave off its fragrance and the dog-rose bore many bright-crimson flowers, around which insects were buzzing. He loved this dog-rose most of all, finding it more beautiful than cultivated roses. Its five translucent, purplish petals revealed the rose's true being. Everything about this rose-bush shone with scent and inwardness. Even the small green leaves had a sweet fragrance.

On his walk he passed a small white villa, which lay a little way outside the village. Its garden was sheltered on one side by the dune. He had often looked into this garden: it had a fairly large lawn, fringed with wide flowerbeds full of sunflowers. The garden ran down into the dunes, surrounded by a thick buckthorn hedge. He heard the sound of voices and as he came nearer saw a small group of children in bright clothes dancing barefoot on the grass. There was an older girl there as well, who was leading the dancing. She wore a bright, lilac-coloured dress. Sometimes she danced with the children, and then stood to one side to see how the whole thing looked. Now and again she said something to the children and

★ From Goethe's *Faust.*

'Anita' (Ingeborg Droogleever Fortuyn, 1915)

demonstrated some movements to them. It was a cheerful, pleasant scene that fitted so well with the sunshine and the summery garden. Bender stopped a little way off, so as not to disturb them. Soon the children sat down on the grass, leaving a space in their midst, where the older girl began to dance alone.

Without thinking, Bender stepped nearer and watched . . . there were miracles in the world, he knew, but this brought his heart to his mouth in wonder. He was overwhelmed as he watched her from close at hand, giving herself up wholly to her movements.

It was as if all the beauty and harmony, all the brightness and inwardness living in her movements penetrated deep into his being, and touched him so deeply that he was lost in its shock-waves. He stood there motionless, without breathing, and a cold shiver ran through him. Something like a violent pain and at the same time a still more violent feeling of happiness trickled through him. Now he could see her face from close up. This face . . . it had something of the still inwardness of the Madonna faces of the great masters of the Renaissance. It was a girl's face, thin and delicate, a slight smile playing around the corners of her mouth. Her eyes were dark, serious in concentration on her dancing, her gaze directed inwards. Her dark-brown hair flowed down over her shoulders. Did he recognize her? Her face seemed so familiar, so intimately known. But how could that be? He had never seen her before. And yet it was like seeing her again, a holy reunion. As though he ought to run to her with arms flung wide and call: 'At last, at last!' He stood there rooted to the spot, motionless as a statue.

She danced calmly on, full of devotion. Her movements were simple but for Bender they were a revelation of the loveliest soul, of the most beautiful being one could imagine. He saw her whole inner nature shine out through her movements: tenderly she bent towards the earth, her hands gesturing a greeting. Then she opened her arms wide to the sky, her head bent back, her lips opening a little, as though wanting to embrace the whole universe. He saw her soul. And in the same moment he knew that it was the soul he had been seeking.

The children clapped and began to talk. He came to himself again all of a sudden. She no longer danced. Quickly she went up to the children and at the same moment caught sight of him. Still deeply moved he took a step towards her. 'I'm sorry,' he said uncertainly, 'I hope I didn't disturb you. I was just passing and could not help stopping to watch.' She looked down at the ground, rather embarrassed. 'That's alright,' she said, 'we were learning some dances for a charity function.'

She gathered the children together, said a few more words to them, then off they went towards the house.

Bender waved goodbye and went on his way.

So it was. She was truly there and he had seen her. The great miracle had happened. For days after he was incapable of thinking about this miracle in any kind of logical way. Then he wrote her a long letter, in which he tried to express what this afternoon had meant to him. It was not difficult to find out who she was. Her name was Anita.

A few days later he received a simple, friendly reply. She did not refer to his description of her and her dancing, but she answered his questions in full. Bender was wholly satisfied. He knew that she was there and what she was like now. She was still very young, and he could wait until fate led them to one another. He was quite certain that this would happen.

In the meantime he thought about her continually. The images which this afternoon had awoken in him gave him enough to ponder. He had seen her as she actually was, and nothing else mattered. He had seen that she was still a child, and at the same time a young, virginal woman too. A child who was still close to heaven, whose dancing expressed heavenly powers, but who also had the innocence and devotion of a child, devotion to all that is good and noble. She bore within her something Bender could hardly find words to express. He called it: truth—light-filled, radiant truth. The way she had moved in her bright crimson dress between the flowering bushes and colourful flowers of the sunny garden seemed to reveal something of the truth of the spirit. In his letter he had written: 'This was no seeking to be set free. Your dancing simply unfolded like simple, clear, eternal truth amidst the mysterious darkness in which human souls live.'

But she was not just a child full of heavenly forces. She was also the virgin, still unknown and mysterious. She had the still smile of the Madonna who knows the greatest wonders, the ultimate mystery of life, the miracle that took place in her when she led the Child down to earth from heavenly paradise. She possessed all the peace and inviolability that go with this: an unshakeable intent to live according to the highest laws she knew.

He became clearly aware of the line that was now drawn in his life. Everything up until now had been preparation for this meeting. The two small girl-friends of his childhood years, Christie too—they had accompanied him like small, bright stars in the sky of his soul, and he had followed the path they showed him.

Now the star which would be his guiding star from that time forth had appeared on the horizon: a radiant star, softly shimmering over the swelling sea.

He need do nothing other than follow this star, and wait quietly until the time came.

The time came. They met three years later. A few words sufficed to unite their souls. Anita had a remarkable, intuitive capacity that can only dwell in a pure soul. She recognized Bender from the sound of his voice, from a single word, a gesture.

Without knowing anything of his outward life, his circumstances, she opened herself to him, knowing that it was right. He could not grasp his joy and good fortune. He tried to express it in innumerable letters which he wrote to her during the hours of the day, when they were apart. Letters and stories, parts of novellas, and sketches, followed one upon another. They were all concerned with love, love in all its forms, love as the mightiest, most inward, powerful and deepest revelation of God's spirit in the human soul. Was there anything else in the world that mattered? Was not all of human life and death, with all its conflict, joy and pain, an uninterrupted, onflowing epic of love? An epic of love's suffering and joy?

One evening on his way home, he beheld an inner image so powerful that it was like a vision: earth and heaven melted and merged with one another into a great sphere penetrated by light, flaming light, that shone pink, crimson, red. Through this light moved figures, angelic beings, rising in lilac fire, moving in rhythmic gestures, approaching one another, embracing one another in heartfelt warmth, chaste, tender, without carnal desire, but full of inwardness; giving one another everything: their brightness, light, warmth and beauty. A pink-crimson world of streaming, weaving light. Earth and heaven had become one: a world of love, of giving love.

In these years Anita's lovely nature blossomed. Until now she had lived in quiet contemplation, only opening herself to the outer world at certain moments, when she danced for instance. It was as if her dancing enabled her to unfold fully upon earth. In daily life she often felt a certain reticence, a slight withdrawal—not from fear, but more because she found it hard to accept much that came to meet her in human souls, at least in the harsh light of day. But she pondered these things and worked through them in her own inimitable way. By nature she was deeply religious, always connected with the real foundations of existence.

Life was for her a long, hard path, but one she pursued with natural joy. She knew that every phase of life must be mastered, and undertook this with cheerful assurance. She knew that suffering can bring greater gains than pleasure, that sacrifice is more valuable than fulfilment. She accepted what she suffered and bore it with inner strength, through which shone a constant, joyful feeling for life. Suffering was for her something which belonged to Creation as much as, and even more than joy.

Her relationship to Bender directed her life increasingly outwards. He was interested in everything, knew much, had seen, heard and read much, and spoke with her of all this. His words brought everything to life for her as though she had witnessed them herself. New worlds began to open for her, which her heart recognized without her ever having seen them before.

For Bender it seemed that his life had only just begun: everything now had sense and purpose. In Anita's soul he saw the deeper sense of all existence. He experienced her being as a delicate but warm, shining reflection of all that the splendour and glory of the world soul revealed. She was an image of this world soul, but at the same time a human soul too. Image of the highest, and an individual entity at the same time, heavenly bride and earth child, Madonna and beloved. Her lovely soul shone like a star in the dark-blue night sky, like a beacon showing the way across the infinite ocean, like the bright eye of an angel from paradise gazing down upon the dark earth.

★

Thus end Willem Zeylmans' recollections of his youth.

In his posthumous papers there was a note on which he had listed headings relating to the book's proposed continuation:

Chap. 4 was to be called 'Love's metamorphoses'
—more about Tristan and Isolde, cf Wagner
—'such a love cannot survive on earth'
—the sting of death
—about Mary Magdalen—'forgive much: she loved much'
—the hetaera: in Buddha
Chap. 5 *Cain*—about Tannhäuser
Chap. 6 *Amphortas*—wounds from sense impressions that penetrate too deep
Chap. 7 *Mea Victoria in Rosae Cruce.*

IV. MY PATH TO RUDOLF STEINER

An autobiographical fragment

When we grow older and look back on our life, and see how certain meetings came about, we may discover that a particular person among many was, in a curious way, connected with those meetings. This one person forms something like a nodal point, a knot, where many threads meet and depart. Such a person may mention a name to us, or perhaps draw our attention to a book or painting, or introduce us to someone; and by doing so he opens up quite new possibilities for us. Our life may take a whole new turn . . . even though he does not have to have a connection with this new development himself.

It was from the student Jan Buys, whom I met in the circle of friends around the painter Briët in The Hague, that I first heard the name Rudolf Steiner. It must have been in 1915. Speaking of one of his friends he said:

'He also knows Pieter de Haan, you know, the son of the publisher. This Pieter de Haan is mad about Rudolf Steiner's books.' I asked: 'What sort of books are they?' 'Oh, about man's origins and suchlike,' he replied, 'but I've never read them myself.'

Although it is certain that I did not at that time form any proper idea of Rudolf Steiner's works, I remembered the name. When I met Pieter de Haan for the first time the following year, our conversation soon turned to Rudolf Steiner and his works. This meeting came about in the following way: among my friends in Leiden was a young student, Veldman, who was a very talented artist, making somewhat decadent drawings in the style of Beardsley and de Nérée. He stood out in student life as an eccentric, and loved to make much of his eccentricity. I mention him here because at this period I was writing a lot myself, among other things some fairy-tale-type pieces, also rather decadent. Veldman and I planned to publish these tales with his illustrations. After a failed attempt with another publisher, I wrote to Pieter de Haan, enclosing a few of my stories and asking to meet him.

Shortly after this he visited me and told me that my stories had received careful attention, and that his father had even read them aloud in the family circle. But he, Pieter, was concerned that they were not really 'fairy-tales' as I had called them. He explained his view that fairy-tales contain deep, instinctive wisdom, connected with former evolutionary stages of the earth. As we discussed this, the conversation turned to Rudolf Steiner, of whom Pieter de Haan told me much. It did not sound very convincing to me however. We could not really agree, but there was a certain human sympathy between us, stronger than our theoretical disagreements; and so we parted on very good terms.

After encountering Rudolf Steiner's name, I soon encountered his picture. Once again Jan Buys was the link. In The Hague there was an exhibition of expressionist painters from the Sturm *movement, which at the time centred around Herwardt Walden in Berlin. Buys was the first of us to have a chance to visit the exhibition; he came back full of enthusiasm and told of his meeting there with Jacoba van Heemskerck. He had, he said, been standing in front of a painting by Franz Marc ('Animal Fate', later partly destroyed by fire), when two ladies passed by. The smaller of the two had nodded to him, and pointing to the painting, said:*

'Wonderful isn't it?'

'Yes,' replied Buys, 'but I find the other paintings hanging beside it magnificent as well.'

'They are by me,' said the lady, 'I'm Jacoba van Heemskerck.'

The upshot of this encounter was an invitation to view the collection of her friend, Marie Tak van Poortvliet, the following autumn, and visit her in her studio.

The two ladies spent the summer in Domburg on the island of Walcheren. As autumn approached they returned to The Hague, and we soon received our invitation. So one Saturday afternoon Jan Buys and I went to Jacoba van Heemskerck's studio. As we entered my gaze fell on an old oak sideboard in a corner of the studio. In one of its compartments I saw the portrait of a dark-haired man of about 55, wearing a fur-hat. I went straight to it, stopped before it and said:

'O look, that's . . . yes . . . what's his name? . . . That's . . . Oh, what is his name . . .?'

'Do you know who it is?' asked Jacoba van Heemskerck.

'Of course,' I replied, 'I know him well, I just can't remember his name.'

'That is Dr Steiner,' she said.

'Dr Steiner?' I asked, astonished. 'No, then of course I don't know him, I've never seen him.'

How I could have thought that I knew this person, even knew him well, remained a riddle to me. And during our further conversation I kept looking over to this portrait that held such fascination for me. This visit took place in 1916, and had important consequences for me.

After we had looked at a number of paintings from different periods of Jacoba van Heemskerck's life, we took up the invitation to tea with Marie Tak van Poortvliet. She had a valuable collection of modern paintings. Besides many by Jacoba van Heemskerck she also had works by Kandinsky, Franz Marc, Campendonc, Feininger, Mondrian etc.

Marie Tak welcomed us warmly, and the conversation flowed as though we had all known each other for years. Naturally we talked about painting, but also about music, social questions and medicine.

'What are you planning to do when you have finished your studies?' Marie Tak asked me.

'I have signed a contract to go to the Dutch East Indies, and I'm looking forward to seeing something of the world. After a few years I'll see what to do next,' I said.

'It's a shame that someone so interested in art is going off to the Tropics to be a doctor', said Marie Tak.

Later she told me that she had already thought at this first meeting: 'This will be the future leader of anthroposophical work in Holland. He must not go to the Dutch East Indies, we must prevent it.' After our conversation she had spoken of this with Jacoba van Heemskerck.

The following autumn and winter Jan Buys and I, and later I on my own, visited the two ladies on many occasions. They were ardent followers of Rudolf Steiner, and our conversations centred largely on his teachings and work. But I was no more persuaded in these discussions than I had been by Pieter de Haan.

Although I was not particularly a 'scientific type', I found it hard to endure the rather dismissive tone in which they spoke of 'modern science'. Many of Rudolf Steiner's adherents spoke like this in those days, and in so doing continually put people off, both young and old, who knew from experience that this science had its failings, but also the amount of ability, hard work and inspiration that was dedicated to it.

But I had so much in common with these two ladies that our disagreements about anthroposophy did not sully the good relationship. On the contrary, we became ever firmer friends.

When I was invited to a meal with them, or had been there to talk with them during the afternoon or evening, I always carried some gift home with me—a woodcut, a painting, a book, not to mention good things to eat—such as honey from 'Loverendale', or chocolate.

The first woodcut which Jacoba van Heemskerck gave me she inscribed: 'For F.W. Zeylmans, as a token of esteem, and in the hope that art and science will unite in him: the ideal of the future.'

During the next months and years they gave me various works by Rudolf Steiner to read: The Philosophy of Freedom, Theosophy, The Riddles of Philosophy, Occult Science, Christianity as Mystical fact, *and many others.*

The following summer (1917) Jan Buys and I were invited to Domburg for a few weeks. On this occasion Marie Tak van Poortvliet suggested something to me that radically altered my life. One afternoon, as we were walking through the garden she suddenly said:

'I wanted to ask you something, but there is a certain condition attached to it. I wanted to propose that you accept from me the sum required to release you from your contract to go to the Dutch East Indies. The condition, though, is that you must never return the money.'

I asked for a few days to think about it, talked it through with my parents, and then accepted this generous gift. It was the first such gift in my life, but I would receive many more, and all of them were more or less directly connected with my anthroposophical path.

Before the third meeting, this time with Rudolf Steiner himself, could take place, certain other things had to occur. I read the books with interest which the two ladies gave me. But I cannot say that I was very gripped by them, or that they strongly persuaded me. It was more that in reading a book such as Theosophy *I had the feeling: 'Yes, that's probably true, it seems likely; there's not really much to object to here.' In those days I held the view that there were a number of significant individualities who appeared in the course of the centuries. Buddha and other great figures belonged to these; and now Rudolf Steiner too most likely. I considered that they all had aspects of 'eternal truth' to reveal. But it did not occur to me that I might have something particular to do with any of these figures.*

Willem Zeylmans later described this stage of his friendship with the two ladies as an 'inner struggle for the truth of anthroposophy'.

Shortly after his first meeting with Jacoba van Heemskerck, he wrote an essay: 'Spirituality in modern painting—Jacoba van Heemskerck' (1917). In it he speaks of human sensibility, examines the nature of 'emotion and rapture in the soul' and discusses the conflict between science and intuition, also characterizing impressionism and the *Sturm* movement. The essay then goes on to examine Jacoba's work, especially that of her cubist period. He develops a kind of psychology of colours in response to her paintings: 'Every colour has a spiritual meaning.'

In later years Zeylmans repeatedly suggested that someone should write a biography of this painter. The Dutch artist Paul Citroen enthusiastically took up the idea in 1960, borrowed Zeylmans' unpublished article, and with its help wrote a poetic description of Jacoba van Heemskerck, of which the following is a brief summary.

Jacoba van Heemskerck was a small, slight, woman full of energy and independence. She was the first to fight alongside Mondrian on behalf of the new art, brave, uncompromising and very dependable. And yet her name has fallen into complete oblivion. Between 1907 and 1912 she began to exhibit in Amsterdam. Subsequently, Herwardt Walden, founder and leader of the *Sturm* group in Berlin, promoted her, publishing her prints and woodcuts, and after her death bringing out an illustrated volume devoted to her work. Her friend Marie Tak van Poortvliet had colour reproductions of her paintings printed.

Her extensive drawings are absolutely unique. Her paintings have a strongly architectonic structure—the tensions in them do not overpower their equilibrium and solidity, their glassy transparency and strongly rhythmical sweep; colours in her paintings are very intensely experienced.

Blazing, burning restlessness in red . . .
sharp radiating yellow . . .
still, cool, clear blue . . .
black—in all its severity,
white—highest and purest beam.

Black and white,
power and higher power,
solemnity and play,
simplicity and abundance.

Striving, clashing forces,
flowing together and against each other,
flaming passion and still, thoughtful reverence
are embraced in
harmonious unity,
great and dramatic,
victorious.

Like every true artist she seeks to free being from appearance, tries to break through into the unity underlying all existence.

Towards the end of her life Jacoba van Heemskerck gained some larger commissions for stained glass windows. In 1923 she died in Domburg at the age of 47.

The poet and critic Theodor Däubler calls her 'one of the leading personalities of modern art', but because she was not involved in the *de Stijl* movement, and had a particular interest in German art, she was, he says, ignored. She is not mentioned either in the *Encyclopaedia of Modern Art* (1955), or in the *Encyclopaedia of Abstract Painting* (1957).

*

In 1917 and 1918, during his medical studies, Zeylmans often stayed with the two friends Tak and van Heemskerck on Walcheren. They discussed questions of modern painting, above all the way that colours were now being used without direct relation to objects. How do colours affect the human soul? They did colour experiments with school children; and Zeylmans researched into such things as the effects of different colour impressions on pulse-rate.

The war ended, and German summer guests came to Walcheren, among them Professor Spalteholz and his wife, acquaintances of Jacoba van Heemskerck. The professor was the author of a well-known anatomical atlas, and suggested that Professor Wundt's laboratory in Leipzig offered the best conditions for undertaking colour experiments. Thus it was that in June 1920 Willem Zeylmans went to Leipzig. On the way he visited Herwarth Walden, the active force behind the *Sturm* movement in Berlin, Jacoba van Heemskerck's great patron, who showed him his collection of modern art.

From July onwards, Zeylmans worked in Leipzig in Professor Flechsig's psychiatric clinic. In the afternoons he did experiments in the Wundt laboratories.

These experiments related to the effect of colours on the human psyche. In a darkened room he exposed a number of people to different colours. Along the lines of Wilhelm Stern's 'tapping method' the subjects were asked to tap out a free but regular rhythm on an electrical apparatus, and this 'psychological tempo' was, together with the regular tempo of a clock, recorded mechanically on roll-paper. Over a certain period, ten subjects were exposed to seven colours of the spectrum plus crimson, and 6 intermediary colours, fourteen colours altogether therefore. Every subject repeated each experiment five times, giving an eventual statistical material of 700 experiments.

In his dissertation Zeylmans gave a summary of the psychological attributes of each subject, their character, level of education etc.

Each could tap any rhythm he liked, as long as it was regular... When we eventually came to compile the results of the test in graph form, it turned out that the colours at the warm end of the spectrum—yellow, orange—had caused a quickening tempo, while the colours at the cool end—blue and violet—had clearly induced a slowing down of the rhythm. Between yellow and orange fell the fastest tapping, and between blue and violet the slowest, while precisely between these, at green, the graph curve passed through zero. On the other side of the spectrum, too, at crimson, there was a similar point of balance. After each test the subjects were asked to give their impression of the particular colour they had just seen. While some gave only a brief reply and others a torrent of words, these personal impressions, too, showed a clear agreement in type of response.

While Zeylmans carried out these experiments each afternoon for six months, he also made an intensive study of Goethe's colour theory, recommended to him by his friends Tak and Heemskerck. In a long letter to them he describes how, for him,

Newton's theory may not be perfect, or explain everything . . . but I believe that it contains a useful core of truth. In my view Goethe's colour theory does not have such a core, yet it can have a very fruitful influence on one's thinking about this subject, through the many important observations and remarks he makes . . . so that my reading was not wasted. (27 July 1920)

★

Marie Tak had asked me to pass on her greetings to the leader of the anthroposophical group in Leipzig, which I did. When I told this lady that I had come to Leipzig to do colour experiments, she asked me if I would like to attend Willy Stoker's course on colour theory. He was a young Swiss anthroposophist studying in Leipzig. I went to his course, but found all that he said fundamentally flawed, and I'm afraid I made the lecturer's life so difficult that one day, in despair, he told me that if I carried on I would ruin his whole course.

*He was right. So I went to the university library and asked for Goethe's scientific writings, and began to read Rudolf Steiner's introduction; and suddenly, lo and behold, a whole bundle of light flashed down from the heavens and struck through me, as I read Rudolf Steiner's sentence: 'Our image of the visible world is the sum of perceptions metamorphosing independently of underlying matter.'**

This sentence gripped me so deeply that, on my daily walk from Brockhausstrasse through the park, I continually had it ringing in my ears as I observed the colours of nature. A whole world opened and showed me colour as a living being.

From the autumn onwards I had many valuable conversations with Willy Stoker. And when I heard that Rudolf Steiner had given a medical course in March—I had had no idea that such a thing took place—and that Professor Römer, professor in dentistry at Leipzig, would be studying this as yet unpublished cycle together with other members of the Anthroposophical Society, I went to Frau Wolfram, the group leader, and told her I would like to join the Society.

---

* 'The Archetypal Phenomenon', from the Introduction to the third volume of Goethe's scientific writings on colour theory, 1890.

'Why?' she asked.

'Because I would like to take part in this study.'

'That is out of the question. What do you know about it?'

'Very little, but that's why I wish to study it.'

The group leader wanted to think about this, since I was, as she said, a decent sort of person. I should come back next week. But when I returned as agreed, she had her dressmaker with her, and opened the door only a fraction.

'Who's there?' she asked

'Zeylmans.'

'What do you want?'

'I'd like to become a member.'

'I have nothing against it,' she replied; and so I joined the Society through a door-crack!

The six months in Leipzig were in some ways very valuable for Zeylmans. When he had time between his studies he could always go to the house of Professor Spalteholz in the Mozartstrasse, where there were music evenings attended by various members of St Thomas' choir school. His friendship with Günther Ramin dates from that time; he was organist for the choir school until his death in 1956.

In December 1920 Zeylmans travels to Dornach.

My relationship to anthroposophy had meanwhile developed to a point where I strongly wished to meet Rudolf Steiner. This became the deciding factor. It happened as follows. On the evening of 17 December I was sitting in the joinery workshop with my fiancée, who was studying eurythmy in Dornach. We were full of joy at seeing one another again, and were waiting for Rudolf Steiner's lecture. It was bitterly cold outside: Dornach lay deep in snow. All of a sudden the blue curtain beside the stage rose, and Rudolf Steiner, whom I knew from pictures, went to the lectern. At this moment I had a clear experience of recognition. This was so strong that a whole series of images surfaced in me at the same time, vaguely recalling former situations—as though I recognized him as my teacher through the millennia. It was the most powerful experience I have had in my whole life. For a long time I sat there, lost in thought, and only later noticed that the lecture had begun: the first of three lectures which were later published as 'The Bridge Between Universal Spirituality and the Physical Constitution of Man', and which he himself later referred to when some young doctors asked what he would recommend as preparatory study.

As I re-awoke from the condition I just described, and saw Rudolf Steiner standing at the lectern, I had the strange sense that I was seeing a human being for the first time! It is not easy to put this impression into words. I had met many well-

Willem Zeylmans, aged about 26

known, even famous people, professors and important artists, had always moved in circles where there was a lot going on—I had by no means led a philistine existence. But now I saw quite clearly: that is how man is meant to be! I began to ask myself: 'What does this mean—I've seen lots of people before?' First of all I had to say that it was the whole way he stood there, like a tree that grows quite freely between heaven and earth. This was not only connected with his straight, upright figure, but above all with the way he held his head—he seemed to float there between heaven and earth.

The second thing that moved me deeply was his voice: this beautiful, mighty voice. I experienced words being born and continuing to exist long after his mouth had spoken them. And the third thing was the ideas expressed. 'I can't understand everything,' I had to admit to myself, 'but these ideas are not just for my understanding, they have a quite other meaning as well.' In professors' lectures it was always a matter of whether one understood everything. Here, whether I 'understood' or not was not the important thing. Nowadays I could speak of the 'seed-force' in ideas, but did not do so then. All that I knew was that something else was occurring and affecting me.

When the lecture ended my fiancée said she would now introduce me to Rudolf Steiner, for he liked meeting young people. I hadn't thought of doing so, but if that was the custom, why not go along with it? I went to the front of the hall with her and was introduced. Then he said:

'I have been waiting a long time for you to come.' I thought he meant that I had already been a long time in Dornach.

'But Herr Doctor,' I said, 'I only arrived late this afternoon.' At this he smiled happily and said:

'That is not at all what I meant.'

Since I had been introduced I thought I would take the opportunity of putting some questions to him that my colour experiments in Leipzig had thrown up, and I asked if I might speak with him some time.

'Please come to my studio at 3 o'clock tomorrow,' he said.

The next day I arrived punctually in the studio vestibule, where a woman was carving a wooden statue. She asked me, in a rather unfriendly way, what I wanted.

'I have an appointment with Dr Steiner.'

'Dr Steiner is not seeing anyone today.'

Ingeborg Droogleever, aged about 20

'But he told me to come.'

'No, he is not seeing anyone today.'

That was a bit too much for me. 'Please,' I said, 'be so kind as to tell him I am here.' Before I was met by any further refusal, the door opened and a lady appeared, a Dutch woman, who said:

'Do come in, Herr Doctor is waiting for you.'

So in I went. Dr Steiner sat by a glowing stove, and there was an empty chair equally close to it. Fortunately I also love heat, and felt very comfortable there.

My question concerned the following: during my experiments in Leipzig I had found out that the so-called active or warm colours evoke a will response in people, while the passive or cold colours induce a slowing and calming of mental and emotional response. When I questioned the subjects about what they had experienced, this was confirmed by the fact that they described active colours in terms relating to the sphere of will or passion, and the blue-violet area of the spectrum in more thoughtful, tranquil or mystical terms. Green lay in the centre of this range, and gave rise to more neutral qualities, nuances purely of like or dislike. In response to crimson, that lay in the middle of the opposite side of the spectrum, also at a zero-point, there was a kind of intensification and synthesis in which all the qualities from left and right merged. Green was a zero-point because all the feeling responses were there in equilibrium; and crimson was, because it represented a balance between the greatest will activity and the highest intensification of thoughtful and reflective qualities. I had found all this out in my experiments, but some of it was still unclear. In particular I still had a number of questions relating to crimson.

'Did you really discover all this?' asked Dr Steiner smiling.

'Yes, Herr Doctor, this all came from my experiments.'

'Then you were lucky. You shouldn't really have found all this from the way you were experimenting. You see'—and here he took pad and pencil—'the spectrum of seven colours is only a part of the whole, is only what is visible in the sun spectrum. To understand the whole spectrum one must draw a circle; and then you have here, on one side, the seven sun spectrum colours, and on the other the five purple colours. And really you should have included these twelve colours in your experiments.' And then he continued: 'One sees these seven colours because the astral body swims in colour, as it were. But crimson is so delicate that it hardly ever appears in nature—and that is where the ego lives in the etheric. Crimson is actually the colour of the etheric realm.

He explained all this very calmly, tore off the sheet and laid it on my knees. It was a very quickly drawn circle, around which he had noted the seven colours on one side and the purple colours on the other. I sat there entranced and found it unbelievable that anyone could talk about colours like that. In one stroke he had answered all the questions that I could not even put, but had carried around with me

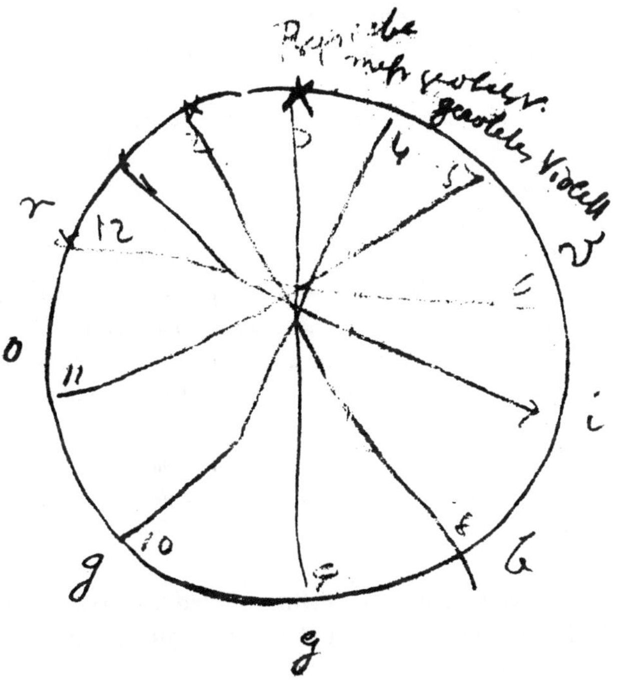

throughout the last six months. Quite suddenly Dr Steiner said: 'You are a doctor aren't you? Doctors nowadays are unaware of the law of reversal, how things turn inside out.' He made the gesture of turning a glove inside out as one takes it off, so that what had previously been outside is now inside, and what was previously directed to a central inner point is now directed outwards to the cosmos. 'Only when one understands this can one understand the relationship of human organs to the cosmos. One should examine this particularly in relation to the spinal cord and brain . . . Goethe had a sense of this, but he did not fully understand it.' He gave a few further examples of organ metamorphosis, then I stood up to depart; and only then noticed that I had sat the whole time with my back to the Christ statue. In terms of my whole previous artistic outlook I did not find it beautiful, but it still affected me, and he saw what I was feeling. 'Yes,' he said, 'that is the Christ, as my spiritual vision perceived Him in Palestine. But it is very difficult to bring everything out, express everything that belongs to it.' He pointed to Christ's robe. 'If it were properly depicted, it should express nothing but streaming love.'

He picked up a chisel and mallet that lay there. 'You see, I had to find my own technique . . . one must always take care that the left hand makes circular movements, while the right hand holds the hammer.'

He worked at it a little as I stood there speechless, and then I took my leave. It was only later that I understood that he was trying to show me certain laws of the etheric realm, movements that, as a doctor, one should come to know.

During this conversation I had, to my astonishment, experienced the greatest inner freedom I had ever felt in the presence of another human being. Given that one knew one was coming to Rudolf Steiner, the great initiate, who could look right through you, before whom one was wholly transparent, I might well have expected to feel highly self-conscious. To my astonishment the opposite was true: I felt freer than ever, taken up into another world in which only the important things matter; in which what one otherwise usually considers important falls away. That gave me a wonderful sense of joy and freedom. This feeling of freedom was helped by the fact that we sat next to one another, not opposite. He looked ahead of him almost the whole time, only turning suddenly, at decisive moments—so that one met the whole sun-force of his gaze. There were moments when, without being impolite, he nevertheless did not listen to what I wanted to say, but was clearly hearkening to something else in my soul.

Rudolf Steiner's sketch, which Zeylmans refers to, consists of a circle around which the colours are noted in letters and numbers (see illustration):

There are no colours next to 1 and 2.
3: illegible (probably 'peach-blossom')
4: 'more reddish' (?)
5: ' reddish violet'
6: 'v' (violet)
7: 'i' (indigo)
8: 'b' (blue)
9: 'g' (green)
10: 'g' (yellow = 'gelb' in German)
11: 'o' (orange)
12: 'r' (red)

Like the spokes of a wheel, Rudolf Steiner connected opposite colours in the circle with diametric lines.

We know that Steiner had given various suggestions for the colours of classroom walls, and other schoolrooms, in the recently founded Free Waldorf School. One can see that the walls start off red in the first class, and then pass through orange, yellow, light green, blue, indigo, violet, and end with light purple in the twelfth class. Thus the question of colours was one to which Dr Steiner had given practical consideration at the time.

Zeylmans was able to stay in Dornach for a week. His fiancée Ingeborg had already heard a number of lectures by Steiner and had in the meantime also become a member of the Anthroposophical Society. She completed her eurythmy training with Annemarie Donath, and had an intense exchange of ideas with her aunt Jeanne Bruinier, who had been working at the Goetheanum since 1914. At this time Willem and Ingeborg also saw performances of two Christmas plays, each briefly introduced by Rudolf Steiner.

On 23 December they travelled to Basle and there attended Rudolf Steiner's lecture on spiritual rebirth, as embodied in ancient times by the poor shepherds and wise men of the Christmas story; and heard how this principal of spiritual rebirth should be grasped by people of our own time:

> My dear friends, we must become devout as the shepherds were in their hearts when they saw the manifestations of nature. In the same way they developed spiritual sight in their inner world, so must we develop spiritual sight through nature...then, when we experience devotion in our outer perception of nature, loving openness of our inner being to the world, we will find our way to the Christmas Mystery, as did the shepherds through inward devotion. We need a new path. Change your way of seeing! Look in a new way at the unfolding of the world, for Europe is hell-bent on its own cultural ruin!

Before we continue describing the further course of Zeylmans' life, let us ask what Rudolf Steiner was tackling in the three 'Bridge' lectures* which Zeylmans heard him give. It won't, unfortunately, be possible to do this in every instance, although the 175 or so lectures which Zeylmans heard Rudolf Steiner give in the following years certainly composed an integral part of his life's spiritual substance.

But it would be good to look briefly at the theme of these 'Bridge' lectures because they are so decisively connected with his life. Rudolf Steiner's introductory remarks, 'I would today like to slip in a theme which may seem to you to be somewhat peripheral . . .' leads one to suspect that this short cycle was perhaps intended by him as a kind of 'special gift'. And reading the three lectures, of which there are transcripts, one can be astonished at the speaker's powerfully enthusiastic tone. One of the lectures is about 'enthusiasm', in particular the effect that enthusiasm for a great spiritual ideal has on a person's physical constitution.

---

* Published as: *The Bridge Between Universal Spirituality and the Physical Constitution of Man*, New York 1979.

Altogether, as the title makes clear, Rudolf Steiner here deals with the effect of cosmic or world spirit on man's physical nature. Among other things we find descriptions of how the elements are connected with the soul and our bodily organism. The four so-called 'ethers' are described and their connection with earthly man, especially during sleep. He says, for instance: 'By leaving our body behind in sleep, we allow the *world spirit* to enter into our warmth organism, and the *world soul* into our air organism.' Later Rudolf Steiner returns to this and shows how, when we are gripped by a high ideal, a 'light source' arises in our organism:

> . . . so that moral ideals, which have a stimulating effect on the warmth organism, thus create light sources in the air organism. These light sources, however, do not shine visibly in our outer perception, our outer awareness, but they appear in the human astral body (the soul) . . .
>
> Such moral ideals have a life-enhancing effect (in contrast to theoretical ideas which are deadening . . . like corpses of the universe within us . . .). And they derive from a sphere which basically does not belong to the earth, but to the spiritual sun being.

This spirit being, he says, is the source of all morality, of all 'moral intuitions'; and these moral intuitions: 'shine out from the human being, from what can live in the human being as moral enthusiasm.'

> Yes, my dear friends, if a sad epoch were to come over the earth, in which millions upon millions of people were to fade into unspirituality, then even if only a dozen people remained with radiant moral and spiritual enthusiasm, *still* the earth would shine with sun-like spirituality.

When Willem Zeylmans left Dornach with his fiancée on 24 December 1920 to go back to Holland, among the many thoughts preoccupying him may have been the words which Rudolf Steiner expressed with such vehemence:

> Europe is hell-bent on its own cultural ruin . . . Change your way of seeing! . . . If only a dozen people remained with radiant moral and spiritual enthusiasm, *still* the earth would shine with sun-like spirituality!

V. RUDOLF STEINER IN HOLLAND

The events of the next three years, from 1921 to 1923, had a very decisive effect on Willem Zeylmans' life. At the age of twenty-seven, on his return from Leipzig and Dornach, he took up his first position as a doctor in Maasoord, the Rotterdam city mental asylum. A few months later he was promoted to section doctor for four women's wards. He also prepared his 'habilitation' or doctoral thesis at the University of Amsterdam, on his colour experiments.

Since Willem Zeylmans later linked his life so closely to the anthroposophical movement in Holland, in this chapter we will examine the history of anthroposophy's development there, to give the reader an idea of where things had got to when Zeylmans first came into contact with it in 1921.

The Dutch had already had a strong interest in spiritual movements in previous centuries. The country had often been a place of refuge for people who fled from their own lands to escape persecution because of their religion or outlook. Strange sects and religious splinter-groups could often find asylum in Holland, so it is not surprising that in this small nation—with its innate tolerance, its many global trade links and its enormous Indonesian colonies—a lively interest was shown in the Theosophical Society founded by Helena P.Blavatsky in New York in 1875. In the first years of the twentieth century one finds, among the 700 or so Dutch members of that society, many well-known names from middle-class and aristocratic circles, as well as officials and colonists in what was then the Dutch East Indies. The latter had a close connection with the motherland, and in those years particular interest was growing in Indonesia for the 'hidden (or occult) sciences'.

The European branch of the Theosophical Society had, since 1904, held its annual congress in a different country each year, choosing Amsterdam as its first conference host—which was a great honour for the Theosophical Society there, and no doubt gave it a great boost. Annie Besant, who later became president of the now blossoming movement, arrived there in person and appeared in the Concertgebouw with the various general secretaries of European countries. As an eye-witness related: 'These gentlemen all looked very grand and ancient, some even had long white beards.'

The young Dutch woman Elisabeth Vreede, of whom we will speak further in this book, and whose mother later did a great deal of very useful work in spreading anthroposophy, had attended the theosophical congress in London the year before (1903). Her account of seeing Rudolf Steiner there for the first time may convey something of the impression which his appearance made a year later on some of those present in Amsterdam:

> A meeting was about to begin when a man entered the room: dark, slim, upright, gaunt, in a long, almost priest-like coat—a countenance full of inner fire, full of intense concentration and mastered will—this is how his image rises in my memory. I was so impressed that I turned to my neighbour and asked: 'Who is that coming in?'
>
> I was soon to learn the identity of this impressive individual. In the course of the gathering, Colonel Olcott, president and founder of the Theosophical Society, introduced him to the assembly as the general secretary of the German section that had been founded shortly before. Dr Steiner went up on to the stage and spoke a few words of greeting in German. The words too engraved themselves deeply into my memory. Dr Steiner spoke in those early years with an extraordinary vehemence, with a force of temperament that far exceeded even the fiery power one could later experience from him. It was as though he wished to convey to the world in every sentence he spoke the whole strength and significance of his mission—from the black hair flying around his fine head to the extraordinarily vivacious gestures of his arms and hands. The enormously powerful accentuation of his speech seemed to make him the actual embodiment of what he had to say.

Another Dutch theosophist recalls the year 1904 as follows:

> At the end of the table of executive council members there sat, very unassuming, a young man with raven-black hair who, when it was his turn to speak, conveyed greetings from the German members in a booming voice. Some of us were very struck by his voice. What can it have been that gave us such confidence, at that time already, in this powerful personality whose name we hardly knew? In the afternoon he gave a lecture on mathematics and occultism. One of us went up to him afterwards to thank him, and said: 'You seem to see what you say.' 'Do you think so?' he asked.

The lecture which Rudolf Steiner gave in Amsterdam at the time was later published several times. There are author's notes of this important lecture, in which he shows that in the same way that a mathematician finds solutions to mathematical problems through his own creative efforts, so the occultist can, in the way the new science of the spirit teaches, make exact observations in the supersensible world, and pursue his researches with mathematical precision through body-free thinking.

A few German theosophists had also come to the Amsterdam congress. One of them later recalled:

> We had the good fortune to stay in the same hotel as Dr Steiner and Fräulein von Sivers (American Hotel, Amsteldijk). We had many personal conversations, at table and on the way to the congress, which were highly stimulating. We also visited the Rembrandt museum with Dr Steiner. In the evenings, in the hotel's drawing room, Dr Steiner generously answered many of our questions. His answers sometimes inspired you for decades. One remark which Dr Steiner made about the fourth dimension has remained engraved in my memory. Someone else had put the question. He replied. I heard the answer. It struck home like lightning, and occupied my thoughts in waking and in sleep, woke me in the night, would not leave me in peace. I made short notes during the night; thought followed thought, living, growing, lightning-like, constantly surprising me.

And Fräulein von Sivers, later Frau Steiner, wrote to her French friend Edouard Schuré:

> The Amsterdam congress was certainly a success. Very good, very large, and very impressive. But these congresses are more outward achievements, while the inner law, of unity, is gravely contravened. When one runs from one lecture to another, it is like passing quickly from one picture to the next in an exhibition—you only get a sense of discomfort. Only Mme Besant is really enfolded in a unifying force. Herr Steiner has the same force, but people have not yet given him the chance to express it here. But Mme Besant has acknowledged him, and his lecture on mathematics and occultism was the only one she honoured with her presence. I myself could not attend it, since I had to take on the role of 'chairman' in another room. The Christian note was struck in this lecture, which is what should now come into its own. At all events, the congress in Holland expressed an elemental force.

> Divisive currents are already making themselves felt, but the strength is there. It is up to us to purify it and lead it in the right direction.

In the meantime the theosophical movement grew in Holland. In 1907 there were already 1000 members, meeting in roughly twenty associations (or 'lodges' at they were called at the time) in different towns. The prejudices against Steiner's ideas, which were 'quite different' from those the theosophists had advanced up until then, changed after his appearance at the Munich congress. One of the Dutch participants reported on it on his return, and one can see from his account how ambivalent was the response:

> The German section bears the very strong stamp of its general secretary Dr Rudolf Steiner. This is probably very much in line with the whole nature of the German people, who place less importance on individual freedom than we Dutch, and who are seen in their best light when under the strong leadership of *one* person. And the fact that in this instance the leadership *is* strong was the inescapable impression of those who attended the Munich congress. According to the German members with whom we spoke, Dr Steiner was the leading light and force behind the whole congress; and we heard brilliant talks by him, which were very clear. It is true they lasted far too long, but this made the great strength issuing from him seem all the more impressive, given the tiredness that such a sequence of lectures inevitably induces. According to Mrs Besant he was by far the best speaker present; and while she radiated great spirituality, Dr Steiner doubtless represented the force of reason. His first address dealt with 'Rosicrucian initiation'; and so as to create a whole experience, the hall was draped in red from ceiling to floor and decorated with rosicrucian symbols. Even our entry tickets and programmes were fire-red, and decorated with a black cross and roses. We naturally regard this as a misconception. The Theosophical Society tries to advance the study of *all* religions, philosophies and mystical societies; and a congress of all the sections is surely misguided in accentuating only *one* aspect in this way. One can also wonder whether it was very considerate towards other sections to focus everything on this one lecture by the German general secretary, when the Germans were acting as host. The red colour was extremely tiring on the eyes (only German eyes seemed to cope well with it, even to enjoy it—are their eyes different from ours? Or do they simply accept everything more than we do?), and the first impression this aroused, of dread and distaste, inevitably reminded one of scaffold and inquisition.

> Everything was blood-red. The delegates' table was covered in a red cloth, on which, as on the lectern cloth, the signs of the zodiac in gold paper still further intensified the strange impression . . .

Shocked, but also impressed, the Dutch members returned home, and when they travelled to Cologne at the end of 1907 to hear Rudolf Steiner's Christmas lectures, all was hung in red again!

In 1908 the Dutch Theosophical Society invited Rudolf Steiner to a first lecture tour in Holland. He initially wanted to give an internal course for members only, at only one location; but he was asked to speak at various other places as well. Thus he arrived in March and within a week gave fourteen lectures in six different towns.

The press reacted positively. Sometimes the halls were full, as in Hilversum where '150 people followed his fiery words with intense concentration'. But besides these public lectures he also spoke in the various 'lodges' about the foundations of spiritual science. Rudolf Steiner himself later said:

> But what was never forgotten at the very beginning of our activity in the Dutch section of the Theosophical Society were the lectures I gave—not dogmatically repeating, as others did, what was written in stone in the dogmas of the Theosophical Society, but speaking directly, from life: this was never forgotten. And those who perhaps still remember that time need only think back to the Munich congress of 1907, when we still lay in the cradle of the Theosophical Society, and recall how the Dutch theosophists were quite furious, were beside themselves about the way this foreign body, as they felt it, had elbowed its way in. They did not sense that something alive and contemporary was standing up against something merely traditional, but experienced it only as a foreign body...Every step for anthroposophy had to be battled for against the traditions of the Theosophical Society. Initially one could only present things to the members of the Theosophical Society. Every step was a struggle . . . It was usual in the Theosophical Society to describe how man passed through what was called kamaloka after death. And so I came to give lectures for the Dutch sections in various towns, about life between death and a new birth; and there, for the first time, right at the beginning of my activity, drew attention to the fact that it is nonsense simply to imagine that we pass through kamaloka as if a piece simply attached itself to a larger whole. I showed that we have to imagine time moving in reverse, and that life in kamaloka is a life in reverse, stage by stage, except that it proceeds three

> times faster than life normally does on earth, or than life spent on earth does. In outer life, of course, no one has an idea that this reversal is a reality, a reality in the spiritual realm, for time is simply conceived as a straight line that passes from beginning to end, and people nowadays have no idea of any reversal of time.

Among the Dutch audience there was an individual who was later of enormous significance for the spread of anthroposophy in Holland: the former commander of the Dutch East Indies Colonial Army, Andries Terwiel, who, returning prematurely to Holland, devoted himself entirely to theosophy. He was highly educated and an excellent translator, and had won the respect of his fellow theosophists by translating into Dutch Blavatsky's very extensive and difficult work *The Secret Doctrine.*

After Rudolf Steiner had left Holland again, this excellent man translated Steiner's book *Theosophy* into Dutch. He had often gone to lectures in Germany, and had gained deep insight into the science of the spirit as taught by Rudolf Steiner. Terwiel knew that very diverse, sometimes disdainful judgements were made about Rudolf Steiner in theosophical circles, and, on his own initiative, added to the Dutch edition of *Theosophy* a biography of Steiner which Edouard Schuré had written. This was a significant deed, for lies about Steiner's life were circulating at the time. Schuré's text was based on authenticated facts, and so Dutch theosophists were now able to learn more, and also intimate, details about Rudolf Steiner' spiritual path. In the foreword Terwiel gave advance notice, in 1908 already, of a forthcoming Dutch translation of Rudolf Steiner's *Occult Science*, which was published in Amsterdam in September 1910 under the title *Het Okkultisme in grote trekken* ('Broad outlines of occultism'), almost simultaneously with the first German edition. At short intervals, Terwiel published further translations of Steiner's writings. After Terwiel became 'lodge leader' in Zwolle, it was decided in November 1911 to 'change the name of our theosophical lodge to the "Christian Rosenkreutz branch": it will in future follow the western theosophical manner of working, though representatives of the eastern method will be free to express their views in speech and writing.' Shortly after this, in March 1912, Terwiel died at the age of barely forty.

The 'divisive currents' which Marie von Sivers described in her letter to Schuré in 1904, at the time of the Amsterdam congress, came increasingly to the fore, and did so with 'elemental force'.

Before Rudolf Steiner visited Holland again in March 1913, he had split from the Theosophical Society. After extremely unpleasant battles he had been expelled from the Theosophical Society together with 3000 of his followers. He now appeared, therefore, in the context of the newly-founded 'Anthroposophical Society' and the lecture cycle he held was the first longer one given on this new footing.

Things had changed in Holland too: a large number of members had left the Theosophical Society there in 1912 and 1913, though only about a hundred of them had affiliated with Steiner's new society. The association which invited him to The Hague was therefore a very small one.

He could now carry out what he had really intended in 1908: to give a longer course for members only, in one location. This course has become widely known as the 'Sheath' course. It consists of ten lectures entitled 'What is the effect of occult development on the human being's sheaths and higher self?'

These 'sheaths' are the bodies of which we are composed: physical, etheric and astral body; and the higher self is our ego, the core of our being.

Anthroposophists came from all directions, from far-away countries too, to attend this course—among them the 72-year-old Frenchman Edouard Schuré. At the end of the course Rudolf Steiner fêted this venerable old man in special terms, as 'an individual here among us, united with us, who has become so precious to us and will remain so: our dear, highly respected Edouard Schuré, who through his enormously valuable writings has done so much for modern western esotericism. The treasure of his presence that this individual has given us during this lecture cycle of the Anthroposophical Society is a gift that we cannot value highly enough.'

The special mood in which Rudolf Steiner gave this lecture course is powerfully clear from his words of greeting. After describing the conflict with the Theosophical Society, he says:

> ...Alongside all the bitterness and pain, I myself feel what has happened as a great liberation too, as a liberation from years of narrow-mindedness in the Theosophical Society, that weighed on us from that Munich congress onwards where we tried to get away from one-sided, national-type prejudice and, on a really broad, contemporary foundation, bring a new, as yet delicate and undeveloped mood into the Theosophical Society. Much that it was impossible to realize in the Theosophical Society because of its prejudices, because of its narrow traditions, will be realized in the Anthroposophical Society; and those who wish to will be able to see that we must aim for the same breadth

> of views that modern life requires, in order for the spiritual wisdom and spiritual impulses of will that are really flowing down to us in our time from worlds of spirit to be able to be put to good account by that part of humanity that has understanding for it. That is why this first cycle I was able to give here for you, my dear friends, which is the first lecture cycle of the newly-founded Anthroposophical Society, seems to be an occasion worthy of particular celebration . . .

This groundbreaking course, lasting ten days, began on Maundy Thursday. In that year there was a remarkable constellation in the heavens, one which occurs only rarely throughout the centuries: the beginning of spring (21 March) fell on a Friday, and the Easter full moon was on the very next day, so that Easter Sunday was on 23 March 1913, one of the earliest Easter days possible. Rudolf Steiner gave an Easter address about this configuration, interpreting what he called this special 'script of the heavens'. In these three consecutive days, he said (the beginning of spring, Good Friday, the Easter full moon on Saturday, and Easter Sunday), three pictures were expressed:

> . . . when they are so close to one another, then to the continuing cosmic *sun forces*, which, in their infinite goodness wish to give the earth ever new life, and the severe *moon spirit* which, because of the being of Lucifer and his forces, must withdraw forces from the merely outward, natural sun, this third, *Easter day* can be added by the human soul in a moral and spiritual sense, like an answer to the great cosmic question . . . When Christ died on the cross at Golgotha and the spirit of Christ united with the earth, that cosmic event occurred in earthly life through which a counter-force was created to all that the moon takes away from the sun . . .

One can understand that when Rudolf Steiner began building the first Goetheanum shortly afterwards in Switzerland, many Dutch anthroposophists moved to Dornach to be near their teacher, and to help work on the great building. There were only a few people left in Holland to work on behalf of the new science of the spirit. In 1913 a hundred people had chosen to follow Steiner. But the few often studied and taught with all their energy and strength. Then came the First World War, and the battling nations drew up their war-fronts between neutral Holland and Switzerland. It is true that people still managed, with great difficulty, to travel between the two, but Rudolf Steiner was unable to come to Holland again until 1921.

★

The lecture tour which Rudolf Steiner undertook in Holland in 1921 was his first trip abroad since the world war. In Holland, in the meantime, efforts had been made to establish a 'movement for the threefold social organism'. Marie Tak van Poortvliet had translated Steiner's *Towards Social Renewal* (Kernpunkte der sozialen Frage).The book was published by the De Haan company in 1919 and contained, as appendix, a list of Dutch people who recommended these ideas to the public. Rudolf Steiner's 'Appeal to the German People and the Civilized World'* had also been translated into Dutch and circulated in Holland. Steiner visited from 19 February to 3 March, and gave 15 lectures in seven towns; and the eurythmists who had come with Marie Steiner gave four performances. The Dutch people who had organized the trip were surprised by the large numbers attending the lectures—over a thousand came to the very first lecture in Amsterdam, and everywhere else there were full halls as well. In Delft six hundred students from the technical college came to Rudolf Steiner's lecture on the economic realm in threefold social life. 'With great warmth,' it was reported, 'they listened and then discussed things with him afterwards.'

On 1 March he addressed the philosophical society of Amsterdam University on the subject of philosophy and anthroposophy. An eyewitness later related what a strange sight it had been when over sixty professors in their black robes entered the assembly hall and listened, very critically and with little understanding, to what Rudolf Steiner had to say. In the subsequent discussion they advised him to go away and study *Kant,* to which he replied:

> Today, at the age of more than sixty, it makes a strange impression on me to be told to ponder Kant's teachings. As a fifteen-year-old schoolboy, because the history teacher bored me, I pasted Kant's recently published *Critique of Pure Reason* into my history book, so that I could read Kant while the teacher gave his history lessons. Since then I have studied Kant, and the advice many of you have given me has thus already been taken.

He had passed the age of sixty a few days before, on 27 February, in The Hague. This was a Sunday and he had given a lecture for anthroposophists in the morning. In the afternoon was a eurythmy performance in the

* Included in *Towards Social Renewal*, London 1999.

Koninklijke Schouwburg, and in the evening he gave a public lecture on questions of education. Those present had been very struck when he presented his idea here of a 'World School Association'. He himself composed the draft for an appeal aimed at enlisting support for such an association, leaving it to others to write the body of the Appeal text based on one-word headings he gave ('*Central aspects—lectures—Goetheanum*'). Steiner's draft runs as follows:

> Those who wish to examine things without prejudice can recognize that our social and economic plight does not result chiefly from economic factors but is the expression of a spiritual crisis, which we can trace ultimately to the nature of our school and education system. The present generation has passed through this system. Those who take the tasks of our time to heart must involve themselves in a thorough restructuring of this education system.
>
> *Central aspects—lectures—Goetheanum*
>
> One can be assured that everyone who really familiarizes himself with these ideas of a free life of the spirit will acknowledge the necessity of doing something of this nature. If, on an *international basis*, people of *all* professions, from *all* walks of life and *all* classes work together to form a *World School Association*, then something will be able to arise out of this mood, out of public opinion, which corresponds to the contemporary needs of civilization. And it is only out of such a mood and public opinion that dead and stultifying cultural institutions can be developed into something *living*.*

From these words of Rudolf Steiner one can see that the 'World School Association' was intended to be a really global society. He thought it should have up to a million members, and that the 'free Waldorf schools' could be financed, independent of government influence, from each member contributing a small sum per year. He was sure that such an initiative issuing from Holland could succeed.

This lecture was greeted by great applause, and at the end a young man rose and urged those present to found such a World School Association. This was Pieter de Haan, who had had a conversation with Willem Zeylmans five years before, after the latter sent his fairy-tales to the family publishing company. In the subsequent period efforts were made to found a World School Association from Holland, but this did not take off.

* This appeal was drafted after the lecture, at the request of Pieter de Haan. Frau Dr M.P. van Deventer made an exact copy of it, the text of which is here reproduced.

Rudolf Steiner's visit to Holland led to people making greater efforts on behalf of anthroposophy. During his visit Steiner had also spoken in eastern Holland, in the industrial region of Hengelo, and had a meeting with Dutch industrialists (the local mayor was said to be an anthroposophist) as well as visiting an infants' school there.

The fact that anthroposophy now aimed to become effective in practical areas of life meant that all sorts of people started to get interested who had not felt drawn to it before. As has already been hinted, Steiner was also subjected to public attack in Holland. He himself said:

> The more our movement demonstrates its inner necessity, the greater will be the opposition. As this opposition gathers momentum, it will become nastier and more underhand. In Amsterdam, on 28 February, for instance, as I was entering the concert hall, there was a man standing there handing out pamphlets which contained the same sorts of things, though in a very smutty and offensive manner, as the pamphlets put about by the priest Kully and others.

That man was Dr de Jong, whom Zeylmans would encounter a year later. The opposition to Steiner gave many Dutch people something of a shock.

Willem Zeylmans only heard some of the lectures which Rudolf Steiner gave at that time. As a newly qualified doctor he could only have a very few days off, and he was due to go to Dornach in April again to attend a medical course there. He also had to work his way into his new profession. From a purely practical point of view it was impossible to return to his lodgings late in the evening since the mental asylum lies on the 'Polder', a sort of island, beside the river Meuse, and he always had to be ferried over in a rowing boat by one of the hospital employees.

It was at this period, too, that Zeylmans wrote a long newspaper article about the Gheel mental asylum in Flanders, from which we quote the following excerpt. The description also gives a good idea of his work in 'Maasoord':

Anyone with a vivid imagination might be tempted to picture this place as a small town through whose streets pass the strangest figures: mad people behaving in the oddest ways, and strangely attired monomaniacs alongside senile people and idiots with dreadfully distorted features. Someone who thinks this would be disappointed by his visit here, for one can hardly imagine a more peaceful country scene. It is very quiet, and at first glance one finds it hard to tell whether the few people one sees walking about are patients or ordinary inhabitants. You only gradually gain a proper impression of the very great number of patients (2,300) who live here and in the neighbouring villages. You start to notice older men and women murmuring softly to themselves, and greeting everyone who passes in an exaggeratedly friendly manner; or you encounter figures who creep past very shyly, with the immovable features and fixed, clouded look of senility. On footpaths outside the villages, too, you meet them, with a cow, or leaning on a gate, dreaming in the sunshine. And as you approach they quickly turn their heads away, and only gaze inquisitively after you once you have passed.

An excerpt from a letter of 8 February 1921 gives an impression of his working environment. He writes to his parents:

The theme 'anthroposophy' surfaced again today, through the singer Antoinette van Dijk, who sang in our hospital yesterday. She is an effervescent, amusing and cheeky Jewish lady, and we had a great deal of fun. This morning we doctors paid her a visit. She immediately said: 'How clean you all look, with your white coats! It is so rare to see a really clean man in white!' Then she related how she had observed us all yesterday evening during the concert. 'Each of you belong to four different types,' she said, and then characterized each of us very humorously and accurately.

'You are the Seeker!' she said to me, 'you're always seeking for something . . . just like my Jeanne (the pianist who accompanied her); she's always doing something new . . . at the moment she's involved in a social reform plan. What's it called Jeanne?'

'O never mind,' said Jeanne, rather embarrassed.

'Come on child, it's something very learned, so learned I can't even say the name!'

'It's what the anthroposophists are doing,' said Jeanne finally. She was very pleased to hear that I also knew about it.

'You see,' said Antoinette, 'I knew at once when I saw the doctor here—now you've found one another, that's nice isn't it?'

And now my colleagues suddenly want to know all about it too. O. and D. are very interested. And H. comes into the doctors' room and says: 'Antolo . . . Antro . . . Oh blast, what's it called again?

★

When I arrived in Dornach again at Easter 1921, the Goetheanum surrounded in blossoms and flowers revealed to me more clearly than three months ago how its structure relates so closely to the laws at work in the plant kingdom, to life itself. To me it felt like a living being, to which I was linked from then on, and I tried to understand how such a large building could appear so organic and alive. When I first saw it in deep snow (December 1920), I only felt that something special was at work here, but could not grasp what it was; now it became a real experience: I became aware of the metamorphosis of its forms, and understood why pillars stood there—which no longer have much of a role in modern architecture. I experienced them as the ego-quality within this form metamorphosis. The coloured light of the engraved glass windows was such a wonderful accompaniment to nature in spring.

If, on entering the Goetheanum, one gave oneself up wholly to the experience rather than making aesthetic judgements as one normally does in other buildings, and waited to see how this living being responded, one could come to a new kind of experience of space. Whereas architectural spaces usually have a certain enclosed quality, the opposite was the case here. The soul was not held back by the walls, was not pulled up short by the walls as it were, but one had the feeling that the forms here made visible were leading one further into the spiritual world. The walls' forms were alive and took up the soul's forces into itself so that these could expand and unite with the cosmos.

Such living forms could arise because they were derived from etheric laws, which are active in the plant kingdom. Thus the forms became organs through which the spirit could directly speak.

The nature of Rudolf Steiner's speaking voice was also very striking in the great hall of the Goetheanum. It was the first time that I heard him speak here, for at Christmas he had addressed us in the lecture room of the joinery workshop, that wooden building which had served in the construction of the Goetheanum. Here it was as if his voice really came into its own for the first time, fully unfolded. His words stayed in the space and continued to exist. In one of the lectures he described—as he had done already in the second medical course that was taking place here at the same time; but now he was speaking before a general audience—how natural science must be developed further into a science of the spirit, and that one should not work magically.

And suddenly he called out: 'Oh, but one could do so!'—and stood there like a magician with outstretched arms. It was a deeply moving moment, for one had a spontaneous experience of the strict integrity which he had imposed upon himself.

This second doctors' course was, like the first, developed wholly from questions people had. It took place in the 'glass house', and there were some who came a few minutes late to the first lecture. 'Punctuality is an adornment which, coming late, you come without', remarked Rudolf Steiner; and from then on no one came late. What he presented was a hard struggle for us. We did not know if we would be able to combine it with ways of thinking learned during eight years of medical study. Yet every sentence he spoke gave one the sense of a door opening into an unknown world.*

---

*The German is a rhymed folk-saying based on a play of words hard to translate: 'Pünktlickeit ist eine Zier, doch später kommt man ohne ihr.'

At the time I also had several discussions with Dr Steiner about particular patients, some from my own practice. My questions were based on the hope that one might now be able to heal all sick people. But Rudolf Steiner gave me certain examples to show how there might be reasons of destiny which meant that nothing could be done. Nevertheless, he gave me advice about remedies that could be administered in each case. This surprised me greatly, for in traditional medicine people do not usually continue trying to heal when a patient is beyond help.

During that week Zeylmans was in Dornach with his future bride, who had had a long illness, and wished to complete her eurythmy studies by the summer. He was able to attend a eurythmy performance in which Ingeborg Droogleever Fortuyn probably took part—of the Ariel scene from Goethe's Faust.

After she had finished her eurythmy training, and the two had attended the 'Stuttgart Congress', the wedding was celebrated. And while the couple travelled to Nuremberg and Munich on their honeymoon, Helene Droogleever Fortuyn, the mother, went to Dornach to invite Rudolf Steiner to The Hague to give a 'university course'.

This course in The Hague was a big undertaking for all those involved. The anthroposophical movement in Holland was still very small: there were exactly 150 members, among whom were venerable older members from the pioneer phase, as well as new, often very young members—a 'new generation', upon whom Rudolf Steiner pinned great hope for the practical realization of his great ideals.

At this time the 'university courses' were held at various locations (Dornach, Berlin, Dortmund, Stuttgart). Such a course was organized as a kind of 'conference of and for university students and graduates': a large number of anthroposophical scholars would arrive with Rudolf Steiner, and speak on all sorts of subjects. He himself gave the main lectures in the evenings.

The Dutch had asked Rudolf Steiner for such a 'UC', but it had been very difficult to get him to make a decision because his programme was already so heavy, and those who accompanied him (mostly Waldorf teachers in Stuttgart who clearly could not stop teaching in order to go to Holland) were also over-burdened. Helene Fortuyn now put all her energy into getting this off the ground, having got an agreement in principal from Rudolf Steiner at Dornach in the autumn of 1921. In her house in Scheveningen she set up a kind of headquarters for the forthcoming UC, which could only take place during the 1922 Easter holi-

Willem Zeylmans and Ingeborg Droogleever Fortuyn, 1920

days. For six months she spent all her time preparing for this conference, travelled to Stuttgart repeatedly to get the ten Waldorf teachers concerned to agree, and corresponded and telephoned uninterruptedly until Rudolf Steiner said to Lili Vreede in Stuttgart (having just come back from Oslo, where he had received a letter from Helene Fortuyn): 'Yes, this UC course in Holland will have to take place. I've had another letter from this lady DF (Rudolf Steiner 'made desperate attempts to say her name')—and it will have to take place between 7 and 12 April—she is so full of enthusiasm for it.'

And so a course for university students did take place from 7 to 12 April in The Hague. Ernst Uehli, one of the speakers, gave his impressions of it in the periodical *Dreigliederung des sozialen Organismus* (Threefold social organism):

> . . . In The Hague no one is in a hurry, not even the numerous bicyclists. Almost everyone cycles, children as well as grown-ups, but they cycle peacefully. I did not see a single cyclist who recalled the race-track. Apart from the centre of town where things are a little more busy, the place seems to breath gently. It reminds one of a quiet, dignified matron with silver-streaked hair. The streets with houses seem to stretch away into infinity, recalling the long lines of dunes that stretch inland. The houses seem as clean and fine-sieved as the sand—all built the same, colourful, with very large shining windows. The streets lie there still and wide-eyed. You walk along them and you feel that they do not lead into life but away from it. You do not dare walk quickly, and involuntarily slow every choleric movement you might otherwise make. Something that hangs over the town like a gentle, imponderable atmosphere enters your legs and slows your step. One adapts to the town's temperament, but one experiences something like a slight melancholy, that is held back, that cannot express itself. I felt something similar when walking through the ruins of Syracuse, Girgenti or the Via Appia, but much more intense and formed. One senses how, as one passes on, one becomes more lost in thought and quieter. The past rises in one's soul. Then one comes to a poster hoarding and straight away sees the great yellow poster announcing our university course. And then one gets legs again, and from there finds one's way out of the past into the future.

The course took place in the assembly hall of a secondary school, and 200 students from all of Holland's universities attended one or more of the events. 60 to 70 of them took part in the whole course, about a third of

PROGRAMMA.

VRIJDAG, 7 April.

10 u. Dr. phil. W. J. STEIN: „Goethes Bedeutung für die Gesamt-Menschheitsentwickelung."
11 u. Dr. jur. et phil. KARL HEYER: „Welt- und Rechtsgeschichte vom Standpunkt der Anthroposophie."
2 u. Besprekingen over geschiedenis, geleid door Dr. Heyer, Dr. Stein en Dr. Hahn.
4 u. Dr. phil. HERBERT HAHN: „Bewusstseinswandel im Spiegel der Sprachgeschichte."
8 u. Dr. RUDOLF STEINER: „Die Stellung der Anthroposophie zum Geistesleben der Gegenwart im Allgemeinen."

ZATERDAG, 8 April.

10 u. Dr. phil. HERMANN VON BARAVALLE: „Mathematik im Lichte des Goetheanismus."
11 u. E. VREEDE, phil. docta.: „Nieuwe inzichten in de Sterrekunde."
2 u. Besprekingen over wis- en natuurkunde, met een inleidende voordracht over het wezen der warmte, geleid door Dr. von Baravalle en E. Vreede, phil. docta.
4 u. ERNST UEHLI: „Dreigliederung des sozialen Organismus."
8 u. Dr. RUDOLF STEINER: „Die Stellung der Anthroposophie in den Wissenschaften."

ZONDAG, 9 April.

10 u. ERNST UEHLI: „Die aegyptische Sphinx als phylogenetisches Entwickelungsproblem",
11 u. Dr. phil. W. J. STEIN of Dr. med. E. KOLISKO: Over een nader te bepalen algemeen onderwerp.
2 u. Dr. phil. CAROLINE VON HEYDEBRAND: „Die Paedagogik der freien Waldorfschule." Aansluitende besprekingen over paedagogie, geleid door de leeraren der „Waldorfschule" te Stuttgart.
8 u. Dr. RUDOLF STEINER: „Die bildende Kunst".

MAANDAG, 10 April.

10 u. Dr. med. EUGEN KOLISKO: „Zur vergleichenden Biologie des Menschen und der Tiere."
11 u. Dr. med. FRIEDRICH HUSEMANN: „Neue Wege zu einer rationellen Therapie."
2 u. Besprekingen over biologie en medische wetenschappen, geleid door Dr. Husemann en Dr. Kolisko.
4 u. Dr. phil. HERMANN VON BARAVALLE: „Bewusstseinsentwickelung in der Geschichte der Naturwissenschaft."
8 u. Dr. RUDOLF STEINER: „Die anthroposophische Forschungsmethode."

DINSDAG, 11 April.

10 u. Dr. CARL UNGER: „Die sozialen Aufgaben der Technik und des Technikers."
11 u. Ing. WILHELM PELIKAN: „Neue Wege in der Chemie."
2 u. Besprekingen over scheikunde, geleid door Dr. Kolisko en Ing. W. Pelikan.
8 u. Dr. RUDOLF STEINER: „Wichtige anthroposophische Resultate."

WOENSDAG, 12 April.

10 u. Dr. CARL UNGER: „Zur philosophischen Begründung der Anthroposophie."
11 u. Dr. phil. W. J. STEIN: „Der Zusammenhang der Erkenntnistheorie mit der organischen Wissenschaft."
2 u. Dr. med. EUGEN KOLISKO: „Freies Geistesleben durch Anthroposophie." Aansluitende besprekingen over „freies Hochschulwesen".
8 u. Dr. RUDOLF STEINER: „Anthroposophie und Agnostizismus".

N. B. De wetenschappelijke besprekingen zijn alleen toegankelijk voor studenten en gestudeerden; de algemeene op Vrijdag- en Zondagmiddag voor allen.

DRINGEND VERZOEK OM IN DE GANGEN VAN HET GEBOUW NIET TE SPREKEN, TEN EINDE STORING DER LESSEN TE VOORKOMEN

total participants. An additional, large public attended Dr Steiner's evening lectures. In all there were 23 lectures, followed by a variety of specialist discussions. All the lectures were in German, apart from one by Elisabeth Vreede (see programme), as were the subsequent discussions. Uehli continues:

> From the very beginning the whole course had a friendly, intimate character. This was in part due to the small size of the event compared to similar ones in Berlin, Stuttgart or Dornach. But it was also because of the attitude of the students attending. Some may have noticed the possibly rather cool reserve of the students to begin with. This was due, however, to objectivity towards the new way of thinking and view of the world which they had come here to learn about. The Dutch student is not blinded by nationalism as is so frequent in Germany, nor so dulled by sport that he does not feel the need to develop spiritually. In Holland there is, it is true, a deeply-rooted lack of interest in spiritual impulses; but those who are interested, and who demonstrated this by attending the course, showed that they were capable of warm enthu-

> siasm as well as objectivity, for after a few days their initially reserved attitude melted into heartfelt warmth which kept increasing up to the end of the course.

On 9 April, Palm Sunday, discussion on Waldorf education took place in the afternoon, and in the evening Rudolf Steiner gave a lecture on the arts which was generally felt to be the most beautiful of lectures, and stimulated great enthusiasm.

Helene Fortuyn wrote to her sister Sanne in Dornach:

> After the most beautiful of lectures on the sculptural arts, I returned home late in the evening. Hardly had we arrived when the telephone rings from the hotel: Can I come back immediately, for the Waldorf teachers are having a meeting and need me? Get on my bike straight away—leaving my guests to look after themselves and find their own way to bed—and there I find the whole crowd: Lili Vreede, Maddy van Deventer, Henk and Erna van Deventer, de Haan and his wife, Knobel, Max Stibbe, Cornelis Los, Daan van Bemmelen, Willem Zeylmans, Walter Stein, Dr Heyer, Herbert Hahn, Hermann von Baravalle, Ernst Uehli, Eugen Kolisko, Caroline v. Heydebrandt, Carl Unger, Friedrich Husemann and Pelikan.
>
> We had an intense discussion about the founding of a Dutch Waldorf school, and everyone was in favour. 'You don't need to worry about getting children and parents ' said Kolisko, 'Mrs Fortuyn will arrange that.' Herbert Hahn gave me various pieces of good advice, his lecturing index finger almost touching the tip of my nose ... what a delightful fellow he is! Do you know him? So lithe and light and funny and spontaneous! Just imagine: the whole 'Drei' around the table! And they *all* started to become friends, more or less ... we didn't finish until midnight.

Thus was born on Palm Sunday, 9 April 1922 in The Hague, the initiative for founding the first 'Vrije (free) School' in the Netherlands.

Willem Zeylmans, who had helped prepare the conference, found several chances of speaking with Rudolf Steiner, mainly about medical questions.

At the time Steiner wanted the doctors to bring out a medical 'Vademecum', a handbook with direct, practical application. He always established a balance between the deepest esoteric approach and the most direct, practical implementation. He demonstrated this, for instance, when he said to me that if Biodoron, Weleda's remedy for migraine, were well-marketed, the Goetheanum could be financed from the proceeds alone. In relation to the Vademecum one of us asked when was the latest it should be ready by, and he replied: 'The latest it should be ready? June 1921!' (It was already April 1922!) During this spring I had been discussing with my colleagues the possibility of opening a clinic. Now I asked Dr Steiner for his view, saying that I was really too young to do this, and knew too little about anthroposophy. He reassured me: 'The fact that you are too young doesn't matter at all, for each day you get a day older. And that you know little about anthroposophy doesn't matter either, for you will understand more as each day goes by.'

But then he grew very serious and told me to consult with Frau Dr Wegman: 'For she has the right courage for healing.'

During her preparations for the UC, Helene Fortuyn had learned how difficult it was to build bridges between the younger and older generations. On the day after the conference ended, she had a conversation with Dr Steiner about this; and on the afternoon of the same day, Maundy Thursday 13 April, he spoke to the assembled anthroposophists about this problem before giving his lecture 'The Teachings of the Risen One'. Then he drove off in the night to England, on the eve of Good Friday. On his way back two weeks later he had a ten-minute stop at Rotterdam, and Helene Fortuyn greeted him on the platform. She writes:

> Have just come back from Rotterdam, where I drove with de Haan to greet Dr Steiner, Frau Doctor, Fräulein Waller and Miss Maryon. They were on their way back from London, and only had a ten-minute stop. To see Dr Steiner getting out of the train and coming towards one in such a friendly way with his hand outstretched! Great heavens, as if one deserved it! 'Frau Doctor is in the compartment—perhaps you would like to quickly say hello?' he said very tactfully. In I went, and there she sat, so fresh, young and rosy-cheeked! If I had known earlier that the train was coming so soon I would have bought flowers for her. I've become firm friends with Frau Doctor. She was simply like an angel to me, so gentle and kind, I love her for ever! Just imagine, as the train left the station she waved to us. It was so strange to feel that there in the train was sitting the greatest figure of our age, the *very* greatest, the only really great one in fact, even counting all ministers of state, kings and scholars! What an unspeakable privilege to belong to this small flock, that is working and wearing itself out for the sake of the future! The fact of being so sure in what one does gives one such a wonderful peaceful sense of confidence. Easy it isn't—good heavens, no! But we don't

> even want it to be, we have no wish to swap places with anyone else, even if we were to go to the wall . . . we'd go gladly! To know that behind this wasteland, where all the poor devils of today spend their lives, there is a living world, and that most of us merely do not *see* it! How I have always longed for what is *alive*, always thought I could find tiny sparks of it here and there—and now suddenly I find myself in 'streams of light'.

As already mentioned, Rudolf Steiner's appearance in Holland met not only with interest, good will or indifference, but with the first opponents also. A combative academic, Dr H.K.E. de Jong, disseminated anti-anthroposophy pamphlets in 1921, which contained an insult he had heard in Germany: 'Rudolf Steiner—what a swindler.' In public talks, too, this Dr de Jong spoke against anthroposophy, intending, as he said, to 'challenge Steiner to a battle', an offer which, to de Jong's great surprise, Steiner did not take up!

When Rudolf Steiner came to Holland again a year later to hold the anthroposophy and science course in The Hague, Dr de Jong once more fiercely denounced him after his departure, among other things in a lecture given to the 'Dageraad' (Dawn) Free Thinkers Society. Many anthroposophists were present and afterwards discussed these issues with the speaker. Zeylmans offered the 'Free Thinkers' a counter-lecture, in which he wished to give an objective portrayal of anthroposophy. Thus he gave a talk in The Hague about the four kingdoms of nature, the human ego and the Christ Mystery—the fifth lecture he had given on anthroposophy.

De Jong was also invited to this, and followed Zeylmans' lecture with one of his own. He accused Steiner of dishonesty and reproached him with altering his opinions in the course of his life. He quoted from esoteric lectures and said: 'I have studied the ancient mysteries for a large part of my life—and everything Rudolf Steiner says about them is a pack of lies. And the higher worlds he speaks of—do they even exist? I do not know, nor do I know how anyone else can!'

Since Zeylmans had refused to respond to de Jong's attacks, the Free Thinkers had invited three more opponents to this event. The first insisted that anthroposophical meditation would induce hallucinations, and he could not understand how any normal human being could waste time with it. Another speaker said that Zeylmans had been mistaken in his lecture when he spoke of the history of Roman law, and that this had actually brought about a great historical transformation. The last speaker expressed astonishment that Steiner and the evening's main lecturer Zeylmans could admire the cosmos for its order and harmony—this was a very naïve view. He himself considered the cosmos to be truly chaotic—everything was all over the place, struggle and battle reigned, and the 'ego', he said, was thus continually falling out with itself. But this might be to do with his own mood, he admitted.

Zeylmans responded to the first speaker by saying that he understood very well what he meant, but asked him to imagine someone who did not know of the existence of the French language, and then suddenly saw someone else studying a French book, and called out: 'He must be mad!' It was just the same, said Zeylmans, with Rudolf Steiner's science of the spirit, whose origins can be found in recent thinkers like Goethe and Fichte.

He asked the second speaker to tell him more about the complete transformation which Roman law had brought about, saying he was particularly interested in this. And he agreed with the third speaker that reacting to the great, eternal laws of the cosmos in the way he did, certainly must have something to do with his own mood!

It is typical of Zeylmans that he sought for positive aspects of his three opponents. He referred to the last speaker as 'a very nice person'!

Thus raising the sword of the word he united himself increasingly with anthroposophy.

*

In 1922 Zeylmans was repeatedly asked to give lectures. And since he had taken part in Steiner's doctors' courses since 1921, he spoke to students about 'anthroposophy and medicine'. He also gave an address to doctors of the Netherlands Society for the Advancement of Medicine; and his audience, we are told, who expected to hear something quite different from what they had heard at their gatherings up until now, were wholly satisfied in this expectation: 'We were introduced to a world view so completely different from the scientific system upon which modern medicine depends (and thinks it can rely) that most of us did not succeed in thinking our way into an approach with such a radically different basis, which moves on paths that are foreign to us.' Zeylmans did not shy away from giving a multi-faceted account of the new anthroposophical approach to medicine and the image of man, as well as a detailed description of the connection between man as microcosm and the whole cosmos. One listener said: 'But the practical application of such a teaching, in which the planets and heavenly constellations rule over the organs of the human body and all its functions, would, in the place of the meagre thimbleful of knowledge we derive from experience, with which we have to be satisfied nowadays, perhaps put a pint-pot of fantasy and speculation into our hands.'

The way Dr van Andel describes the end of the evening is symptomatic of Zeylmans' gift for maintaining warm human relationships in such a situation: 'The manner in which our colleague Zeylmans has led us into this strange realm of thinking deserves high praise. He easily overcame the difficulty of holding the interest of an audience not necessarily sympathetic to the views he was defending, and of compelling rapt attention. We can be grateful to him for the lecture he delivered with clarity and conviction, in which the great outlines of the anthroposophical system became clearly apparent. The debate which followed reflected this impression, and was distinguished—despite the great differences of opinion expressed—by a tone of respect and politeness.'

★

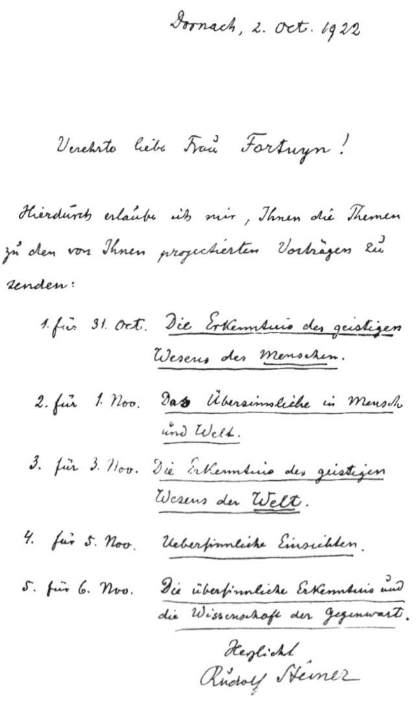

Dornach, 2. Oct. 1922

Verehrte liebe Frau Fortuyn!

Hierdurch erlaube ich mir, Ihnen die Themen zu den von Ihnen projectierten Vorträgen zu senden:

1. für 31. Oct. Die Erkenntnis des geistigen Wesens des Menschen.
2. für 1. Nov. Das Übersinnliche in Mensch und Welt.
3. für 3. Nov. Die Erkenntnis des geistigen Wesens der Welt.
4. für 5. Nov. Uebersinnliche Einsichten.
5. für 6. Nov. Die übersinnliche Erkenntnis und die Wissenschaft der Gegenwart.

Herzlichst
Rudolf Steiner

Letter from Rudolf Steiner to Helene Fortuyn

In November 1922 Rudolf Steiner gave some more lectures in Holland, which were rather poorly attended. In Rotterdam in particular, so few people came that we were quite depressed. But he himself viewed things differently, for in conversations with members he remarked: 'There was a very good audience in Rotterdam.' One had the impression that he saw certain souls who were valuable to him, and it was not so important to him whether there were larger or smaller numbers of people in the hall.

I was still a doctor in the mental hospital on an island in southern Holland, inwardly pleased and satisfied that I had found the Goethean-anthroposophical direction and Rudolf Steiner, whom I experienced as my teacher from the distant past. But now several older anthroposophists got together, who thought that the work was not going well, that a circle should form to take spiritual responsibility and put itself at Dr Steiner's disposal. I was urged to participate too, although I said that I knew little about the problems in the Society. But I welcomed the chance to meet with Rudolf Steiner. Each time I met him it was a joyful, festive experience, whether I was discussing a patient or something else, whether the conversation lasted half an hour or only two minutes—and this, I am certain, was how others also felt.

At one such meeting, something that one of the participants presented seemed not to please Rudolf Steiner in the least. He sat there listening calmly, jiggling his foot about a bit. I waited in tense expectation to see what was coming.

'You see, as long as our Society has a sectarian character, we won't get anywhere,' he said. A cannon ball could hardly have had a greater effect. He continued. Our Society as it now was, he said, could not yet be taken seriously by the rest of the world. And then he reported that a Catholic priest had recently asked to talk to him, and that he, Steiner, had at long last been able to speak with someone about important world affairs. The priest had also been pleased and invited him to visit, and he regretted that he had not had the time to take up this invitation. He would also have liked to invite this priest to Dornach, but had not done so because he did not know how the members there would behave. Finally he asked whether there was no one in Holland who could give public lectures about anthroposophy. There was embarrassed silence, for some had tried this without success—hardly any audience had turned up. I had made some beginner's efforts in this direction, only because members had asked me to. They thought that someone with a doctor's title would make more of an impression, and a few more people had appeared, though always under a hundred. One of those present now said that I had given some well-attended lectures; and it was a surprise both to me and the others when Dr Steiner responded:

'Well, then all you need to do is make Dr Zeylmans free for anthroposophy and offer him a generous salary.'

He turned to me: 'Would you like that Dr Zeylmans?'

Well, I did not think that my lectures were much good—I felt they were of little consequence, even rather incompetent, and that I had just cobbled together my small amount of knowledge with great toil and effort. But I said:

'Yes, Herr Doctor, if you think that I can do this, I will of course be glad to do it.'

He repeated that I must then at all events be free for anthroposophy. Then there was silence. People had expected something else of him. Only one of the members there, Pieter de Haan, pursued the matter, and I said to him, though rather ashamed, that I would try to move to The Hague, perhaps to found a clinic and live from my practice. Pieter de Haan's input at the time did in fact have a decisive effect.

On the day before his departure, Rudolf Steiner gave a lecture for the small anthroposophical circle in The Hague, on 'Hidden aspects of human existence and the Christ Impulse'. After this he gave a short address, which paints a deeply distressing picture of the despair he felt about the situation in the Anthroposophical Society and at the Goetheanum.

First he expressed his deep concern about the lack of money for completing alterations to the Goetheanum building:

> ... in only a few weeks' time we will have reached a point where we cannot get any further in Dornach... The building of the Goetheanum was begun with enthusiasm, but those same people who had such enthusiasm to begin with have now lost it. And now they have simply left it to me alone to find the way forwards... Why does one have to say that the Goetheanum may, in a few weeks, be unable to continue? You can have all sorts of things at the periphery, Waldorf schools etc., but of course nothing has strength when the centre is missing. And the right heart is missing from this centre.

And then he described how more and more institutions devoted to practical work had emerged from anthroposophy, and how these were developing at the periphery:

> But people ought to see that the need increasingly to deepen spiritual science has been accompanied by a less and less well-organized Society, a less and less enthusiastic will for making the Society itself into an instrument. And that is what I ask our friends for again and again, as a priority; for we now face the urgent need to make the Society an active being that works in the world.
>
> That, my dear friends, is what we need. It would of course be

> very desirable for the centre at Dornach not to collapse, but for friends to be found who can help . . . If the Dornach centre collapses, everything else will collapse as well. And I would simply like people to be aware of this, for they have largely lost sight of it. And this is, I have to say, an extremely heavy burden of worry for me, a deep, pressing concern.

Eight weeks later the Goetheanum went up in flames. Zeylmans was still working in the mental asylum at Maasoord, and was unable to go to Dornach. Although he got more 'study leave' than others, he had already had more than his quota.

With his young family he moved to The Hague the following year, where he started his own practice. A small clinic at Prinsevinken Park opened in the autumn. In September of the same year he was awarded his doctorate in Amsterdam. The Free Waldorf School in The Hague began during the same period.

Lively collaboration with Pieter de Haan, who had so enthusiastically taken up and supported Rudolf Steiner's suggestions, soon developed into a friendship that lasted for decades.

The idea for a clinic had arisen in August 1917, when Marie Tak van Poortvliet invited Willem Zeylmans to her summer residence on Walcheren island. As we have already seen, Marie Tak intended to win Zeylmans over to the anthroposophical cause. She went very decidedly to work, but not without a certain diplomacy. Zeylmans was still fully occupied with his medical studies, and she saw that she would still have a few years in which to pursue her goals.

At the time she offered to take over the financing of his studies so that he could free himself from his contract to be a doctor in the tropics, she also mentioned her sister, who had been severely mentally ill for a long time. Her case was hopeless, and that is why Marie Tak had the ideal not only of giving her sister a dignified future, but also of doing something positive for all mental patients. She spoke to Willem Zeylmans of her hope that he might later specialize as a psychiatric doctor. And in conversations with the two ladies (the painter Jacoba van Heemskerck was also present), plans for a future sanatorium were mentioned.

Zeylmans had a natural aptitude for psychiatry. Already as a student his fellow students sometimes consulted him about their emotional or mental problems; and in his letters to his parents one cannot help hearing a gentle, caring tone directed towards his mother, who sometimes suffered anxiety attacks, and was subject in later years to a certain degree of mental strain. It is therefore understandable that once Zeylmans had completed his practical doctors' exam in 1920, he set about seeking to qualify as a specialist. Marie Tak followed his progress from a distance. She urged him to study at university level, so that he would later have the right academic qualifications; and they repeatedly discussed the possibility of him opening a clinic of his own.

In the letters which his wife wrote home from their honeymoon trip there is also mention of his 'own sanatorium': 'But Willem does not want to settle in the country, since he would like to have his private practice in a large town, alongside his other work.'

The founding of the Dutch Anthroposophical Society was planned for November 1923, and all the other national Societies were to be similarly re-founded. Rudolf Steiner gave a cycle of evening lectures in The Hague: 'The supersensible being of man in the light of anthroposophy', as well as two public lectures in the newly founded clinic (I myself had now moved to The Hague). There were also a number of members' meetings, so the programme was huge. Both the little clinic and the small school had their own opening ceremonies.

I collected Dr Steiner and a few friends from the station. As the train slowly drew in, and I saw him sitting at the window, I got a severe shock from seeing him look so tired and pale—and at the same time perceived a quality in his features which went beyond temporal things. It was as if his countenance was carved from a rock-face, and this impression went right through me.

Then came normal things again. I helped him alight, greeted the friends who had accompanied him: Frau Dr Steiner, Mieta Waller, Frau Dr Wegman, Dr Wachsmuth. And as I went down the steps from the station with him, I asked whether he had had a good journey. In the middle of the flow of other travellers he stopped, turned to me and asked, astonished:

'What do you call a good journey?'

I suddenly realized what he meant. I had seen him arrive, our eyes had met, I saw who he was and he saw that I saw it—and now I asked if he had had a good journey. He meant: 'Wake up. Don't be a philistine!' We still stood there unmoving in the stream of passers-by.

'I only meant to ask whether there had been any outward inconvenience,' I said finally.

'I see, that is what you meant! Yes, in that case I did have a good journey.'

He visited the small school, which consisted of no more than a couple of rooms in a private house, and very few children in three classes. Yet he treated the founding ceremony with as much seriousness and care as if it had been a large school, observed the children, gave advice about each one of them, sometimes also medical advice. This medical advice in particular I, as school doctor, often found very surprising. For instance there was a thin little fellow with pale, greyish skin, a working class child.

'He is anxious right into his inner organs,' said Dr Steiner, 'he must practise a curative eurythmy "I", by leaping over a rod . . . and then of course Prunus spinosa . . .'

I had never heard of Prunus spinosa, for at the university I attended next to nothing was taught about plant-lore, and now I felt like a stupid ass—everything was new and surprising.

'Hypericum perforatum . . . you know that don't you? Its leaves are full of holes in which you can see drops of oil,' he said to me as I wrote all this down in a notebook.

So it went on for three mornings, with the two teachers van Bemmelen and Mrs Mulder, and the eurythmy teacher Miss Hoorweg.

The clinic was only a private house, where I worked together with a nurse. To begin with we only had a single patient, who actually regarded herself as a paying guest. And once more Rudolf Steiner behaved as though he were attending the opening of a large hospital. I brought together about thirty-five doctors and older students for the two medical lectures he gave. These were extraordinarily well received, although it was the first time that many people had heard anything about anthroposophy. After the second lecture an older doctor stood up to speak, saying that the whole thing had made a great impression on him. It was, he said, a unified system; and although there were still many gaps, he could see that these would be filled in the course of further lectures. 'My scientific approach is also a closed and complete system,' he added, 'which also has gaps that can be filled. Which should I decide to follow I wonder?'

The doctor who asked this sat right at the back. Dr Steiner walked slowly through both rooms until he came to his chair, then said:

'You are quite right. One cannot get further than that. But the heart decides.'

The next day this doctor phoned me and said that although he was not wholly convinced he would like to give anthroposophical medicine a fair chance, and asked me to treat his Angina pectoris.

After the evening lectures we—a group of friends—used to go with Rudolf Steiner to the Oude Doelen hotel. After he had eaten, we sat in the lounge around an open fire, and often stayed up talking until the early hours about new literary works, political events and other such things. Dr Steiner was usually cheerful, related anecdotes or answered questions. Mr van Leer, for instance, asked:

'A rabbi like Baalshem, who does so much, such amazing things—can one regard him as an initiate?'

'No, it's true such a person can really achieve a great deal, but he is not even a semi-initiate,' was the reply.

That year following the Goetheanum fire was marked by the re-founding of the Anthroposophical Society. Dr Steiner, who until then had expressly wished not to become a member himself, seeing his task only as that of teaching anthroposophy, expected enough strong impulses and efforts to emerge among members to give rise to new social forms. A first step in this direction was the founding of independent national Societies in different countries.

In Holland too we had many preparatory meetings for months on end, which gave me the chance of getting better acquainted with the Dutch Anthroposophical Society. I had been asked to lead it, since the view had circulated amongst some members that Dr Steiner wished me to become the Dutch General Secretary when the Society was re-founded. Later on, in the autumn, another view became current, namely that I had too little connection with the Society, and it would be better if I just gave lectures.

People tried to understand what Dr Steiner, who had only given general hints, was actually expecting. But not much progress was made in all the preparatory meetings, apart from the idea that an organism rather than an organization should arise. Various fairly profound ideas along Goethean lines were put forward in this connection, but basically no one knew what to do.

Now too, when Dr Steiner was in The Hague in November 1923, we had some meetings in his presence, where reports from various areas of work and study were presented. I also gave a report, which I thought I delivered very poorly, so that I felt it necessary to apologize to Dr Steiner. He laughed very cheerfully and said:

'That's nothing to worry about. You have to give a hundred lectures before you can count on one of them being any good.'

I found this very encouraging.

During discussions about the new founding of the Society, Dr Steiner mostly sat there in silent expectation. He wanted members themselves to find out what to do. While sitting there he examined, for instance, the mechanism on a writing slate belonging to a lady beside him, with which one could at one go erase what had been written. From my hand he took a tobacco pouch which I had taken out of my pocket by mistake, carefully examined the—at that time newly-invented—zip-fastener, and said to me:

'What a shame one of us didn't invent that!'

On the evening before the actual founding, Saturday 17 November, when we were sitting in the hotel lounge once more, Dr Steiner was so pale, grave and sad as he entered that none of us dared say anything. At last Frau Dr Wegman asked if something was wrong. Very sadly, and as though to himself he then spoke words which showed how difficult he found what he experienced as members' lack of understanding for actual spiritual necessities, despite their subjective good will:

Er lachte ganz heiter und sagte: „So etwas ist gar nicht schlimm, wenn man einmal hundert Vorträge gehalten hat, ist es auch möglich dass einmal ein guter dabei war". Dieses fand ich recht ermutigend.

Während der Besprechungen, studierte Dr. Steiner sorgfältig den Mechanismus der Schreibtafel einer Dame, die neben ihm sass — man konnte das Geschriebene mit einem Griff auslöschen — nun nahm er den Tabaksbeutel, den ich zufällig in der Hand hielt, ab und betrachtete eingehend die damals neue Erfindung des Reissverschlusses und meinte dann: „Wie Schade dass Unsereiner so etwas nicht erfunden hat!"

Nach den Abendvorträgen gingen wir, eine kleine Gruppe von Freunden mit Rudolf Steiner ins Hotel. Nachdem er etwas gegessen hatte sassen wir in der Halle um ein offenes Feuer und man redete oft bis tief in die Nacht, über literarische Neuerscheinungen, über politische Ereignisse und manches andere. Dr. Steiner war meist heiter, erzählte Anekdoten, wie er gerne bei solchen Gelegenheiten tat oder gab Antwort auf unsere Fragen. So z. B. wollte einer der Freunde wissen: „Ein Wunderrabbi, wie der Baalschem, kann doch ungeheuer viel. Muss man in ihm auch einen Eingeweihten sehen?". „Nein. Es ist schon wahr, so ein Mann kann wirklich sehr viel, aber er ist doch noch nicht einmal ein halb-Eingeweihter."

Am letzten Abend, dem 17 November, als wir wieder in der Halle sassen, kam Dr. Steiner blass und ernst und so traurig, dass keiner von uns wagte das Gespräch zu eröffnen. Schliesslich fragte Frau Dr. Wegman, ob etwas passiert sei? Ganz traurig und wie für sich sprach er dann Worte, die zeigten wie schwer es ihm zu schaffen machte, was er als Unverständnis der Mitglieder, bei allem subjektiv guten Willen, für die eigentlichen geistigen Notwendigkeiten erlebte.

'The members do not want . . . they are full of good intentions but . . . What should I do . . . ? Am I supposed to found a religious order?!'

We sat there devastated, sensing the deep pain that filled him and the heavy burden he had to carry. The conversation only gradually started again, and Dr Steiner explained more clearly why he was repeatedly disappointed in the Society, no matter where he went, and what it was he found lacking. He also said that he had made certain suggestions, and also hinted at the person he regarded as suitable to lead the work here. And now, instead of taking up these suggestions, people were coming along with other, quite inadequate proposals.

It was late at night—the next day, Sunday 18 November, was to be the day of the founding—before the discussion ended after much deliberation. I told Rudolf Steiner that I was prepared to accept the office of General Secretary of the Dutch Society, despite opposition from a number of older members.

The gathering next day was, quite unexpectedly, the happiest event imaginable. Now and then we made fools of ourselves, but Dr Steiner sat there quite confidently, and finally sketched out draft principles for the Dutch Society. We were to work through these and later bring them into harmony with the General Anthroposophical Society to be founded in Dornach at Christmas.

The founding gathering was not minuted, but Rudolf Steiner's remarks were taken down in short-hand. He wanted an Anthroposophical Society to form what would function in just as down-to-earth and objective a manner as an anthroposophical hospital, a Waldorf school, or Weleda. In such anthroposophical fields of endeavour, he said, a purely objective, matter-of-fact spirit held sway, whereas the *Society* (he repeatedly made a distinction between movement and Society) was quite 'sectarian'. But it would be catastrophic, he went on, if the *Society* failed to keep pace with further positive development in the practical fields of medicine, education, business and art etc.—in other words what he called the *movement,* for:

> Many who approach us will then sense there is something sectarian going on, something penetrated by all sorts of things like fanaticism, self-righteousness, abstract idealism, hazy mysticism etc., by all kinds of things which stink of sects and cults, which have a certain soul-spiritual stink about them. I only say this, naturally, because we need to call a spade a spade, not because I want to hurl accusations at people. I also only say it so as to put the other side of the picture, as it were, the sect-like side of the picture, for I want to stress that things in the Society should be how they are in these different fields of practical endeavour, which have achieved such positive results. A really down-to-earth, objective spirit should reign within the Society, and show itself as such before the world.

And he described how the Society should, for this reason, be completely renewed and re-founded as a structured and differentiated organism, an 'international anthroposophical Society', with a central executive committee and 'headquarters' in Dornach:

> But such an international Society can only be founded in Dornach at Christmas if the various different national Societies have been founded

> beforehand, and then send their delegates to Dornach. Then the international Society can form from the national Societies. That was why national Societies have been founded in various countries in my presence. In Sweden there has been one for a long time. In Norway one was founded during my stay there. The Swiss and English Anthroposophical Societies have been founded, and in Italy the attempt was made to do so. The German Anthroposophical Society has been founded, as has the one in France. [A national Society had also been founded in Austria.] Thus all these national Societies have been formed and founded, and while I am present here I ought also to be able to count on the founding of a Dutch Anthroposophical Society, which will then send its delegates to Dornach at Christmas to represent all the possible will impulses of the whole Society here. By such means an International Anthroposophical Society can come about, which will at last really start working.

After these words the attempt was made to formulate the 'statutes' of the new Dutch Society, and Rudolf Steiner once more pointed out that the Anthroposophical Society could be represented *objectively* before the world:

> Of course to do this it is necessary that those who lead the national Societies take pains to work as objectively as happens in individual fields of practical endeavour. One cannot say that those leading the work in these fields of endeavour do not get beyond their subjective views. They do, they enter into the objective reality of their work. That must also happen in the overall anthroposophical sphere of the Society.

And that, he said, should be clearly enshrined in the statutes:

> For the Anthroposophical Society it is a real question of survival to avoid the impression of anything sect-like . . .

In the statutes, he said, one should speak a 'worldly' language, give them a down-to-earth, worldly style, and he went on:

> I have thought carefully about these things . . . It is not right to say that things should first be sorted out in Dornach, and that there is no point in fixing anything before that happens. The individual national Societies should arrive in Dornach with their statutes already drawn up. The right thing is to draw up the statutes in their final form, down to the last dotted 'i'.

Rudolf Steiner also spoke about the new position of 'General Secretary':

> It seems to me that if I myself, for instance, was a Dutchman here among you, and someone asked me whether I was willing to be elected General Secretary of the Dutch Society, I would say: 'Well, first I must hear what this Society is going to be, what it will look like. Until I know that I cannot decide whether to accept this post or not...'
>
> The role of General Secretary of a national Society is an eminently important one; and even if this were not yet true, it would have to become so. The General Secretary has two responsibilities: 1. To represent the whole anthroposophical national Society to its own members; 2. To represent the national Society to the leadership of the International Anthroposophical Society in Dornach.
>
> To these two are added a third, something absolutely necessary if the Society is to continue to thrive: the General Secretaries of separate national Societies must become people who are known, whom one mentions in the same breath as the Society. A General Secretary therefore cannot be nominated for a short time only, but must serve for as long as possible. Now you have today elected Dr Zeylmans as General Secretary in a way that, it seems to me, should even be enshrined in the statutes.

Zeylmans later wrote:

Rudolf Steiner's presence brought great joy to people, of a kind that comes about when they feel themselves united and of one spirit. But his presence at the same time represented a continuous appeal to slumbering forces of consciousness. This phenomenon often meant that the meeting took a rather strange course. The unspoken call to awaken was so strong that those whose task it was to lead the meeting became extremely uncertain and unsure. An ordinary kind of chairmanship was wholly inadequate. A different, more spiritual kind was sought but not found. This repeatedly resulted in chaos, in which Rudolf Steiner then intervened with the greatest understanding and kindness. With a few words he pointed out the right way to proceed. The contrast was striking—and increasingly felt throughout the course of the day—between our helplessness and his cheerfulness and good mood. From later conversations it became apparent that this cheerful mood was due to his great trust in the good will which shone so strongly through the chaos.

After the executive committee members of the new Dutch Society had been elected, they all remained sitting where they had been. Those who were speaking merely stood up, and then sat down again. Neither Rudolf

Steiner nor anyone else had had any kind of official 'chair' or place. Rudolf Steiner was clearly not happy with this. He stood up, pointed to the small rostrum in the hall (on which were arranged a small table with a few chairs), and said he thought the General Secretary and the executive committee should sit there, and thus *show* themselves clearly to the meeting. Then he remained standing and began to clap. The meeting joyfully followed his example, and accompanied by this clapping the whole new executive committee ascended the rostrum.

In his last lecture Rudolf Steiner then said:

> Anthroposophy is after all connected with the actual progress of human civilization. But the misery we can nowadays see within this civilization should be a call to us to approach a supersensible vision of man and the world. Yet we can only do this when we remain fully aware of what is going on in the world. So, my dear friends, please regard today as the beginning of something more than just gathering in your anthroposophical branches and closing yourselves off from the world. Look out instead to what is going on in life. Please take seriously the word I have used so much today [in the founding meeting of the Dutch Anthroposophical Society], a word I have more or less 'done to death' by now, the word 'worldly'. Try to grow together with the world, and that will be the best and most important 'programme'. We can't enshrine that in statutes, but we can nurture it as a flame in our hearts. I cannot serve you best with programmes and points, but rather by directing you to the right feelings and attitudes that should accompany anthroposophical life. And if you warm to these right feelings and attitudes through what I say, then something of what I intended with my observations on supersensible man, and how one can comprehend him anthroposophically, has been fulfilled.

We had lunch with a larger group of members; and Dr Steiner related such merry anecdotes almost the whole time that Marie Steiner, almost choking with laughter, asked him to stop, for she couldn't take any more.

After lunch I went to him and he spoke with me about my role as General Secretary. 'Remember,' he said, 'that from now on you have complete esoteric and exoteric responsibility for all anthroposophical activity in Holland.'

He took both my hands and looked at me for a long time. That was the last thing which happened in 1923 before the Christmas Foundation Meeting.

VI. FROM THE CHRISTMAS FOUNDATION MEETING TO RUDOLF STEINER'S DEATH

When we came to Dornach at Christmas 1923 for the founding of the General Anthroposophical Society, it was clear to me from the moment that Rudolf Steiner performed the 'Foundation Stone' ceremony that we were witnessing a Mystery deed of significance for all humanity, the first Mystery rite to be performed in public. Although the eight hundred or so people present were members, they were people of such different kinds and at such different stages of development that one really could say that this deed took place in public. A few members felt, as I did, that this was at the same time a kind of personal moment of birth—and that from then on we were born as spiritual individuals.

It also gradually dawned on me to what extent this Foundation Stone ceremony was connected with the laying of the First Goetheanum's original foundation stone on 20 September 1913. On that previous occasion the foundation stone had been laid in the earth in the form of a double dodecahedron, upon which base the forms of the Goetheanum had arisen. Now, after the Goetheanum had been destroyed by fire, all its forms and powers and colours, all the condensed imagination it had embodied and made visible, returned in the words of the Foundation Stone ceremony at Christmas 1923, as inspiration from the world of spirit.

The second impression I had was connected with Rudolf Steiner's plans for a School of Spiritual Science with three classes. This too involved a manifest secret, for Rudolf Steiner wanted this School to be regarded as something that stood publicly in the world, which could be openly discussed, although one could only complete the School's classes by undergoing actual inner development. Here too, then, what was public went hand in hand with what was secret: a manifest secret in Goethe's sense.

A seed was planted for real, contemporary initiation, which each individual must first pass through alone, but in which it is essential for this individual, as he comes increasingly to know himself, to experience himself more and more as a part of all humanity. Thus is the human ego prepared for becoming the bearer of the ego of humanity. Man becomes humanity; the whole of humanity lives in the individual.

Zeylmans stayed in Dornach for almost three weeks (from 23 December to 9 January) and, besides the new Society's foundation meetings, also attended Rudolf Steiner's great lecture cycles, the doctors' lectures, eurythmy performances and Christmas plays. Rudolf Steiner gave more than 40 lectures during this period.

In his book *The Foundation Stone* of 1956, Zeylmans summed up his thoughts about this Christmas Foundation Meeting. The book contains very condensed summaries of hundreds of lectures which he himself had given on this theme. Those who wish to understand his life can find in that book the 'inner thread' of his highest ideals. And by studying his youthful writings one cannot help sensing that the experiences he went through as a child and young man, to which his early work bears testimony, were a kind of preparation for this 'Foundation moment'.

During these days I also had various conversations with Dr Steiner, which I would like to reproduce here as far as I am able. First I asked him about a member who had died, a painter, and the possibility of maintaining a connection with her.

'One can approach her,' he said, 'by recalling a particular moment that was significant, for instance when one stood in front of one of the pictures she was painting. One needs to imagine such a situation in full detail, and once it has become very alive and vivid, one should dampen down wakeful consciousness and continue the inner content of this image, then raise it up to her in the world of spirit. Then one should wait for a response in calm and quiet. Thus a conversation can come about.'

Another time I asked him about the work which I would now have to undertake in Holland. It was very difficult for me, I said, to continue my work as a doctor, to work on behalf of anthroposophical medicine, and now also to take on the large tasks involved in being General Secretary. Especially this last, working for the Society, I said, was very difficult for me, for I had less interest in this than in anthroposophy.

'That's your karma, and there's nothing to be done about it,' he said smiling. We talked further, and he said again:

'You see, the tasks on behalf of the Society are simply your karma.' And then he said it a third, final time, still smiling.

To my comment that I would find it hard to combine my work as doctor and General Secretary he replied:

'As a doctor you are especially fitted to be General Secretary, for the Society will increasingly need the therapeutic aspect.'

And in relation to anthroposophical work:

'Everything will develop, but first the School must be sorted out. And as far as Society questions are concerned, you can see it like this: the Society sets inner tasks; solutions appear in the soul's loneliness.'

During these days Zeylmans also asked Rudolf Steiner for advice on the themes he should deal with in his lectures. Steiner said: 'You should give lectures on health care and morality, diet and so forth. That is the finest thing you can do.'

During the Christmas Foundation Meeting Rudolf Steiner had discussed with Zeylmans how the Society's journal should be organized: each national Society should publish an additional 'insert' to the weekly magazine *Das Goetheanum*, written in the relevant language. 'The best thing,' said Rudolf Steiner, ' is for such news to arise as far as possible from the individual perspectives of each contributor. A person finds certain things going through his mind—and he writes them down. Absolutely no categories or headings. If it's all over the place, never mind. Four pages, just written however one feels like it.' And so this 'Holl. Bijblad van het Goetheanum' ('Dutch insert to *Das Goetheanum*) was produced every two weeks from January 1924 onwards, initially edited by Zeylmans and Stibbe, and containing a colourful collection of articles, news and reports.

As early as the second issue Zeylmans published an article on 'Science and Wisdom', in which he describes the threefold nature of man: *Science should become wisdom,* he exclaims, *and to achieve this, knowledge should be saturated in warmth of feeling and permeated by scintillating impulses of will . . .*

And a few months later he writes: *The mighty Foundation Meeting has taught us that anthroposophy is from now on something which must not exclude anyone. Now we know that anthroposophy must be proclaimed throughout the land, as a message of joy. And that is what we have tried to do!*

In Holland there now arose a flurry of public activity—courses and lectures throughout the country. Among other things, for instance, a course was held in Rotterdam on history and social economy, pedagogy, music and medicine.

. . . To recount something symptomatic, there was an old gentleman who said on the first day that a great deal of all we were saying was very fine, but he could not accept the 'spirit' we kept talking about, for there was no such thing. But he stayed for the second day and listened very attentively. After the concluding lecture he came up to us with pleasure on his face and said: 'Now I am convinced. There is a living spirit!'

It became clear to many of us that anthroposophy must be proclaimed rather than proven through a contemporary scientific approach. And those whose task it is to do this must struggle until the forces of their hearts completely conquer their intellectuality. One speaks *through the intellect, but only from the heart's forces can one* proclaim!

The youth conference on 29 June was a lovely event: a number of younger members gathered from The Hague, Amsterdam, Rotterdam, Utrecht and Bennekom, and there was a good feeling in evidence: the will to serve anthroposophy with heart and soul! One young member spoke movingly of the new human being that must arise through anthroposophy. It is through the warmth and strength radiating from individuals, from the loving way in which one approaches others, that people outside our movement must gradually recognize the being and working of anthroposophy! Through this love we must start another crusade!

Let us carry this crusading spirit into the whole Society, and from there out into the whole country.

★

I would also like to mention the meeting I had with Rudolf Steiner in Paris in May 1924, where he gave a wonderful lecture in the Salle Solferino, Boulevard St. Germain. Jules Sauerwein, the well-known editor of Matin, *translated for him, and old Edouard Schuré sat in the audience. In between the members' lectures and all the other claims on Rudolf Steiner's time, I was able to have a long conversation with him about the work in Holland, which greatly inspired me—a conversation that was at the same time profound and joyful. Then, one afternoon, as I was walking near Notre Dame, Rudolf Steiner and Frau Dr Wegman came towards me across the large square. They had obviously just been in the cathedral, and I went up to them.*

'Have you been in the Sainte Chapelle?' I asked, meaning the thirteenth-century chapel that had once been the scene of fiery dispute between professors of the Sorbonne, the Dominicans and those who were called Arabists.

'We want to get into the Sainte Chapelle, replied Dr Wegman, 'but how does one get there?'

Since I had just come out of it, I pointed to the gate, and the little tower one could see from where we stood—and that was all. Yet it seemed to me more than can be expressed.

★

During the Christmas Foundation Meeting I had already asked Dr Steiner whether he would be prepared to give a pedagogical course in Holland, and he immediately gave me dates for this.

'And what would you like me to do there?'

I presented him with my list of wishes: firstly a public course on education, secondly a few public lectures with a medical theme; and then three members' lectures also. Without pausing for thought he accepted the whole programme. Later two classes were added for School of Spiritual Science members, and an address for young people.

We had long pondered where this course should take place, had visited many locations to find something suitable, and finally had chosen Arnhem because there was a large conference building there, by the Rhine, which was available to rent. In the surrounding area there were also reminders of ancient Germanic culture, of historical traditions which one only seldom finds on Dutch soil. Thus we were sure we had found the right thing. But when Rudolf Steiner arrived and drove to his hotel, he looked around him a little and then said:

'Ah, this must be some kind of holiday place. It seems to be becoming the custom to combine anthroposophical study with a summer break.'

We all looked rather embarrassed.

Shortly before this I had had to make one of the hardest decisions of my life. Dr Steiner had telegraphed to say he would be arriving late, and would therefore be unable to deliver his first lecture; and when I collected him from the station at the appointed hour together with Pieter de Haan, Michael Chekhov and another Russian actor—it was 17 July 1924—I was frightened to see how exhausted and ill he looked. We went to the car, and before it drove off he said to me:

'Yes, I was unable to give my first lecture this morning. What do you think, Dr Zeylmans, should I catch up by giving it this afternoon instead?'

I had been compelled to give the opening lecture myself, because various important guests had arrived to hear it.

Dr Steiner knew of this. Marie Steiner declared that there was no question of still giving the lecture, for Herr Doctor was worn out from all the meetings in Stuttgart, and he must definitely rest this afternoon. This was completely understandable. But Dr Steiner still fixed his gaze on me and repeated that I must decide, for I was responsible for the conference.

'What do you think—should I give this lecture or not?'

Frau Steiner once more exclaimed, out of her deep concern, that it was impossible; and once more Dr Steiner stressed that I should decide for it was my responsibility. Everything in me was crying out: 'Rest, forget the whole conference!' But on the other hand I was thinking: 'Other laws are at work here.' Terribly tormented I said at last:

'Herr Doctor, I believe you should give the lecture.' And he replied calmly that that was fine, and he would give it.

(Zeylmans later added: *I only mention this incident because I know that many other friends in the anthroposophical movement have found themselves in more or less this same situation, in which Rudolf Steiner left decisions, even when they affected himself, to the complete freedom of another.)*

One could not help seeing how ill Rudolf Steiner was during the conference. When other people gave lectures—Dr Schubert, Dr von Baravalle, van Bemmelen, Stibbe and I on pedagogical themes—it was distressing to see how exhausted and absent he appeared. When I sat next to him I was also alarmed to see how emaciated he had become. But it always turned out that nothing had escaped him, despite all tiredness; and when he stood on the rostrum once more, he was as vivacious as ever, enthusiastic, full of life, so that one could hardly believe that this was the same person. It made a deep impression on us to hear him talking in the pedagogical lectures and also in the address to young people about Schiller and Schiller's death, about the enthusiasm which can consume one, about Schiller's heart, of which there was hardly any physical substance left by the end. We had the impression that what he was talking about we actually saw before us: the flame that consumes the body.

Pieter de Haan later recalled: 'I witnessed moments after the lectures when he collapsed completely.'

Marie Steiner described the pedagogical lectures as ones in which Rudolf Steiner 'spoke quite freely to his audience, taking account of their particular soul configuration, and speaking in a way as close as possible to the character of the people of that region: a distinctive, spontaneous, straight-talking quality'.

The well-regarded newspaper *Nieuwe Rotterdamse Courant* published translations each day of almost all of these lectures.

In his *Rudolf-Steiner-Studien* (Rudolf Steiner Studies) Emil Bock described Rudolf Steiner's karmic researches, which were later published in six volumes, and showed the particular importance of the three lectures given in Arnhem. In his view these are quite distinct from previous lectures on this theme. I would like to quote this description here, despite its length, for it illumines the special quality of the classes which Dutch anthroposophists, including Willem Zeylmans, experienced at the time. Emil Bock writes:

> Nowadays we have the third series of lectures on karma, 1–6 and 7–11, in one volume. One simply reads on from the sixth to the seventh lecture, noticing at most perhaps that these were separated by the space of a few weeks, in which Rudolf Steiner travelled to Holland and gave lectures in Arnhem. But if one becomes aware of the strikingly new element that suddenly appears, one can begin to understand everything in a new light. The members who were in Rudolf Steiner's proximity in Holland during this period say that he was often so close to the limits of his strength that they were deeply anxious and concerned about him. If one remembers this, one can realize that in the three Arnhem lectures he meets this problem head on, rather than avoiding the dangers which seem to threaten. From Arnhem onwards the karma lectures gain a new quality. From this moment on the theme of Michael enters the

karma lectures. Until then Michael had not been mentioned, but now this name enters like a stroke of lightning. First the two main karmic streams are summarized—but no longer so tentatively. One stream, which takes its character from the first centuries of Christianity, is that of the Platonists, while the other, which harks back to pre-Christian centuries, contains the more Aristotelian souls. The expression 'old' and 'young' souls is also used for these two groups. The old souls have been incarnated a larger number of times, the young ones not so many. Everything is given in an enormously intense and concentrated form, and it becomes clear that we are actually dealing with the stream of human souls who belong to Michael. A wholly new theme!...

And now a motif suddenly and surprisingly lights up, one that has not yet surfaced in previous karma lectures. When the Platonists from Chartres and the Aristotelians who wish to become Dominicans come together to hold discussions around 1200 AD—what do they discuss? They agree to cooperate in guiding mankind's destiny, leading to a culmination at the end of the twentieth century, when a decision must come. And Rudolf Steiner adds that this shows that a large number of those who genuinely approach anthroposophy will come to new incarnation on the earth before the end of the [twentieth] century, after only a short interval, so as to be present when the great spiritual confrontation of our time occurs.

Bock goes on to say that the cosmic intelligence mediated by Michael should be grasped nowadays by human beings on earth:

But it is not possible for this to happen without ahrimanic powers trying to wrest it from us. And so the present Michael age is imbued with Michael's struggle with ahrimanic forces, in which the archangel can only prevail through the human beings assigned to him.

Rudolf Steiner himself described his Arnhem lectures in the following way:

In the members' lectures I described the way in which observation of the supersensible element in human evolution leads to recognition of the tasks of the anthroposophical movement. I presented what one can call the 'Michaelic' guidance of mankind in its supersensible course from the seventh century BC to the time of Alexander, and then again in our present age. Such a description should give rise to the kind of spirited enthusiasm that must penetrate the Anthroposophical Society.

At that time we were together with him one evening in a smaller circle of friends. We were discussing the need for the 'International Laboratories', which produced medicines in Arlesheim, to have a proper name at last. We sat around the table and made suggestions one after another—humorous ones, clever and not so clever ones. Dr Steiner sat there with his pad open before him, pencil in hand, and listened with a gentle, almost mischievous smile on his face. Then he began to move the pencil around in the air above the paper. Suddenly he made a wave-like motion, which descended closer and closer to the pad; and finally he said, as he wrote it down: 'Welle-da [literally 'wave-there'] *... that is the name of the Germanic priestess of healing.' And that is how 'Weleda' got its name.*

I was also able to have some conversations with him during this time in Arnhem, and asked advice about the dilemma of having to speak about anthroposophy in public, yet with so little real experience of it. 'You can speak about anything in my cycles and lectures as long as you ensure that you do not do this until a year after you first studied it,' he replied.

We also discussed another basic problem: that I had always been fascinated by all modern cultural developments, in painting and literature for instance, and that I found it very difficult to push this all to one side. 'You should look at it this way,' he said, 'always have the greatest tolerance for everything in the world, yet practise the most rigorous honesty in representing anthroposophy.' I knew that this would become an important thought for me, to which I would continually return.

★

In September 1924 all of us attending the new courses in Dornach had the feeling of living far beyond our normal consciousness. We felt lifted into other spheres: we all looked different, were all seeing and hearing beyond our own capacities. When we looked at one another we said to ourselves: 'Is that really him*?' This was an incredible and indescribable experience. We were already living in a world of spirit, which was of course far beyond our own powers. There were moments during the last lectures of the Pastoral Medicine Course when Rudolf Steiner emanated nothing but love and spirit—to such an extent that it was hard to listen to his actual words. The audience was also no doubt one to which he could wholly pour himself out.*

The audience consisted of doctors, and priests of the Christian Community founded two years before. A 'Speech and Drama' course also took place, to which the doctors and priests were invited too. Each evening he held the great lectures on individual karmic connections. The one in which he spoke about Otto Weininger (21 September) was the last I heard.

The same afternoon we—a few doctors and Frau Dr Wegman—had been with him. He lay wrapped in a blanket on his bed, and gave us some last instructions. Then I had to return to my practice in Holland.

★

In the months after Rudolf Steiner fell ill, from October 1924 to March 1925, Zeylmans came to Dornach a few times, and was also there at Christmas 1924.

And then, on 30 March 1925, after an illness lasting seven months, his death called us to Dornach. We divided the vigil between us, and I would like to tell what I remember of my immediate experiences on this last night:

Rudolf Steiner lay on his death-bed in the Studio. I want to try to express what his spirit revealed to me in death. This will be nothing better than stammering, for only an inspired poet can find words for the inexpressible . . . The image I received was one of divine joy and human suffering.

The 'friend of the gods and guide to mankind', as Albert Steffen called him, was dead. Outside in nature the gods celebrated as the great guide of mankind returned to them. Within, by the death-bed, human beings mourned, for the friend of the gods had been taken from them. Spring was coming outside. The birds suddenly began to sing. The joy of resurrection lived in plant and beast. The joy of resurrection sought its path to the human being, entered his senses and sank down into his heart.

. . . Within, by the death-bed, stood the mourners, and looked in pain upon the dear face. Memories surfaced, the noblest and most beautiful of their lives. Pain flashed through their souls and welled up in their hearts . . .

Joy of resurrection and the pain of death encountered one another there: divine joy and human suffering.

How wonderful he looked on the first day after his death! As though gently sleeping, so peaceful and thoughtful. As though he might wake up at any minute to tell us what his spirit had experienced up in the heavens. His death had been like prayer, we were told. For hours he lay enfolded in deepest thought, gazing into far distances. Then his thoughtfulness increasingly became prayer. He lay immovably still with folded hands, speaking only a few loving words to his friend and nurse Frau Dr Wegman. After some hours he closed his eyes and died. Without a death struggle, his prayer on earth fulfilled.

But to us it seemed his spirit continued to pray, as though his mighty prayer passed through our mourning souls. And where joy of resurrection and death-pain found one another in our hearts, something blossomed and floated aloft, borne on his prayer, ascending. And what was, for each individual, a prayer of thanks, became a trusting picture of the future for one and all.

On the second day it seemed different to me. There was now a shadow of pain across his spirit-penetrated countenance. As though some of the pain of the many hundreds of friends gathering from all countries was reflected in his face. It was harder to experience joy of resurrection now. But solemn, rejoicing thoughts arose from his illumined forehead.

Then came the third day, and once more something had changed. Now I saw the face of a saint before me, without pain and without sin. A face that seemed greater than an ordinary human being, but at the same time contained, in miniature, all that is beautiful, good and true. Unreachable, far away from us, but at the same time very close. Divine, but the epitome of human. His noble brow shone brighter than before. His deep eyes concealed world secrets. His beautiful mouth spoke a cosmic language. Never before had one seen such hands. They were powerful like the hands of someone used to hard work, but spiritualized right into the last fibre of muscle. He had carved hard wood with them. He had used them to write his clear, light script. He had given his hand in greeting to countless people, and each person felt this as a blessing . . .

Six doctors and four others, all people who had been close to Dr Steiner, were allowed to keep the vigil in that last night, two at a time. The hours we passed there were unforgettably beautiful and sacred. It was a still, peaceful spring night. The moon shone like a sun. Black, demonic cloud-shapes kept trying to conceal its light, but it reflected sun-light more and more brightly down to earth. In the Studio, now in his coffin, the incomparable man in death. Around him burned candles, casting their glow on the black coffin. The fragrance of flowers floated up, speaking a delicate language of the soul. Great and silent stood the statue of Christ at his feet, with its world-destiny-guiding gesture. On either side of the coffin we held our vigil, watching over the candle-flames to make sure they burned evenly and peacefully. How strange and mysterious everything looked, yet familiar at the same time. Images of the long-gone past arose, glittering like silver in the candle-light, then vanishing. This had happened before, some other time . . .

And then we suddenly knew: this event reaches beyond time. It points back to the far distant past, and forwards into the far future. Past and future here melt into one, and thus united form an eternal macrocosmic image. An image of the divine guidance of human beings and of human cosmic destiny!

Then friends entered and made a death-mask. We stood there silently. And when we saw that the mask was a good one, we thought joyfully: God be praised, now many will be able to see this expression of deepest wisdom, inmost love and greatest holiness for centuries to come. The birds sang in the early dawn. We know that hard times will come. But each one who, in his mourning heart, shared in the experience of this festival of resurrection, will find that the hard times are no more than probations, probations of the soul, in which he will prevail.

VII. A PIONEER OF ANTHROPOSOPHY

During the first years after Rudolf Steiner's death, up to about 1930, work on behalf of anthroposophy in Holland developed and expanded fast. In 1924 Zeylmans had spoken of a 'crusading mood' which he wanted to spread through the country. Ita Wegman encouraged this same kind of mood globally. She often came to Holland, worked with the doctors and gave 'esoteric classes'.

A Dutch eurythmy group was founded, there were courses for children and adults in many places, and artistic performances on special occasions. Training courses for doctors and medical students were held at regular intervals in different towns. Study groups for young doctors and biologists had formed.

The so-called 'Anthroposophical Science Course' had already started in 1924. This was a kind of weekend event in various different towns, at which the practical and scientific basis of fields such as pedagogy, medicine, agriculture etc. were studied over a two-day period.

The new Waldorf School in The Hague became very active. In the second year it had 45 pupils, in the third 90. Most of the teachers were also busy as lecturers. There was Henri Zagwijn, for instance, the gifted composer. Decades later Mieke Lagewaardt recalled:

> Zagwijn's introductory courses were a unique experience for me. I came to him in Rotterdam as a young, interested person, and first found out about anthroposophy through him. We all sat there, crowded together. There was a great blackboard on which were drawn interweaving yellow, red and blue circles to introduce us to the human being's threefold organism. To begin with I understood nothing at all of all this. I had the greatest difficulty in taking it seriously. But our great friend Zagwijn knew how to grip us with his own fiery enthusiasm and love for Rudolf Steiner. If we interrupted him to ask for further explanation he replied: 'Oh yes, we'll come back to that later,' and then calmly carried on with the thread of his presentations—which we only later learned to value for their thoroughness and an enormous underlying knowledge of anthroposophy. It was a fascinating chaos that he poured over us. I felt giddy from it all, and I really needed a *vademecum* to provide me with some kind of guide to the whole thing.

> When I asked him about this, he grinned and said: 'Just leap in, there's no beginning or end!'

Then there was the stormy, brilliant teacher Max Stibbe, who later in life founded many Waldorf schools, and who at that time was very active as a speaker; or the teacher Daniel van Bemmelen who, as an Arts Academy student, had been working in Dornach in 1920. There was Elisabeth Mulder too, who later studied astronomy with Elisabeth Vreede.

The Prinsevinkenpark clinic already mentioned was developing into a therapeutic and clinical institute. The medicine manufacturer Weleda had also begun at this time. And every active anthroposophist supported the new medicine as a matter of course, as is clear for instance from a letter which Susanne Bouricius wrote to Willem Zeylmans:

> I am no fervent propagandist, it is true, but every now and then I let fall a word or hint among my acquaintances, and that helps. On Saturday evening a friend of mine, for whom I had prepared a Weleda remedy, gave me a great vase-full of flowers to thank me, because it had worked so well. I will see to it that I spread news of this cough-syrup around, in the same way that I have done for Infludo and Everon. I may send you a patient in the spring who suffers from hay-fever . . . I will certainly do all I can . . .

She also did all she could by donating money when, in 1926, the first plans were laid for a specially designed clinic. Zeylmans' friend from his student days, Jan Buys, who had meanwhile set up practice as an architect (and to whom Zeylmans owed his first contact with the two ladies Tak and Heemskerck), was commissioned to design it. The two friends, who as students had been so enthusiastic about modern art, disagreed a good deal about the best shape for the building. Buys was no anthroposophist, and a few years later came to pursue extreme modern functionalism. Zeylmans had become acquainted with Steiner's buildings, and had a quite specific conception of his new clinic's outer form. Their friendship was sorely tested by this, and Buys was close to despair, failing to understand what his friend Willem really wanted. At last, in a moment of some agitation, Zeylmans picked up a blue pen and sketched the form of the building and its roof in a few decided strokes, saying: 'That's the shape of the hill, and that's where the path runs along underneath, and that's where it runs up above . . . and that's how the roof's profile should be.' Suddenly Buys understood the idea of the whole, and said: 'Ah, that's what you meant—now I see how it's supposed to be!' From that moment on Zeylmans gave his friend free rein, and the new Rudolf Steiner Clinic quickly arose on the most beautiful dune-hill between The Hague and Scheveningen, with a wonderful view of the newly-established Westbroekpark. At the building's opening ceremony in July 1928, architect Buys expressed his great gratitude to the builders for putting no hindrances in his way during construction. This, he said, had enabled him to put his deepest humanity into the building, and it had been a liberation for him.

This clinic was financed through the gift of Susanne Bouricius (1872–1934), who also made great financial contributions to building the first Goetheanum, and the Waldorf school in The Hague.

Previously, in a solemn address at the foundation stone ceremony in November 1927, Zeylmans had called upon the help of high spiritual forces, speaking of them as the powers of Mercurius/Raphael whom he asked to support the efforts of doctors and therapists in this new clinic. He spoke of the ideals of what was from then on to be called the Rudolf Steiner Clinic, which would strive to work in the spirit of the medical section of the School of Spiritual Science in Dornach. Into the foundations was placed a foundation stone verse which Rudolf Steiner had written for Elisabeth Vreede's home:

May soul live in this house,
Penetrated by spirit
That seeks in the depths
For certain will,
So that it may acquire
Sense of the devout
In all this building's rooms
And that from above
Can unite
Blessing of the spirit
And God's grace
In all who live within.

The building had two façades: one facing the West, towards the park and the Scheveningen coast; and the other towards the East, where the entrance was.

The doctor Rob van Houten had been part of this project for some years already, also the young doctor Dr Galjart, who became especially active in the laboratory and cancer research. Sister Johanna Spruyt also worked with them, dying a year later after a long illness. Sister van

The laying of the foundation stone of the Rudolf Steiner Clinic, Nieuwe Parklaan 26, Den Haag, on 13 November 1927. Ita Wegman (centre), with Willem Zeylmans (holding hat with both hands) to her right. Far right, Elisabeth Vreede. To her right (with folded hands) Suze Bouricius, who donated the building costs.

Doorn, who had been there at the beginning, did not live to see the new building.

In The Hague and throughout Holland the clinic's opening excited a certain interest, not only because of its unusual architecture but also because of the ideals at work there: the founding of a new, anthroposophical medicine. One of the ladies present at the opening expressed this as follows: 'This building gives the impression of being a strange boat, a gift from unknown waters that has sailed to the Dutch coast. May many people find healing here and then go out into the world with a sense of gratitude for this new art of medicine.'

Zeylmans now had the opportunity of realizing a wish he had harboured for years—putting his new, Goethean psychology of colours to therapeutic use. All thirty-five patients' rooms, as well as the other rooms, were painted in different colours. Thus one could exert a healing influence on certain illnesses by exposing patients to a particular colour through their immediate environment. As one can imagine, this was at the time a very new and unusual form of therapy, and repeatedly came to public attention over subsequent years. Since the clinic lay on the road which linked The Hague with the spa town of Scheveningen and public trams ran past the strange building, passengers repeatedly began talking about the treatment methods used in the clinic's coloured rooms. This led to the most wayward speculations, and workers at the clinic had a great deal of amusement from the new anecdotes frequently overheard on the tram. One Dutch professor even used these rumours in a book he wrote:

Rudolf Steiner Clinic at Scheveningen

> Each room has its own colour. If a patient is very agitated, he is accommodated in a red room (where everything is red); then he becomes still more agitated until a reaction sets in and he cannot bear the red room any longer. Then he is put in a purple room; and thus passes through a sequence of different rooms until he is at last calm and normal once more.

As early as 1930 the clinic opened an outpatients treatment centre in another area. At the instigation of Dr van Houten, who had always had the ideal of carrying anthroposophy's practical applications into the wider world, away from the narrower circles of the original idealists, a kind of private health insurance scheme was founded, which could assure those who paid a few guilders per year a bed in the clinic when they needed it. It soon became apparent that this was not enough: the practical ideas at work in the clinic needed to become better and more widely known. Lectures with popular appeal were held on medical themes in a local hall. Zeylmans spoke about: 'Why do we become ill?', van Houten gave lectures on the theme: 'What can I do to improve my health?' and the teacher Stibbe addressed the question: 'How can a school contribute to children's health?'. Thus a circle of about a hundred people gradually grew up around this new treatment centre—people who otherwise would not have found their way to the Rudolf Steiner Clinic. Between 140 and 170 listeners attended these evening lectures, and so-called workers' annual subscriptions were increasingly given for people to attend this outpatients centre, which enabled seriously-ill patients who otherwise could not have afforded a bed in the Rudolf Steiner Clinic to be treated for little or no money.

In 1937 there were so many new patients applying for a place that the nurses living in the clinic had to move out to allow for a drastic increase in the number of patients' beds. This followed years of severe financial difficulty. Susanne Bouricius' help had come to an end because she had lost her considerable wealth in about 1931. 1934 and 1935 had also been difficult years.

Nevertheless patients came from England and Germany in order to be part of the intense therapeutic and artistic life imbuing every aspect of the clinic's work. All branches of artistic therapy were practised and for the nurses too there were regular training courses. The co-workers and friends of the clinic formed, over the years, a truly idealistic human community.*

---

* After the second world war the building was used for general medical purposes. There were plans to use it for anthroposophical therapy again from 1980 onwards, and to add a hospital building with up-to-date facilities.

★

Willem Zeylmans began to develop his lecturing activity. From 1922 until his death he delivered close on two thousand lectures. Nearly seven hundred lecture-notes survive, which list the main points of his lectures on long, folded pages. He used these notes to fix in his mind what he first saw as image before him. When speaking he no longer referred to them—he always spoke without notes, saying that after practising the 'accompanying (or "subsidiary") exercises' given by Rudolf Steiner for two years one no longer lost the thread of one's thought.

It was probably his lectures' vivid imagery which chiefly struck his audience. In 1954, when he was describing Holland to children in an Australian school, one of the pupils afterwards asked: 'Are you a painter?'

One can see how he himself thought about the art of lecturing from a 1929 essay written for Dutch anthroposophists. There he says:

We can perceive much around us which shows that questions that are waiting for answers come towards us from the world. Are we ready to do everything necessary to meet properly this interest coming from the world? There is probably no need to say that simply giving as many lectures as possible is not the answer, for good will alone does not convince. The only thing that really speaks is what we have inwardly attained. At a time when man has forgotten how to distinguish between truth and appearance, mere teachings do not win people over. The only really convincing thing is what we attain through struggle and effort, the way we transform ourselves through a spirit-imbued world picture. What convinces is someone who not only knows about spirit but also has a deep inner experience of spirit, and above all lives by it and through it.

This view of giving lectures means nothing less than regarding their actual content as a matter of secondary importance, as a 'vehicle' for something still more important—the actual experience of the speaker, what he has himself become.

Apart from giving lectures in his mother-tongue, Zeylmans also lectured in German and English, and was able to speak fluently in both these languages without notes. He only seldom lectured in French, having little to do with French cultural circles (apart from his collaboration on the psychology of different peoples). As far as we know he did not publish any writings in French either.

Fate dictated, rather remarkably, that his lectures were almost always given to full houses.

His ability to speak publicly about anthroposophy soon drew a large audience in Holland. In The Hague, in later days, he often gave lecture series on Sunday mornings. He regularly participated in the 'Round Table Conferences' organized by the priest De Jongh in Haarlem, in which people of very different persuasions took part. He himself described how strange it was for him when, as a doctor and psychiatrist, he kept returning to Christianity, while the priests who gave lectures often ended up talking about psychiatry! He was often asked to give the concluding address at these gatherings, ably summing up all the discussions of the conference in a synthesis and overview. This gift of summing up all that different people had contributed over several days gave many people the impression of an eagle who, circling calmly at a great height, looks down upon a whole landscape. Such power of synthesis gave his lectures an artistic element. As he spoke he often made vigorous gestures (of which he himself was unaware); his voice was not especially powerful or deep in tone, but one could always easily understand what he said. He seldom spoke for more than an hour, and in latter years usually no more than fifty minutes. He once said to a colleague: 'One should speak about the basic principles of anthroposophy in such a way that the audience experiences the train of thought as an etheric healing process.'

His courses for the Amersfoort International School of Philosophy whose director Professor Mennicke often invited him, allowed him to develop a theme over a whole week: in the mornings he presented the chief ideas, and in response to subsequent discussions and written questions he then composed his evening lecture.

It is natural that over the course of his life, during his extensive lecturing, he experienced many remarkable and also funny events, which he could relate in a very humorous way. For instance he told of a listener in the front row who shook his head most decidedly from time to time, at which Zeylmans made greater and greater efforts to convince this listener in particular—but the head-shaking just grew stronger. At the end the listener in question had come up to him and thanked him—he had agreed with everything! And why had he kept shaking his head? That was just an involuntary tick...

But he also experienced difficult moments, for example in Helsinki in 1929, when two of his anthroposophical friends had to break off their public lecture soon after they started speaking because of some kind of strange hypnotic disturbance. They told him that their words had been hurled back at them like bricks! Warned by such experiences, Zeylmans began to speak very quietly and without any 'pressure', and soon discovered from which corner the opposition came: at the back of the hall stood two rigid figures with crossed arms, who fixed their gaze upon him. From the moment he discovered them he was able to carry on and finish his lecture without disturbance.

In 1925 Zeylmans and Dr Eugen Kolisko were invited to London to address English doctors. The invitation came from the General Secretary of the English Society, Daniel Nicol Dunlop. This was the first time that either speaker had lectured in English, and both naturally had a bit of stage-fright. But Dunlop, as chairman of the conference, radiated such impressive calm, and warm, honest trust towards the two young doctors 'from the continent', and introduced them so warmly, that 'the lectures were a success before they had even begun' as Zeylmans later related.

These lectures resulted, a few years later, in Zeylmans going to London once a month, and then every two months. Consultation sessions were organized in which he worked together with English anthroposophical doctors, thus helping to get the medical movement going.

Dunlop's invitation to England affected Zeylmans' own destiny, and also had far-reaching consequences for the spread of anthroposophical ideas in the English-speaking world. Zeylmans thus learned at an early stage to lecture in English, and this later enabled him to lecture effortlessly all over the world, in the USA and finally also in South Africa. During these years Zeylmans and Dunlop often met, and a deep friendship developed between them. Zeylmans said:

Discussions with Dunlop had their own charm. To begin with he usually spoke little, but instead listened most intently. Towards the end of the conversation he loved developing his viewpoints in a wide-ranging panorama, in which he referred to everything that had previously been touched upon. At the end he often expressed very deep, intelligent ideas, in a somewhat chanting, almost ritualistic tone of voice.

Dunlop had grown up with his grandfather on an island full of the remains of Celtic holy sites. One night he found his grandfather dead in the bed beside him; and as he gazed through the window over the sea, he fell into a kind of trance in which he saw images of himself and his grandfather in a previous life. These images came and went as in a kaleidoscope. Later he met the writer and philosopher George Russell ('A.E.') in Ireland, and for the first time heard of reincarnation from him. Russell became one of Dunlop's most intimate friends. He died a few months after him, in July 1935.

Dunlop had come into contact with Rudolf Steiner some time before, and since he spoke no German, Jo van Leer made the introductions. Like van Leer, Dunlop was an international businessman, and like him too had an irrepressible idealism for anthroposophy.

In later years he saw it as his particular task to organize gatherings and invite other speakers. He was unequalled as a chairman. With his deep respect for human freedom, and broad overview of the whole scope of a conference, he structured things in a way that allowed every speaker to realize his full potential, and yet also to feel part of the whole. This was a very important task since anthroposophy was coming more and more to public attention through these many international conferences, and drawing an increasing number of people towards it.

With Mrs Merry, Dunlop organized the Summer Schools in Penmaenmawr and Torquay, where Steiner gave his great lecture cycles.

Dunlop had a great sense of humour, and particularly in difficult situations could highlight a whole complex of difficulties with a single, humorous word. He kept himself in the background, yet gave participants a feeling of enthusiasm and trust. In the summer of 1928 an anthroposophical World Conference was held in London, in which many anthroposophists took part—not just from England, but from Holland, Germany and Switzerland too. Dunlop felt very connected with the economic ideas of the threefold social organism, which aimed to create the right relationship between producers and consumers. He had organized a World Power Conference on this theme in Wembley in 1924, the first international conference after the First World War in which German technologists and scientists could participate on a truly equal footing.

It was not until later that Dunlop said how hard he had had to struggle to bring this about. This conference was followed by further ones: in Berlin in 1930 there were 4000 participants; and group meetings on the same theme took place in Basle, London, Barcelona, Tokyo and Scandinavia.

The founding of the periodical *The Present Age*, edited by Dr Walter Johannes Stein, was also one of Dunlop's ideas.

Dunlop suffered a great deal from the difficulties in the Anthroposophical Society. He was deeply hurt not so much by the difficulties themselves, but by the way they were handled. He was one of those who signed the Statement of Intent, which led to the signatories being excluded from the General Anthroposophical Society in 1935.

Dunlop died, following an operation, on Ascension day 1935. Zeylmans wrote:

In my memory he lives on as a great, mighty individual, a true Westerner, someone whose soul is wholly united with the earth, but who at the same time discovered truth and morality in the depths of his soul. An 'observer' of the world-stage, who recognises what is truly needed, and then proceeds to action with unwavering will. A man in whose soul lived old Celtic wisdom like a delicately shining light, a light in which the Christianity of the future can be born.

If we want to imagine Zeylmans during this time, it is as a 33-year-old, fiery idealist putting all his strength into the task which destiny has given him. The fire with which he represents his view of the world can be seen, for instance, in his response to the visit of the well-known Dr Johannes Müller, who enjoyed great regard at the time with his movement for 'non-denominational culture'. The latter gave a highly acclaimed lecture in The Hague about the Sermon on the Mount. His thesis was that this had been completely misunderstood, and the main thrust of his argument was that people ought not to strain and strive so much in religion: he called this the 'broad road' to ruin. People should realize, he said, that inner effort does not bring them a single step further, but leads them instead to despair and inner death. Only through pure, god-given grace does resurrection to a new state of being come about. Zeylmans listened to this lecture by the 60-year-old theologian, and immediately afterwards wrote the following review:

Is there anything worse for our age than this? Müller thinks that the Sermon on the Mount and modern culture have nothing to do with one another. But for anthroposophy the Sermon on the Mount and modern culture have a very great deal to do with one another. In the profound decline brought about by the power of all things material over our time, the light of the Sermon on the Mount shines out like the annunciation of a new kingdom, and thus becomes commandment for us. Whether or not we can transform modern culture depends on the powers we can develop in our soul. To someone unaware of the soul's evolutionary possibilities, the Sermon on the Mount seems to demand the impossible. But those who know of the divine powers living in the soul, feel the duty to develop these forces in order to make possible what is desired by God.

A fiery idealist, yes indeed—but this did not mean he was unrealistic. We only need to remember the concluding words he wrote about the deathbed of Rudolf Steiner: 'We know that hard times will come. But each one who, in his mourning heart, shared in the experience of this festival of resurrection, will find that the hard times are no more than probations, probations of the soul, in which he will prevail!'

These probations came sooner than expected, connected with the following:

At Rudolf Steiner's first visit to Holland after the war, in 1921, Willem Zeylmans had attended the public lecture of 27 February in The Hague, in which Steiner spoke of the great questions facing education and teaching. This lecture was one of the first which Zeylmans had heard Rudolf Steiner give in Holland. It made a huge impression on the young doctor to witness Rudolf Steiner describing the ideal of founding a World School Association. Six months later Steiner stressed again how necessary it would be to found such a World School Association, and that he had pointed to this need several times during his Dutch trip. The plan had come to nothing, he said, although he was sure that this would have allowed people to continue building the Goetheanum in peace.

Steiner apparently expressly said that Holland seemed to him particularly suited for founding such an Association. Later he also said that the countries of Central Europe could not have done anything about it at that time, but:

> I wanted to appeal to those forces which could have existed in the Anthroposophical Society. Perhaps these forces will still gather themselves one last time to found something like the World School Association. It is dead and buried at the moment. One cannot just talk about such a thing, but it must be practically taken in hand. And a number of people must be there to do it.

Perhaps Zeylmans saw, even five years later, that Holland, as a small, neutral country with an international outlook and a number of very capable, self-sacrificing anthroposophists, would still be in a position to realize the ideal of a World School Association. There had been previous attempts to do this in June 1921, in other words shortly after Steiner's talk in The Hague. Among others, Zeylmans' publisher-friend de Haan and his father-in-law Pieter Droogleever Fortuyn, had made efforts on behalf of this idea. The latter, as a city councillor in The Hague and later as Mayor of Rotterdam, would certainly have been able to do much to help it forwards, but the plan came to nothing at that time.

In the meantime Zeylmans had got to know Daniel Nicol Dunlop in London, and seen in him a man of the world who wished to make the ideals of anthroposophy into practical reality. Zeylmans had also been on his travels, and an international quality had entered into his whole mood and approach to life. He had just completed a lecture tour of Copenhagen, Oslo, Stockholm and Helsingfors (Helsinki), and there naturally encountered the need for Waldorf schools to be founded. It is understandable, therefore, that in November 1925, on a trip to Glastonbury and Stonehenge with Ita Wegman, Günther Wachsmuth, Maria Röschl and several other friends, he grasped the impulse to make a practical start with founding the World School Association on the fifth anniversary of Steiner's lecture in The Hague—which would also have been Steiner's sixty-fifth birthday—and thus to realize Steiner's ideals. In a certain sense, therefore, he put himself under pressure of time, and although he travelled about a lot he did not properly calculate how much time and how many tactful conversations with all those involved would be required for such a founding. In the first few days of 1926 he sent a good number of friends out everywhere with a 'founding statement'. But Zeylmans had to witness the powerful inner opposition of which Steiner had already spoken in 1920 and 1921, which, against his intentions, repeatedly reared its head. And now it led to the collapse of a valuable initiative. This was a severe test for Zeylmans, a terrible experience which made him wiser.

In early November 1926 the Dutch anthroposophists had organized an international pedagogical conference. There were public performances of work from the Waldorf curriculum; and from Germany, Switzerland and England came outstanding speakers to support the young teachers of the Waldorf School in The Hague in giving an impressive series of lectures. Hermann Baravalle gave a lecture about the new way of teaching geometry; Schwebsch spoke about artistic ideals in education; Eugen Kolisko lectured on 'How the art of medicine can become fruitful in education'; the renowned teacher Caroline von Heydebrandt spoke about Rudolf Steiner as an educationalist; and Count Fritz Bothmer, with his pupils from Stuttgart, gave a performance in the Koninklijke Schouwburg (a theatre in The Hague) of the new Waldorf gymnastics.

The conference was very well received in Holland. The newspaper *Telegraaf* printed on the front page of its Sunday edition a large photograph of the 29 initiators of this event.

The Dutch doctor Bernard Lievegoed was present at this conference, and wrote:

> This was my first meeting with the broader context of anthroposophy. As I entered the lecture hall I was introduced to Dr Zeylmans. He was 33 at the time, but in my memory no different then than in the last years of his life. Despite his young years he seemed a mature person. He

soon began to speak in a quiet voice, but with such clearly formed consonants that one could hear every single word from the very back of the hall. During the following days the great teachers of the Waldorf School spoke too: Kolisko, Stein, von Heydebrandt; and round all of them wove something like the aura of Rudolf Steiner's still-present spirit. For me as a medical student it was an inexplicable experience—to witness such differences and yet such unity. The die was cast: I belonged here too.

I invited Zeylmans to give a few lectures on anthroposophy to students at my university town of Groningen. He came and gave two lectures full of humour. He seemed in the best of moods, and had long conversations with us between the lectures. As he took his leave something occurred that had a decisive effect on my life. My fellow students had given me the name of 'Fire-ball', not just because of the red hair I still had then, but also because of the fiery way in which I sometimes spoke. When Zeylmans heard that, he took me by the upper arm (we were already at the station) and said: ' Now then, how do things stand with you—will you willingly sacrifice yourself to the dragon or . . . ?' Then he left me with this riddle of a question. That was his manner of calling people to inner activity and awareness. Still today I can feel his firm grip on my upper arm. 'Sacrifice myself to the dragon . . . ?' I kept asking myself, 'what did he mean?' Why did this image engrave itself in my soul as so characteristic of Zeylmans? Later I heard how, in medieval times, people underwent inner transformation through a single meeting in the middle of a crowd, when another looked at them and spoke only a few words. These 'others' were rosicrucians, and this was the way they found their pupils. During the next months I came to see that I must ask Zeylmans how I might find the way to my own self. That was the beginning of an intimate friendship and pupilship that was to last 35 years.

The great event of 1928 was the World Conference which took place in London in the last ten days of July. The General Secretary of the English Anthroposophical Society, Dunlop, had previously spoken with Rudolf Steiner about holding this sort of international conference. It was Dunlop's ideal, as we mentioned already, to bring anthroposophical ideas into the spheres of human work—and he had the gift and capacity to do this! His position as General Director of an international business company allowed him to place such a conference on the right footing. After Rudolf Steiner's death, therefore, a plan had gradually formed to hold an international conference of this kind. Representatives from the fields of trade and business, science, sociology, education and the arts were to enter into dialogue with representatives of the new spiritual science.

The various speakers who participated in the conference gave short introductory addresses. A brief address by Zeylmans has survived, in which he describes his feelings, as a Dutchman, on arriving in London from Holland:

Foreigners keep telling us that Holland is a strange land. It is indeed, not because the inhabitants wear wooden clogs and smoke long pipes, but because of the nature of the ground. When you go walking in England you feel that you have solid rock beneath you. Foreigners who come to visit us in Holland often say that they feel as if they 'had no ground under their feet'. And that is true! It is a fact that in many parts of Holland one treads on a surface that floats on water. Just look at a town like Amsterdam! The houses all look solid enough, yet they are not built on solid ground but on a kind of wooden raft, an enormously big one, that stands on thousands and thousands of piles. These piles are driven into the swamp-like ground until they stand solid in it. Imagine a town of almost a million inhabitants built on a sort of wooden raft which more or less floats on water! The surrounding countryside is also unusual. The fields and great stretches of grass are interspersed with many canals and ditches. These meadows too are floating on water. You will be able to imagine that in such a country the element of earth has rather less importance than it does in England, for instance. Holland is a land of water, air and light. The fields float on water between canals and trenches—the sun's light breaks in delicate colours through the low-lying clouds: a watery mist, light-permeated, floats above a swimming soil. We Dutch get to know a land in the state it is when new-born—composed of water, air and light. For hundreds of years the land has been won back time and time again from the water, in arduous toil and struggle, and protected from water and wind. So you can imagine that the Dutchman's gaze is more attuned to the forces that form the earth than to the earth itself. We have more of an eye for the formative forces of nature than for what has grown solid. The creative, formative forces of nature are very closely connected with water! How can we understand this? . . .

Then Zeylmans goes on to describe the significance of Rudolf Steiner's ideas about the so-called formative forces, the etheric forces, which form and create everything—and speaks of plant and animal worlds, of how the embryo swims in fluid, and how man and beast begin to breathe at birth. Then he describes the elements which have formed the whole human being, and which affect him. In such brief addresses Zeylmans could create a sphere of images and pictures which is characteristic of his lectures.

On 24 July he then gave a full-length evening lecture on the human soul in relation to waking, dreaming and sleeping: a very fine lecture, clearly structured, which he worked on further for his book *De menselijke ziel* ('The human soul').

We also have a lecture which Ita Wegman gave at this conference: 'The art of healing in the light of anthroposophical spiritual science'. Ita Wegman made a great impression on her contemporaries at the time. As both doctor and member of the *Vorstand* or executive council of the General Anthroposophical Society, and particularly because of her close collaboration with Rudolf Steiner in the last years of his life, many people found their way to anthroposophy through encountering her.

Rudolf Hauschka, who later founded the Wala medicine firm, arrived at this conference on his boat. It tied up in the London docks and was visited by many of his friends, for he had discovered a way of processing shark-skin to use it for manufacturing shoes and other items. It was hoped this would mean a great revolution in the leather industry, since shark-skin is clearly much tougher than the leather derived from mammals.

⋆

1929 was a very active, busy year. An event of great personal importance was the death of Zeylmans' mother on 15 February. He had been very close to her and she had followed his development from close at hand, with great interest and involvement. He continued to feel her close to him after her death.

The professional high-point of this year was probably the so-called Science Congress in Amsterdam.

He also undertook various journeys: he was in Dornach on four occasions, in Berlin three times, twice in London, and then in Paris and Stuttgart. From mid-April to mid-May he travelled through the Balkans, giving lectures in Jena, Prague, Brunn, Pressburg, Vienna, Linz, Salzburg, Innsbruck, Gnadenwald, Zagreb, Belgrade and Munich. This was the first time he had been to these cities, and he must have been surprised to meet with such interest everywhere. He also saw ancient cultural monuments and landscapes that particularly interested him: for instance on his journey through the region where Steiner had spent his youth, his visit to the famous antimony mine near Bernstein and the St. Florian monastery, as well as a pilgrimage to Bruckner's grave. In Belgrade he met a whole circle of doctors with whom he gathered several times at the university, under the chairmanship of Dr Stefanowitsch. His lecture themes in Belgrade were: 'Science and liberation of the spirit', and 'Destiny and illness'. In October he was once more invited to give a longer series of lectures: he spoke in Berlin and then travelled on to Riga and Reval to give lectures there too. Then he flew to Helsinki (still called Helsingfors at the time) for a few days, where he had given lectures before, in 1925. After this he returned to Reval, and also gave a lecture for the medical faculty at Dorpat. It was here in the Baltic states that he first met Valentin Tomberg, the mystic who lived in Holland for a while before settling in England.

At Easter he had given a lecture in Dornach about the Easter experience in Goethe's *Faust: 'A poetic work like Goethe's* Faust *contains a great, inspiring force for a doctor.'* He describes how a doctor can draw inspiration from the scene where Faust, in despair, lifts the cup of poison to his lips, and then, as he suddenly hears the Easter bells ring out, has an experience of the force of resurrection in the world. Zeylmans:

In our time one can feel that all of humanity stands at the threshold of a Faust-like experience . . . one can experience how this in fact applies to human beings today, how they must all suffer from forces that are full of the forces of death. Particularly as a doctor one can experience this, when one studies the way in which the degeneration of life forces is making itself felt in mankind . . . If one tries to follow human life as it presents itself to a doctor, one becomes witness to a dire need. One senses suffering everywhere, coming towards one from man's body, soul and spirit. It is a terrible suffering one observes in contemporary human beings, who wish to develop but are hindered by the weight of degenerative forces . . .

And at the end of the lecture:

The first thing one needs to do in order to help mankind today is to bear witness to all this need and misery. In future a time will come when all that is ugly, sick and full of suffering gains the upper hand. And only when one feels inwardly prepared to accept all this and transform it through the forces which come from anthroposophy, will one be able to say that one is practising a 'healing of the future'. All those who can relate to this should see it as their task to take this 'healing of the future', which is spiritual science, out into the world . . .

This was a thought which became central in all of Zeylmans' further life, and of which he spoke time and time again in many different ways.

For a good few years already, in fact ever since Rudolf Steiner had addressed the graduates in Amsterdam and Delft, Dutch anthroposophists had been aware that little progress would be made in their work if the scientific aspect of anthroposophy was not thoroughly described and presented to academics. But there was hardly anyone in Holland able to do this. A young Dutch medical student called Hans Grelinger had also been to the World Conference in London. He was a very enthusiastic man and had formed a deep affection for Willem Zeylmans. He had been so inspired by the appearance of so many prominent anthroposophical scientists and professionals in London, by the multiplicity of their interests and the innovative way in which they spoke about their fields, that he wanted to try to organize something similar in Holland. This is what led to the Science Congress which many worked to prepare throughout the whole year. On 8, 9 and 10 November 1929, roughly five hundred participants gathered in the lovely Colonial Institute in Amsterdam. The scientific world listened with commendable openness to what the anthroposophical world view had to say about modern science. Many may have been surprised at the festive mood in which the 'illustrissimus Senatus Studiosorum amstelodamensum', the council of elders of the Amsterdam student body, entered the hall. Zeylmans opened the congress with a very fine, very carefully-structured talk on the relationship between science and anthroposophy. The audience listened to him with great expectation and a certain excitement. And one of the participants observed how serious were the discussions after each lecture. The mood intensified even more when it became clear that the hall initially set aside for these dialogues was too small and the participants had to move into the great assembly hall. Many people stayed talking together after the lectures, long into the night, then adjourned to the American Hotel and carried on debating. The speakers from Germany and Switzerland had to discuss their lectures with the students and defend their points of view. Günther Wachsmuth was there lecturing on man, earth and its formative forces; Frau Kolisko gave a lecture on the connection between sun and gold, and on sun and moon eclipses; Ehrenfried Pfeiffer gave a talk, with slides, on his crystallization method and the experiments he had done to reveal otherwise invisible formative forces in nature; and finally there was Hermann Poppelbaum, who compared anthroposophy's new teachings about evolution with the accepted scientific view of evolution. Elisabeth Vreede and Ita Wegman were also there, and got involved in intense discussions with the students. On the Sunday evening Zeylmans gave the concluding and summarizing talk, and spoke so vividly of Rudolf Steiner that Grelinger said: 'Such a thing was only possible because people had spent the last few days studying together. One could read in the faces of those present that this final address had found its way straight to their hearts.'

In fact this congress led to a large number of young scientists beginning to occupy themselves with anthroposophy. And it was partly thanks to this initiative that a whole series of academics—doctors, physicists, engineers, agriculturalists and teachers—later came to work in the anthroposophical movement in Holland. In the last issue of its seventy-third year of circulation, the grand and venerable magazine for medicine gave a broad overview of the principles underlying Goethean science and an objective summary of the lectures that had been given.

But a quite different experience had also arisen during this gathering: that younger people in particular took up ideas of a new spiritual direction almost exclusively through establishing human contact with a person or people who presented them. Many anthroposophists had experienced this for years, and saw it in relation to a strong urge to form community. It was this that gave rise to the plan to organize a large-scale youth-camp, which would offer an opportunity both to study together for ten days, and also participate in a life of shared community. The young Hans Grelinger was the initiator of this plan.

★

The Stakenberg Camp not only made a great impression on the participants at the time it was held, but also remained in their memory years and even decades later. Many different factors worked together: 1930 was one of the most eventful and, behind the scenes, most dramatic years in European history that century. It was still possible, for someone who wanted to, to be free to organize a gathering of 1000 people, and disseminate his ideas. People could still travel wherever they wanted. But a mighty, threatening cloud hung over Europe, of which we can hardly have an idea now. Great vacuums opened up in the economy, in cultural life, in politics, in the whole social structure; and not only did younger and older generations fail to understand each other, but it was also very arduous for different nations to approach one another. What did a young Englishman understand of a young German's despair? Did the younger generation in Germany have any idea what was going on in the West? This was one of the chief ideas underlying the Stakenberg Camp: to bring young people together from East and West so that they could get to know one another through mutual study and conversation.

Particularly for anthroposophists the beginning of the 1930s was a time that brought a great sense of expectation, but also disquiet. Almost seven years had passed since the re-founding of the Anthroposophical Society, when most countries had formed their own Societies; and people still remembered Rudolf Steiner's repeated warnings that appalling chaos and great despair would enter human souls if no steps were taken to oppose materialism with a spiritual outlook: 'The materialistic world-view will only sustain people for two generations—the third generation will be destroyed by it.'

Steiner had placed special emphasis on the importance of the early thirties as a time when a new Christian spirit might enter the soul. And one can understand how a young generation, in particular, looked to anthroposophy as the start of a world-outlook that would renew everything.

We can see that the year 1930 was of special significance in Willem Zeylmans' own life. He was 37, and had been General Secretary of the Dutch Society for almost seven years; and had a deep sense of the breadth of possibilities and growing interest, but also of the first signals of an approaching spiritual battle.

The Stakenberg organizers turned emphatically towards 'young people'. They were young themselves and experienced the longing of their generation and a still younger one for new forms of work and community. Never before had anthroposophists had the idea of camping with 1000 people for ten days in the open, and of studying, discussing, experimenting, engaging in artistic activities and games in big tents. A great ideal underpinned preparations for the Stakenberg Camp. Zeylmans and his friends appealed to young people, and knew how to speak their language. In other words, Stakenberg was an attempt—and a very successful one!—to reach out openly and publicly to fellow human beings.

At the beginning of the year Willem Zeylmans and Hans Grelinger drove through Holland for a few days in search of a suitable site. Close to Harderwijk in the beautiful Veluwe district—a place steeped in legend, often mentioned as early as the Middle Ages—they found an estate of 40 hectares with a beautiful country house.

Grelinger was the son of a well-to-do tropical fruit importer, and was able to devote a whole year to the preparations. He also had great flair as an organizer (in later years he was commissioned to set up a psychiatric service for the armed forces). The whole thing had rather a military air, somewhat like the Scout movement which was widespread at the time. Terms were used such as reveille, return to barracks, tent commander, night-watch, camp doctor, Red Cross tent etc.!

To prepare the public, too, for the Stakenberg Camp, a kind of newspaper was produced, the first issue of which appeared already in March. This was printed in a large edition and distributed to all students in Holland. Grelinger undertook journeys to Germany, Switzerland and England, and enrolment offices were set up in all large cities. The Stakenberg paper also appeared in English and German, and contained a series of articles, preparatory descriptions and brief underlying observations written by a dozen prominent individuals of various nationalities in the anthroposophical movement. Thus, within a short time, this considerable amount of effort enabled a wealth of anthroposophical ideas to spread among young people in Europe who were looking for a new conviction and way forward in their lives. Some of these newspaper articles are still worth reading today.

Elisabeth Vreede came especially from Dornach to look at the site. She describes how, on Ascension Day 1930, she wandered in all directions through the Stakenberg landscape with an eye to the camp that was to take place in the first weeks of August. She quotes movingly from verses by Rudolf Steiner which tell of nature as it can be experienced in the month of August: of the spirit that speaks to us from nature, from the blue dome of the heavens, from the singing of birds, from the blossoming heather; and, at night, from the glorious majesty of the starry sky. This was a poetic but also very thoughtful and in some ways sober attempt to get a conscious hold on a rather daring—because very new kind of undertaking.

In the first issue of the Stakenberg newspaper there appeared a fiery appeal by Willem Zeylmans, which is printed in the appendix to this volume.

The campsite was intended to cater for about 600 participants with their own tents. Grelinger had borrowed a few very large tents from the Dutch army. There was a large kitchen tent with cooks, a Red Cross tent with a small ward for people who fell ill, a tent for the secretariat and one for study purposes with a library. In short, everything had been well prepared for the arrival of participants, these preparations having been done in a 'pre-camp' in which lectures and introductory courses had also been held for the helpers, over 8 days. But when the camp itself was due to start, not 600 but 1000 people arrived. Some had come on foot from Germany, some also in large lorries, others on bicycles. Many participants came from England too. It was clear that the young people were relying on being able to take part even if they had not enrolled beforehand! So the organizers had only a few hours to ensure that more food and provisions were brought; and a group of sporting Englishmen got down to work to peel potatoes for four hundred more people than had been envisaged. This unexpected influx also naturally led to a particularly happy, open mood. And on Saturday evening, 2 August, when Willem Zeylmans gave his welcoming address in three languages to 1000 people in the large lecture tent, there was a particularly attentive atmosphere. The newspaper reported next day on the harmonious, almost devout mood.

The great wealth of lectures and courses began the following day. Each enrolling participant had previously been sent a small booklet which enabled him to choose the study groups he wanted to take part in. The first series was a scientific course, led by Ehrenfried Pfeiffer and Dr Eckstein. This was held in German—with a parallel course in English—and addressed general science, chemistry and physics, botany and biology, earth evolution and geology as well as agriculture. An experimental laboratory had been set up in a separate tent.

Elisabeth Vreede and Joachim Schultz held courses in astronomy. There was also an observatory.

Great efforts had also gone into a study course for young doctors and medical students, led by Ita Wegman. Teaching in it were Karl König, Eugen Kolisko, Suchantke and other doctors. There was an extensive pedagogical course, and one on business and social economy. Then there was a study group for history and art. Hermann Poppelbaum led a special course on 'Man and Animal'.

A large number of eurythmists taught eurythmy in three languages. There were courses in speech formation, painting and modelling. Rhythm games were organized and there was a choir. Count Bothmer, whom we mentioned before, gave a course in gymnastics.

The courses were mainly set up in response to participants' wishes, which they had been able to express in questionnaires distributed in the months leading up to the camp.

Alongside intensive study, there were lectures two or three times each day which addressed all the great themes of anthroposophy. Yet more than the content itself, the participants were struck by the *way* these lectures were given! A final-year student later looked back on the camp and said:

> I know exactly what it was that at the time so impressed us students at Stakenberg who were close to completing our studies. Apart from the excellent organizational collaboration, it was the way people worked together in spirit. They spoke and acted out of a unity which, however, did not strike those observing it as something that had been agreed beforehand or organized as such. What we had missed as university

students—universality, an all-encompassing world view—was present here. We discovered how all sorts of new possibilities and perspectives for our own studies, and also for the future, arose through spending a week listening to lectures on history, medicine, science, pedagogy. We did not mind in the least that this anthroposophical camp for young people was also full of grey-haired people whose 'youth' was less of a physical than spiritual nature. This camp for 'young people' rejuvenated all of us—adults and students, foreigners and Dutch people. When we went to our little tent among the pines after the evening music (Kalevala songs played on lyres), not only had a little bit of 'cosmic consciousness' come closer to us, but we also felt more strongly rooted in the Veluwe soil under our feet, for we had found the place and evolution of the earth anew in a way which would enable us to serve it 'in the true spirit of the time'.

And a female student later told how, on her bicycle journey across the Veluwe towards Stakenberg she had asked herself: 'What will we find there?':

Yes, how was it? In my memory it was like the waves of an ocean, which now and then lifted you high up so that you were graced with a surprising vision; and then carried you back down into your own wave-trough, to float about on hesitant or fierce counter-arguments. Later it became apparent that mighty pictures remained behind from our experiences at the peak of the waves. How could we fail to remember Walter Johannes Stein evoking images from world history for us during a storm of rain that pelted down on the great tent? His descriptions of the temple of Ephesus made the greatest impression on me. My plodding secondary education suddenly made sense. And when something makes sense, doesn't everything alter in your life? But certain experiences in the wave-troughs were no less influential. For instance I remember the following: I knew how little ordinary science can do to help epileptic children, and so I was looking forward with high expectations to what Werner Pache's lecture might offer. What he said was a disappointment for me at the time, for I could not yet grasp it at all. But that moment lived on in me as an important one—as I only realized years later—because of the unaffected warmth with which he spoke of epileptic children. The performance of Eduard Schuré's drama *Persephone*, directed by Max Gümbel-Seiling, had a similar effect on me. Everything was almost shockingly different from what I had imagined the classics to be, and yet the performance made me value this play very highly.

If the images we thus received began their hidden, transformative work, the conversations and discussions we had gave more direct nourishment. Though to begin with one might just sit and listen, these conversations provided food for thought for many subsequent years . . . we were taken up into a mighty stream that flowed towards the future!

On the second day a storm blew the great tent over, though luckily when no one was inside it, and the 1000 participants had to listen to the evening lecture squashed together in the dining tent. The weather was not very good—it kept raining, and one can imagine that the participants sometimes spent less than comfortable nights in their tents.

In his welcoming address Zeylmans had expressed the underlying theme of the conference as follows:

When we look at anthroposophy as Rudolf Steiner gave it to us, we can say that it is not a teaching but a deed . . . We regard ourselves as pupils! . . . We hope that direct dialogue between people will come about here, so that from this can grow something like a new spiritual working. This is what our time needs. Today there are many people who say 'Things must change', who say this out of despair. One can feel that they want to turn everything upside down, and can understand this very well, especially when one meets them face to face. But this is not the way forward. For what, one can ask, will be born from an impulse of devastation, and what will it look like if it is? We believe that what is coming towards us can only live when we learn to understand the forces our civilization needs. Then one arrives at spiritual knowledge, and out of this knowledge we will be able to say: 'Now we understand that a metamorphosis should come about. Not new systems, but new people is what we need' . . .

The whole Stakenberg undertaking met great opposition within the anthroposophical movement. Many of Rudolf Steiner's pupils found this way of appealing to the public too superficial and lacking in dignity.

VIII. DEVELOPMENT AND SPIRITUAL CONFLICT

In the spring and summer of 1931 Zeylmans underwent an intense period of inner trial and testing. A small diary from this time testifies to the need, for the 'very difficult times to come', of forming right judgements and clear insights. This is why he now wanted to note down his reflections and experiences, so as to create for himself '*as great a certainty as possible in relation to the inner development which must be undergone in connection with all this*'.

On Sunday, 28 June, by a lucky chance, I had the opportunity to wander through an old wood. It was a lovely, sunny day, and the wood was deep and still. Far-off one could hear the faint sounds of people talking and laughing, celebrating Sunday in the near-by park. I met single walkers only every now and then.

In an isolated spot I noticed a few old trees: a high fir towering up into the deep blue sky, a stout birch, and somewhat lower oak-bushes round about. The stillness emanating from this group of trees was so complete for a moment that I almost took fright. I overcame this vague fear, approached these trees and was suddenly seized and moved so strongly that tears sprang into my eyes, and I was filled with the sense of deep suffering. With gasping breath and pounding heart I encountered the overwhelming workings of nature. The stream of sunlight illuminating everything round me with a golden glow, the flood of warmth that penetrated my whole soul, the blue sky with the towering trees, the brown and the silver tree-trunks, the dark fir-needles and the pale-green leaves—all gathered into an incomprehensible unity, an inwardly integrated image that appeared to me like a door into a higher realm.

A feeling of the deepest reverence for the holiness of that moment filled me. It was as if my soul was separating from my body and I entered through this door; then my soul stayed at rest, uniting itself with the colours and forms, with light and warmth.

And then the miracle happened: in the air trembling with warmth my soul perceived swiftly moving, inexpressibly delicate beings in human form, vaguely resembling dragonflies, flowing along shafts of light, continually changing, revealing themselves then vanishing. At the same time other beings appeared from trunks and roots, equally delicate and changing just as swiftly in form and shape: beings that seemed composed of a head alone—not like human heads and yet similar to man.

I realized that I had seen elemental beings, sylphs and gnomes. I wanted to form these words but something in me said with terror: Don't say it, do not break the mystery. But already it was too late—the image had faded. Lovely old trees stood before me again under the blue sky. I felt a deep and painful loneliness, the tears came to my eyes once more. Unwillingly I walked on, hoping for the miracle to repeat itself, but it did not.

This experience, accompanied by other similar ones, contrasted with the despairs and doubts he felt at the time in relation to the conflicts within the Anthroposophical Society.

A short time ago the thought came to me with dreadful certainty: 'Resign as General Secretary—not only that: resign as a member too! Free yourself totally, do not fail in your task!' Who is it, though, who makes these thoughts resound within me? That is the agonizing question. One needs to become clairvoyant to distinguish such things properly. But even then one has to be able to wait patiently.

Sometimes the nights were hard to endure because of the violent struggle *'which must be fought with demonic powers'*.

This is where his little diary ends. We know that he woke up every morning for three years asking: *'God, let me die now!'*

★

A short time after the Stakenberg Camp, the publisher Philip Krusemann from The Hague approached Zeylmans with the request to write a book on Rudolf Steiner for his series 'Helden van de Geest' ('Heroes of the spirit'). Volumes on Goethe, Hegel, Kant, Nietzsche, Plato, Schopenhauer and Spinoza had already appeared in this series. He accepted the commission in June 1931.

He worked on this book at a time in his life when, as we have seen, he was battling with the temptation to resign as General Secretary of the Dutch Society and to leave the Anthroposophical Society. It may be that working on this book helped him to overcome the crisis.

As a young man Rudolf Steiner had once written:

> There are four spheres of human activity in which man gives himself wholly up to the spirit, and renounces himself completely: knowledge, art, religion and loving devotion in spirit to another individual. Anyone who does not live in at least one of these spheres does not live at all. Knowledge is devotion to the universe in thoughts, art is devotion in perception and vision, religion in emotion and feeling, and love is

> devotion of the total sum of all our spiritual forces to something that appears to us as a precious being of the whole universe. Knowledge is the most spiritual, and love the most beautiful form of selfless devotion. For love is truly a light of heaven in daily life.

Reading Zeylmans' book on Steiner one can feel that it is written out of this kind of devotion. What may the Dutch public of the thirties have felt in response to the following description, in which Zeylmans tells of his first impression of Rudolf Steiner?

. . . A few hundred listeners sit on simple chairs. On a small platform covered in blue cloths, before curtains of the same blue which separate the stage from the hall, stands Rudolf Steiner. As he speaks everything is quiet as can be in the hall. All eyes are continually fixed on the dark figure in front of them.

Rudolf Steiner is of medium height and thin, almost delicate. This strikes the listener immediately, for his voice is heavy and powerful. A voice whose sound one will never forget. It has something moving about it, as though the speaker shares in the suffering of all humanity.

Sometimes his voice sounds warm and enveloping. The hearkening soul feels borne up by it into worlds inaccessible to normal consciousness. Then it resounds more powerfully. One experiences a strength which can only belong to higher powers. Words ring out like warning trumpet calls over the earth. Then again one hears in the sound an inward, delicate quality that deeply moves the listener's soul, giving him the sense of waking into an inner world, in which shines a hidden light. But it is always as though each word spoken unfolds a life of its own. These are not words as abstract symbols clothing thoughts, but they are born as living beings and live on in the listeners' hearts . . .

. . . It sometimes happened that people who saw Rudolf Steiner for the first time could not conceal a certain disappointment. They had imagined a 'world-renewer', a prophet with a corresponding outer appearance and gaze. And then they saw this remarkable, lively man, who was continually born anew, appearing to them now as an artist, now as a scientist or priest, but who remained a human being above all, without any pose or façade. A man who lived out of the deepest depths of the spirit, who wanted the spirit to triumph, not removed from earth and mankind, but as a creative earthly power working on earth, working in human souls. This spirit was made manifest in Rudolf Steiner's life work, there for all to see. He embodied it in the purest humanity, made it visible in his own person.

Rudolf Steiner! For many this name signifies their purpose in life. Meeting him was for many the beginning of a new life. How many years will pass before the mystery of the man who bore this name is plumbed to the depths? . . .

After a vivid characterization of Rudolf Steiner there followed a description of his life. The book's main content, however, consists in the subsequent three sections: an account of German idealism ('The dawn of a spiritual consciousness'); 'The birth of a new image of man'; and 'Resurrection of the forces of the soul'. This structure brings the whole of Rudolf Steiner's life's work—anthroposophy—to expression in a clear and telling overview. Zeylmans worked on this book at the same time as his many other tasks. Besides his medical practice and daily hospital work, he had to give 65 lectures in that year, undertake three trips abroad, and was involved in a nine-day Goethe memorial festival too.

Herbert Hahn, the well-known Stuttgart Waldorf teacher and scholar, moved to The Hague in the same year. An active and fruitful anthroposophical collaboration began, and one can imagine that Zeylmans and Hahn, who had known Rudolf Steiner well and who brought spiritual riches with him, formed a reassuring and mutually inspiring connection with one other. Hahn later wrote a long review of the book, in which he made the following notable remarks about the chapter on German idealism:

> Any German who, like me, has perhaps heard and read well-turned lectures and essays on German literature for years, will read this chapter with a sense of joy—but also deep pain. Pain, because such full and profound thoughts are still so rare back home. These observations culminate in a description of the spiritual significance of the friendship between Goethe and Schiller. Underlying the friendship of these two heroes of the spirit stands, as its higher sense, what it truly means to be human . . .

When Zeylmans departed for Indonesia in 1932, he left his wife the task of editing the extensive manuscript and preparing it for publication. Beautifully illustrated, the book appeared shortly before Christmas 1932 and sold well.

But that was not the end of this book's destiny. In 1961, on the occasion of Rudolf Steiner's centenary, it was re-issued without additions, and minus all notes and references.* This version formed the basis for the German-language edition which was published in Stuttgart in 1961. This latter had a strange fate, which I would like to mention here. More copies were printed than sold; and so, in the seventies, several thousand

* These included a significant paragraph on the 'Christian Community' which was only later re-inserted in the work *The Reality in Which We Live.*

'remaindered copies' ended up with a mail-order bookseller, who advertised the volume, together with many other titles, at half-price. It then became so popular that two more editions were printed, and thus Zeylmans' book on Rudolf Steiner found purchasers in Germany for many more years!

*

Zeylmans' relationship to Goethe is more profound than one might think. His great effort to explore the truth of the latter's Theory of Colours in Leipzig in 1920 was of momentous significance for him. In July of that year he had written in a letter: 'I have now studied Goethe's theory of colours from beginning to end, and as far as I can see it has nothing useful to offer.' Then, compelled by the conflict with Willy Stokar to read Rudolf Steiner's introduction to Goethe's work, he experienced a real revelation ('A whole world opened to me—of colour as a living being').

Three years later he presented his doctoral thesis at Amsterdam University, and each chapter of it was headed by a motto from Goethe's work! From 1926 onwards he gave lectures on Goethe's importance for anthroposophy, his ideas on metamorphosis as Easter revelation (1928); and a year after that on 'The Easter revelation in Goethe's Faust'.

At a public conference in Amsterdam in the same year, Zeylmans gave the introductory lecture on 'Goethe's importance for the sciences'. One of the other lecturers, Dr Günther Wachsmuth, later wrote:

> Zeylmans masterfully resolved the great difficulty of introducing an audience, that had mostly heard nothing of anthroposophy before, to both this and a specialist area of study at the same time...

Only a few years later Zeylmans had the opportunity to go into much more depth on Goethe than is normally possible in a single lecture, in a programme organized to commemorate the hundredth anniversary of Goethe's death (1932). For a whole week he was able to hold a seminar on Goethe's colour-theory with the Hague Waldorf teacher Frits Julius, and this was an event which gave many participants their first gateway into anthroposophy. It was at this time too that he first referred to a law apparent in Goethe's biography: word—life—light—darkness. In 1959 Zeylmans still expressed surprise that none of Goethe's biographers had seen this connection between these four phases of Goethe's life and the four phases which appear in the prologue to St John's Gospel.

First, as poet, the word awakens in him; then he discovers an underlying principle of life with his 'metamorphosis of plants'; after this he grasps hold of the world of light with his theory of colours; and then, in his friendship with Schiller, according to Zeylmans, he begins to confront the 'darkness' in human consciousness:

A life in which the primal laws of divine humanity are so revealed must be called Christian in a deeper sense. Underlying this life one continually recognizes, against a deep-blue sky, golden letters spelling out the words of the greatest and deepest poem of human love: 'In the beginning was the Word, and the Word was God and a God was the Word. The same was in the beginning with God. In him was life. And the life was the light of men. And the light shone in the darkness, but the darkness comprehended it not.'

On one occasion, during a lecture tour in Leipzig and Jena, he spent a week in Weimar in October. The only thing known of this visit is the simple diary entry: '*Meeting with Goethe in his study.*' He did truly meet him, in visible form.

Immediately afterwards, on his journey through Indonesia, Zeylmans was able to highlight Goethe's significance for our time, as he did in later decades until his death in hundreds of lectures throughout the world. In California in 1950, for instance, on his second trip to America, he spoke the following words at a Goethe-lecture he had been invited to give:

I have to speak a good deal about Goethe here. Here people call him Goethie; and since a conference in Aspen, Colorado, last year, everyone has heard of Goethie. This Aspen conference (Aspen is a kind of deserted mineworkers' township, 2000m up in the Rocky mountains, which has now been turned into a vacation resort) was organized by Robert Hutchins, and a rich industrialist donated the money for it. Albert Schweitzer was one of the guests of honour, and in the mind of many Americans Aspen is now more connected with the name Schweitzer than Goethie. Never mind . . . For me the question about Goethe began in La Jolla, California, where I gave a lecture on the colour theory to some academics from Scripps' Oceanographic Institute.

⋆

Willem Zeylmans was invited to Indonesia by several anthroposophists, who lived in what was then the Dutch East Indies, also called *Insulinde*, a wonderfully beautiful island-kingdom where ancient cultures had flourished. Ownership of this colony had provided Holland with much wealth since the seventeenth century.

Already as a student Zeylmans had planned to move to Indonesia to practise medicine in the tropics—a plan prevented, you will remember, by the offer of Marie Tak to finance the further course of his studies. Now he could travel there, and in the space of three months get to know the islands of Java, Sumatra and Bali. His travelling companion, Frau Elisabeth Knottenbelt, secretary of the Dutch Anthroposophical Society, organized roughly forty lectures while they were en-route.

In the Dutch East Indies the local inhabitants enjoyed relative prosperity at that time. The management of the colony was largely in the hands of experienced native officials. (Ten years later Japan conquered Indonesia; after the Second World war the country ceased being a colony and established its own sovereignty.)

The few anthroposophists who had invited Zeylmans hoped his lectures would awaken the interest in anthroposophy of both the Dutch settlers and the Indonesians, and also stimulate their own studies. During his stay about two thousand people did in fact attend his lectures, and many discussions and encounters took place. This trip also meant a great deal for Zeylmans in his later work in Holland. Dutch culture had been deeply influenced by contact with these colonies. Many anthroposophists had either spent their youth in the Dutch East Indies (such as Dr Ita Wegman) or had family there (such as Elisabeth Vreede). Zeylmans had the chance to experience for himself an aspect of the Dutch character in the form of three hundred years of 'colonial management'. Holland's task in respect to Indonesia over those centuries became clear to him, as did the degree to which it had succeeded. He wrote about this in 1940 in his book *Die Aufgabe unseres Volkes* ('Our people's task'). In 1945 he visited Indonesia again as part of a world-trip.

The voyage by ship, lasting nearly three weeks, provided him with a peaceful transition to the East. He had a deep experience of the ocean. He later wrote about this voyage:

. . . For me the sea was a place imbued with Christ forces, penetrated and illumined by Michael. My thoughts and meditations formed themselves more strongly and clearly on the sea than anywhere else. As I sailed across the Indian Ocean, hosts of souls in the world of spirit travelled too, very close to me. The 'thin wall' of which Rudolf Steiner speaks, between the physically visible and the spiritual world, was nowhere so thin as here. And how could it not have been so? Christ penetrated the

earth with all its 'sheaths'—light, air, water, earth, right into the inmost core of earth. So where would one have a more direct experience of his working than at a place where the forces of metamorphosis—light and water—themselves hold sway? Everything is thinner, more transient, more fleeting, more fluid. I think that destiny probably takes a hand in where we experience Christ most strongly. For me it is the world of light, colour, water and landscape (and of this last particularly the physiognomy, the gesture, the language as it were). And then above all, man as bearer of the spirit—each person as a (however weak) Christopher, Christ-bearer. And so we all enter the dome of the cosmos, coming from different directions, and continually see other, different aspects.

Willem Zeylmans felt he was on a mission. On the evening of the first day after landing, before falling asleep, he beheld the tropics as though in a vision:

A dark, gloomy plant-world, animals and tropical blossoms, Hindu-figures, bronzed bodies with white head-dresses, everything heavy and sultry, suddenly split and struck by a powerful light. In this light appears an angel in knight's armour, his wings shining white. The armour is silver, with bright-blue diamond shapes upon it. The angel holds a mighty sword before him, offering it to me. With a sign he shows me that I must take the sword so as to bear Michael's message to the East. He tells me from whom this sword comes, but I do not understand. I think to myself: Perhaps he means Godfrey de Bouillon? But I do not know if that is right. Then the angel stands to one side and another appears, dressed like an eastern, Persian statue: a golden, richly embroidered cloak, as in ancient Persian or perhaps Babylonian statues. 'That was my past form' the first angel tells me. Behind this one appear other figures again, an endless succession of angels.

In Sumatra he had his first profound meeting with the Orient:

My first experience on coming to Indonesia was an intense sense of liberation. It is like being relieved of a heavy burden. The warmth, the sunshine from six in the morning until six in the evening, the world of light almost continually enveloping one, gives a feeling of new trust in everything celestial (even during the rainy season).

Then there is the luxuriating vegetation, the fairy-tale forces of growth, the endless wealth of colours and forms! In the jungle you think you are back in long-gone mythical times: ferns, giant palms, gigantic trees, all wound round with flowers and orchids. It is as though the soul streams out into eternity in a hugely magnified summer-experience. One starts to understand why people there live in a dream rather than being wide awake, given up to and embedded in powerful, intoxicating natural forces. They have drunk in the peace and calm of this nature, and are never in a hurry. Does the plant hurry when it unfolds, the tree when it grows? Everything occurs in accord with the laws reigning in nature, the interworking of earthly and heavenly forces—also in human life. We may become agitated or rebellious, but things simply are as they are.

He soon encountered Islam when he paid a visit to the sultan of Deli. On 12 July the crown prince Amirudin received him in his palace in Medan.

. . . We speak about Holland, where Tengku Amirudin was with his brother. Then we sit in the front gallery, behind us the great hall with much marble and gold inlay, here and there ugly, expensive objects, but the whole having a certain magnificence. The sultan comes towards me in a very friendly manner, makes a deep bow and gives me his hand. We sit down at the table, and cigars and cigarettes are passed round. The crown prince acts as interpreter, but it turns out that the sultan understands Dutch quite well, though he does not speak it.

The conversation begins on the subject of anthroposophy (people have read about my visit in the newspapers). For the sultan the great question is: Is this a belief or a science? I try to answer by describing German philosophical idealism: he listens politely but does not understand. Then I speak about man as both a physical and a spiritual being, and our connection with stars and planets. This is very well understood. The ice is broken: 'Ah, so it is a faith.' Then I talk about anthroposophical pedagogy and medicine, and they seem very interested. Then about infections and those who infect themselves intentionally for scientific purposes (leprosy and cholera). The sultan considers such people heroic. He believes that ultimately human life is in God's hands.

We change the theme of conversation and begin to speak about Islam, and the relationship between Islam and Christianity. They regard Jesus as a prophet like Abraham and also Adam. For them Christ is no God—what do we base his divinity on? That is the question. On the fact that he had no father? That is nothing remarkable really. One can be born in four ways: created by God alone (Adam), by God and a father or a man (Eve), by God and a mother (Jesus) or by God and two parents. I mention the relationship of Jesus to Christ and the Jordan baptism: 'This is my beloved son, in whom I am well pleased.' * *The sultan thought this was only a loving way of speaking, but no proof of his divinity. Then*

---

* In the German translation of the bible, this passage reads: 'This is my son, whom today I have brought forth.'

we talk about the redemption of humanity and the Fall; they do not understand how Christ can redeem humanity since everyone must bear responsibility for their own actions. I try to explain the relationship between humanity, earth and individual. How do they regard the idea of reincarnation? This is altogether rejected. Then we speak about the esoteric path of development, about which they know (or say) little. After an hour I make it obvious that I would like to leave, but the sultan says he has plenty of time, having set aside the whole morning for this conversation. 'This may be the only time that we see you. Let us use this opportunity well.' We continue to speak, about agriculture and biodynamic methods of manuring. They see this method as very important for tobacco in particular, for it is very difficult to preserve the quality of tobacco. They are completely in agreement with my views on artificial fertilizers, believing the cosmic influences of sun, moon and stars to be of the highest importance.

Then we speak about the possibility of raising the instinctive path of wisdom to the level of a conscious training; they think this would be possible, but only in the future.

A servant brings cool drinks. The first drink is accompanied by much ceremony.

The conversation continues again, on the subject of western civilization. The crown prince expresses his regret that he has never found any westerners who were interested in talking about this: 'One cannot talk with them about anything, not even on journeys.' He believes this is due to the fact that they have no faith, even Christians and Jews. He only knows three true religions: Judaism, Christianity and Islam. These come from God. Brahmanism and Buddhism came about through human beings. The Messiah of whom Jews and Christians speak will one day come and preach Islam to all. The sultan tells me in a fatherly way that he finds me far too peaceful and serene for a European: 'The European is nervous, but you are not.' Two hours pass and I try to take my leave. The sultan holds a small farewell speech: it has been a great and very rare privilege to talk with someone about the things that are closest to his heart. He is very grateful. Although I have different views on life, I have shown interest in him. Everyone is touched and moved, the crown prince also; he says many kind things about me and speaks of friendship. In the West nowadays, he says, people don't have friends any more, only 'business friends'. He also uses the image of the sword that becomes rusty and can only be honed again through conversation: 'Such conversations are necessary . . . we always need one another.' He regards such a conversation, he says, as a gift.

From the bottom of my heart I reciprocate with many compliments. The sultan again greets me with many bows and mumbles all sorts of things, bending over my hand. I descend the stairs between the two young princes and am driven home in the sultan's car. The few pennies that I give the driver (for five minutes' drive) send him ecstatic with joy. I had in fact heard that people have to scrimp and save a lot there and are fairly poor.

The long car drive across Sumatra introduces him to the most wonderful landscape. He notes down many phrases to try to record the overwhelming impressions in his travel journal. With a painterly eye he describes the many colours he sees. For instance, when driving along the edge of Toba lake, at a height of one thousand metres:

. . . Undertones of a deep grey-green; at the edge of the lake a bright emerald or a dark green that becomes pale as emerald. Some parts of the landscape are blue to indigo. In contrast very bright, delicate colours edge the mountains. Some places on the mountains are formed in waves and folded like cloths. Others rise out of the water or nestle close to the lake. Some places are covered in green while others are bare and, at a distance, appear a delicate purple and blue. The clouds change, but mainly everything is bathed in blue light with white clouds . . .

During his lectures and many visits he becomes more familiar with the eastern way of life:

The Indonesian is far removed from the problems that beset westerners. He lives in the world and with nature as a matter of course, his soul streaming out into the macrocosm. He senses his connection with stars, sun and moon, but also with gods, nature spirits and demons, with all good and bad powers in the world. His space, roofed by stars, is a space still truly heaven. He dwells there outside time, imbued with eternity.

When a European gives himself up to such dreaminess, he senses his rigidity dissolving, feels himself streaming out into the world; stars and heaven come close again. We become one with the unending cosmos, the sharp outlines of our western soul start to fade . . . but we rarely dare to give ourselves up consciously to this state of mind—and rightly, for the danger of losing ourselves is great.

Imagine the front courtyard of a temple in Bali. The richly ornamented temple portals with sculptures that seem like a continuation of nature: plants, animals, nature spirits and gods—all combining in a single, lavish, fairy-tale beauty and unity. Does it not seem as if the whole temple is growing up out of the ground? The Waringin tree brings this earth connection to expression: its runners hang down in hundreds from the air, reach the ground and become new trunks, linking heaven and earth with one another. The tree grows in two directions, from below upwards, but also from above downwards.

Then there are the people who move through this unity of nature and spirit, the women who actually walk as only dream-priestesses otherwise do, their many-coloured offerings piled high on their heads. The Indonesian still lives in a paradisiacal, timeless state, embedded in the breadths of the heavens, untouched by the contradictions of our western civilization.

People were especially grateful for his lectures in small towns and isolated villages—these always led to much discussion and liberated people from the ordinary course of their daily lives. It was spiritual food for them. Sometimes he stayed several days in one place, and new invitations would arrive out of the blue. Numerous conversations and some medical consultations took place, and on a few occasions he held discussion meetings with other doctors.

Zeylmans' chief lecture themes were:
The importance of colours for the human soul
Goethe's Faust
What is anthroposophy?
Sleeping, dreaming, waking in our life of soul
Earthly and cosmic image of man
The idea of reincarnation as the fruit of western thinking
Steiner's anthroposophy as a further development of Goethe's idea of metamorphosis
What is the importance of illness for the human being?
Goethe's esoteric significance and his poem 'The Mysteries' (Die Geheimnisse)
The evolution of human thinking
From Buddha to Christ
The earth and the evolution of man
Man's relationship with the various arts

Among the most striking experiences of his Indonesian journey was his visit to the Borobudur temple on Java, one of the largest Buddhist monuments in the world.

On Java, Buddhism has only been able to play a role for a relatively short time. It probably arrived from Sumatra, where a mighty Hindu kingdom existed in the fifth century, the rulers of which cultivated Buddhism. This impulse quickly led to the creation of magnificent monuments, including those on the Kedu plain where Borobudur is also to be found. It is not so much a temple as a structure built over some of Buddha's ashes. The building itself has the form of a 'stupa'—a square foundation upon which a round, bell-like structure rises up, with a decorative tower as spire—and bears 72 smaller stupas above, each one containing a statue of the Buddha. Borobudur is built in nine terraces above a hill. The lower six are square, the upper three rise up in circles. The galleries have a total length of 3 km and everywhere there are images of the Buddha. In a sublime peace they express various gestures and stances like a living language. They gaze in all the different directions of space. In ancient times those who visited this temple could also enter on a path of schooling, intensifying their experiences to the highest wisdom.

On Saturday evening, 18 September, we reach the small hotel directly below the temple. The sky is cloudy and in the darkness we can see the temple's vague outlines. Later on, when the moon breaks through, we walk up there. The sky becomes brighter. As we pass through the galleries, we find the dimensions become ever greater. At the top we have a wonderful view over the moonlit landscape with its forests of palms. One can just make out the volcanoes Merapi and Merbabu. The next day at 5 in the morning we are up there again. The moon still shines brightly and a first pale pink aura bathes the volcanoes. Over the mountain slopes plays a continually changing, rich and delicate veil of colours. At sunrise the plain is covered in white mist, with green palms rising up out of it here and there. The volcano peaks of Merapi and Merbabu are coloured a delicate pink and a pale sheen of light becomes visible between them.

Suddenly a wave of golden light breaks through and streams over the plain. The mist is interwoven with gold and silver rays of light, and dissolves in the rich abundance of light that now floods everything. The palm forests now become visible, dressed in a delicate, damp morning green. The influx of light colours the mountain slopes opposite pink, purple and bright grey. The radiance of the fast rising sun grows ever greater. The whole plain is bathed and sustained in these waves of light, seeming to float between the delicate colours of the mountain slopes all around. Standing on the upper terrace of the stupa we gaze speechless at this miracle of light's birth and feel our souls grow one in deep awe with the silent statues around us. In all directions the Buddhas gaze over the awakening plain, their gestures seeming to liberate themselves from rigidity. An inner motion of soul breaks through the whole immobility of the statues. A divine dialogue begins between the bearers of light and the one who, in many other lives, brought the teaching of healing to earth.

Towards five o'clock in the afternoon, after lunch and a midday rest, we return once more: the first twilight arrives, then sunset—a miracle! The landscape becomes a place of imagination. The volcanoes float away into the heavens in violet, purple, pink and gold. This, together with Toba lake, is one of the mightiest sights of my life! We do not come down again until it has grown dark, and are deeply moved by what we have seen. We have met Buddhism—after previously studying it and valuing it, we have now truly encountered it!

As he falls asleep, the hundreds of Buddhas surround Zeylmans as though in a dream:

From the fixity of their gestures a movement is delicately born, a kind of eurythmy. Only their hands and lower arms move in a celebratory way, their faces stay motionless. The whole choir of them floats around me for a long time. Then the image fades into another: the Merapi volcano as a coloured image floating above the clouds in the most delicate, unearthly colours.

Where Zeylmans had met Islam through the sultan of Deli, and a fairy-tale kind of Buddhism at the Borobudur temple, so he now encountered a very ancient and venerable Hinduism at the 'Wajang' performance, a shadow-play with colourful puppets, that was presented in village market places in the evenings.

This was a large festival for travellers and tourists, but also for the hundred or so Javanese men, women, boys, girls and infants.

The orchestra of six or seven people plays the 'gamelan', a child bangs on the gong, and amongst them lies another, smaller child sleeping.

The audience, sitting on the ground in the open air, watches the performance for half the night in great excitement. The often very complicated stories which they see performed are very well-known to them.

The shadow-play tells of the adventures of Rama, an incarnation of Vishnu, and the audience is wholly involved as he wages his mighty battle with giants and demons. Then, breathless, they watch the battle of the Titans between Pandawi and Kanrawas—above whom, as a wise, helping power Krishna (another incarnation of Vishnu) continually floats—and the story of Hanoman, the monkey king, in battle with lower orders of gods and men. Clowns appear. Silent dialogue, stirring battle, humorous scenes: all this comes to expression with modest means and effects, in the puppets' simple arm movements. The expression of pondering, the gesture of expectancy, of aggression, of resignation, argument, the gesture of being 'at death's door'.

As Zeylmans asks his neighbour about a certain puppet whose name he did not hear, he gets the reply: 'Him? He's a mortal!' This answer shows him the state of consciousness in which the Javanese watch such a play: the gods and heroes as the truly real, while man is only a 'mortal'.

Finally let me tell of the meeting which Willem Zeylmans had in Solo (on Java) with the prince or Mangku named Negoro VII. He had been invited to this prince's palace to give a lecture on 'Experiencing spirit and spiritual consciousness—a problem of East and West' to a study group whose members consisted primarily of Hindus, but also included some Chinese people and a few Dutch priests.

In his lecture Zeylmans describes eastern consciousness, then western, and characterizes the mid-point between these as the event of Golgotha, speaking of the possibility of a synthesis once both types of consciousness have developed further through training in thinking. The twenty or so listeners react very differently from one another. The prince listens very attentively; he is dressed in European clothes and makes an elegant impression on Zeylmans, almost like a predator in his movements. He has a sly and unlovely face. The subsequent discussion turns into a real battle for Zeylmans. The Mangku regards the gulf between East and West as unbridgeable. He cannot bear the idea of 'thinking meditation', except possibly as it appears in Samadhi philosophy. What Zeylmans has presented, he says, seems to him like scientific materialism. The main goal of all inner training is to know: 'Where have I come from and where am I going?' Ultimately this is a question of light. (The Mangku clearly has no sense for the spiritualization of matter.) One of those present finds all this far too complicated. Surely the ultimate goal is the same for everyone? The prince cannot accept that spiritual training also has social implications. He believes that acting as an example is sufficient. A Dutch priest interposes that one ought to come closer to God, then everything would come by itself. One of the other priests asks: What are we giving to the masses? Then the discussion passes on to the question of whether the development of our spiritual powers is available to everyone. Zeylmans describes the possibility of also experiencing the great spiritual truths through feeling. One of the doctors present wishes to know more about the philosophical basis of anthroposophy. The mood in the group is very engaged and Zeylmans has the impression that people are taking these questions very seriously. '*But the Mangku, untouched by all this, is a one hundred percent oriental: he goes his way and acts. "The man with two faces!"*.'

When Zeylmans meets his old student friend Sumitro again shortly after this, the latter tells him that the present 'Mangku Negoro VII' once lived as a poor student in Sumitro's student lodgings, at the time of the 'INA' Leiden dispute. Whenever Zeylmans came to visit 'Sum', his room-mate had withdrawn to the kitchen. So, sixteen years before this battle of words, the two of them had once been in very close proximity to each other!

Before he left the Indonesian archipelago, a newspaper asked Zeylmans to describe his impressions of his travels. He gave an overview of his experiences and activities and finally said that he had been troubled to see '*how little westerners and easterners know about each other in this country*'. It seemed to him, he said, '*as though the gulf between them is becoming ever more distinct, also because the two groups have such differing experiences. How many*

Europeans know about the Wajang figures, familiar to every Indonesian? And how strange European family life appears to Oriental people'.

And the spiritual sword which Willem Zeylmans received, as it were, on his first day on Indonesian soil? He certainly did not allow it to 'rust' in the conversations and discussions he held as he journeyed through the Indonesian archipelago!

★

But in Europe a drama was being prepared that took place in 1935, when Willem Zeylmans was expelled against his will from the General Anthroposophical Society, along with many others. He wrote a booklet about this in July 1935 (translated by Dr E. Vreede into German) entitled 'Development and Spiritual Conflict'.

Those who manage to read this text without too much emotion will find many valuable thoughts in it on the Anthroposophical Society. One can also discover in it elements which point to the way he was able, in later years, to become a person of the 'middle' realm, i.e. someone capable of encompassing and combining the most painful contradictions and oppositions.

Those who executed this 'expulsion' in 1935 were the same who rescinded it again in 1948. Twelve years later some sort of 'reintegration' occurred.

The ideal of founding a common, international, all-encompassing and globally active Anthroposophical Society, such as Rudolf Steiner hoped to realize in 1923, and did indeed do so at Christmas of that year, was one of the deepest experiences of Zeylmans' life. This took place only three years after he had first encountered anthroposophy as his life's work, and for him Rudolf Steiner's various descriptions of such a wholly new world society assumed the nature of a sacred, esoteric task of the highest order.

In founding the Dutch Anthroposophical Society on 18 November 1923 Rudolf Steiner had made many passing remarks about things of decisive importance for the Dutch. (In the relevant chapter in this book we have reproduced the most important of these so far unpublished remarks.) The idea of such a world society is basically an esoteric one: it can only become visible through the living, moral action of human beings. Its basis is not an 'organization' but the mystery of a living being, whose name is 'Anthroposophy'. '*A spiritual society will simply have to continually renew itself, will have to continually be reborn, and will have to find the courage for this "dying and becoming".*' And: '*One really only has such a society if one continually strives to create it.*'

Rudolf Steiner said that this society should, for the first time on earth, encompass all human beings of the most varied destinies and orientation who seek anthroposophy. As Zeylmans said in 1935:

It seems obvious that when such a Society is formed, the Goetheanum directors (i.e. the executive council or Vorstand of the Society) need to turn with great openness towards all those who have joined it or who are still destined to join it; and that they must continually ask themselves how all the forces, all the impulses that are born from spiritual will can stream together into the whole.

When he wrote the booklet 'Development and Spiritual Conflict' in July 1935, he basically set himself the task of reviewing the time during which he had known of anthroposophy: a period of 18 years and close on 7 months, since Tak and van Heemskerck had first introduced him to anthroposophy in the autumn of 1916.

Willem Zeylmans suffered unspeakably from the 'spiritual conflicts' between anthroposophists, as did many others who were affected. But one would be wrong to think this applied primarily to the year 1935 and the expulsion. He was caused greater pain than this in 1930–31, when he believed that Rudolf Steiner's ideal of the 1923 Christmas Foundation Meeting was no longer alive. The fact that the General Society later expelled several thousand anthroposophists and two of its council members, and was therefore no longer able to embrace all the streams within the anthroposophical movement, was merely confirmation of his view. In conversation he once said that while one might lose one's membership of the General Society, one could never depart from one's spiritual stream. This conviction was connected with the deepest impulse visible in his life, which he described in his book *The Foundation Stone*, and to whose realization he continually devoted himself. Here I would like to add that, as he often said, the practice of self-knowledge requires us to refrain from criticising others when we have difficulties with them; instead we need to raise to awareness our *own* part in such dispute, observing and learning from it.

We younger ones, often impulsively striving to conquer the world for anthroposophy, took too little account of the older generation of anthroposophists. Our behaviour was sometimes tactless and unnecessarily wounding. Many of my friends from that time do not wish to look at this.

Perhaps the title of his booklet gave expression to the essential issue in this whole question. It is, after all, called 'Development and *Spiritual* Conflict'.

These words might almost suggest a secret formula—perhaps even a formula for the future.

★

The difficulties within the Anthroposophical Society that ran parallel with the rise of the Nazi movement in Germany led to Zeylmans working more intensively in England. In London he had already held consultations at regular intervals and also been involved in ongoing medical collaboration with anthroposophical doctors there. From 1933 onwards the annual summer schools began, in which he usually participated (at Bangor, Westonbirt, Harrogate, London and Cambridge); and he also went to England to give lectures on other occasions. Cecil Harwood, later General Secretary of the Anthroposophical Society in Britain, described in a 1961 obituary how he had experienced Zeylmans over the decades of their collaboration. Let me cite the following from it:

> Dr Zeylmans was an outstanding friend of the Anthroposophical Society in Great Britain, so much so that his loss is hardly less felt among us than in Holland. For very many years no major event in our movement was complete without his presence. On these occasions his unique social gift was of the greatest value to us. He always found the right word to say, and human difficulties melted away in the presence of his genial wisdom. He was exceptionally capable of being all things to all men yet he always remained eminently himself.
>
> I remember more than once hearing him say that to be a universal man meant not to reject but to fulfil the characteristics of your country: that Shakespeare was accepted by the entire world precisely because he was essentially English, Goethe, because he expressed so perfectly the genius of Germany. We in England experienced Dr Zeylmans as a typical Dutchman with a Rembrandt richness of soul, but one who had raised the natural qualities of his country to the height where it was acceptable to all. He loved to speak about the psychology of nations, but he did more than speak about it, he enacted it. As befitted the nature and history of his country he was both a European and a Citizen of the World. I was once privileged to follow in his footsteps in America and I can testify to the profound impression his lectures and his personality made in the New World as well as in the Old.
>
> He spoke the English language with wonderful clarity, fluency and charm, and his manner of speaking immediately won the hearts of his audience. We shall not soon forget his characteristic voice, the mobility

of his body, and the gestures with which he seemed to be gathering the spiritual events he was describing into the focus of the room in which he was speaking. On less formal occasions than lectures, when we sat with him in a small circle, he never obtruded himself and yet he always remained the centre to which everyone instinctively turned. It was somehow taken for granted that the final word, the ultimate judgement would rest with him. Everyone felt that he would be able to see the matter from all sides. For both by natural genius and (as I believe) by long practice he combined in himself a great variety of powers which he kept under conscious control. It is perhaps a mark of a great man in our modern age to unite qualities which may even appear contradictory to each other. This Dr Zeylmans certainly did. In him were found dignity with affability, authority with modesty, enthusiasm with cool clarity, gravity with lightness, knowledge with simplicity.

His lectures engaged all the powers of the soul, thought, feeling and will, for it was out of these powers that they were born. In his last visits, when he revealed to us some of the secrets of the Foundation Stone Meditation, he seemed to have reached the climax of his inspiration. We shall long remember the way he spoke of the fivefold repetition of the word Light in the last stanza of that Meditation, and how he revealed through it the vision of the five-pointed Star which led the Kings to Bethlehem. We felt he was himself speaking with kingly authority and wisdom.

★

Willem Zeylmans visited Egypt with enormous enthusiasm. The trip lasted only twelve days, from 24 December to 5 January. But it filled him most profoundly—indeed it was a fulfilment for him.

On his journey through the Suez canal three years earlier, on the way to Indonesia, he had already had a glimpse of this landscape. From the steamer, as it glided past Bedouin villages at night, he watched the moon rising over the desert: *'A wonderful sight, like an Egyptian with a fez on his head!'*

A small company of nine people had met up for this Egypt tour, under the leadership of Professor van Bemmelen, whose son David was also coming. The latter had already prepared himself intensively for the journey by writing a number of insightful articles on ancient Egyptian culture.

Zeylmans, together with his friend Herbert Hahn, had been invited on this excursion by a businessman from The Hague, who had recently become treasurer of the Dutch Anthroposophical Society.

Things augured well for the trip from the outset: as the ship passed through the Straights of Messina, they caught sight of Orion above them, according to ancient tradition the constellation of Osiris; and before them, bright and clear, stood Sirius, the star of Isis! After leaving Cairo on Christmas Eve and travelling along the Nile in a luxurious Pullman train towards Aswan, the company decided to hold a festive reading of a Christmas lecture by Rudolf Steiner. Packed together in one of the sleeping compartments they listened with emotion and surprise to a passage describing the Egyptian lion god Sachmeth as representative of the sentient soul, a soul body of the human being whose origin lies in ancient Egyptian culture.

Before falling asleep Zeylmans noted in his travel journal: *'The ancient Egyptian Osiris Mysteries celebrated their initiation festival in this period of the year, between 20 and 30 December!'* And when he awoke early next morning (*'never before in my life have I slept so well in a sleeping compartment!'*), he hears his travelling companions already stirring too: *'As though it had been agreed we all awoke at the same time, and on opening the small curtain saw the red disc of the sun gleam up over the desert horizon, with two outstretched wings of bright pink clouds—an overwhelming sight of the Egyptian sun.'* From the hotel in Aswan they marvel at the sight of the Nile cataract: *'Indescribable . . . this is how things must have been in ancient Biblical times! The Mystery of light: here all becomes symbol, and that is how we must also surely understand the hieroglyphs!'* After this they travelled in sailing boats to Elephantine, and found themselves at the place where the capital of Upper Egypt had been in ancient times.

'Towards evening we crossed the Nile together in a small rowing boat. Suddenly a deep stillness spread over the whole landscape. Silently we observed the sun vanishing from the glowing red sky in mysterious colours.' Without a sound they glided between cliffs and felt *'touched by the delicate hands of Aton. A Mystery journey . . .'*

The next day, led by their 'Battleaxe Mohammed', they visited the first cataract and sailed across the reservoir, deep below whose surface lies the ancient capital Philae. Ancient tradition says that this place is the Nile's earthly source, and that is why the temple of Isis is here. The ancient Egyptians felt that everything beyond the first cataract was dangerous, for there lay the land of the gods, the Nile's heavenly source.

'With my heart in my mouth' Zeylmans took leave of this place the next day and travelled with the others to the Horus temple in Edfu. They crawled through the passages of this best-preserved building of ancient times, and arrived at the crypt: *'Paths which the neophyte had to take . . .'*

Willem Zeylmans (on front camel)

In his notebook Zeylmans recorded little sketches and numerous words and phrases on his journey, which he used in later years in his lectures on Egypt. He must have become aware on this journey of countless insights into the mysteries of the hieroglyphs and images in ancient Egyptian art and religion. Intense conversations between the travellers also continually gave him food for thought, and they also studied Baedeker. In his notebooks for instance, one finds: *'Sun and moon are regarded as the eyes of Horus, the eye altogether. The eye of Osiris: loss of the old clairvoyance . . .'*

From Aswan they travelled north along the Nile and visited temples and royal tombs. In the Osireion of Abydos he walked along the 110-metre passage and, deeply impressed, noted with a great exclamation mark: *'Resurrection of Osiris in heaven!'*

By now the year 1936 had begun. They reached Cairo and rode to the tombs and sphinx at Memphis. They entered the inside of the Cheops pyramid, about which their tour-guide, Professor van Bemmelen, had written a short book. In those days the Cheops pyramid was frequently the subject of all sorts of speculation: people thought they had discovered prophecies of the future in the measurements and dimensions of this gigantic structure! The company naturally spoke a good deal about this and Zeylmans was able in later years to tell of this visit into the pyramid's interior, where they stood in silence around the pharaoh's sarcophagus in the king's chamber.

A surviving photograph by the desert photographer Gabriel Choueri shows Willem Zeylmans amongst his companions, all sitting on large camels. The pyramid stands in the background and the nine camel-leaders occupy the foreground in their breeze-blown robes. *'On a camel at last!'* he notes in his travel journal for this day.

Passing through Malta, where they witnessed a moon eclipse and visited the stronghold of the order of St John of Jerusalem, they travelled home via Chartres.

'Seeking the soul of humanity' Zeylmans once noted when searching for a motto for his autobiography. These words are on a page where he also mentioned his Egyptian trip. The series of phrases he lists are remarkable:

'N. and S. Egypt, papyrus and lotus, Osiris and Isis, the two crowns, larynx and womb, birth of the Word *from the soul, sentient soul.'* It is not too hard to make the connection between this 'life motto' and the figure of the goddess Isis. The country which he has encountered has, through the Nile's unique geographical form, a similarity with the human form: north and south Egypt, a human being as it were, and within this rests the figure

of the goddess Isis, for: *'she is the being of true humanity who slumbers within us . . . the human being who is reborn out of the spirit.'*

Thus Zeylmans, in coming to Egypt, came also as it were to the land of the ancient goddess Isis herself, where her archetypal image sleeps.

'Larynx and womb' refer to our natural birth and the birth of the spiritual human being of the future from the power of the Word, of the Logos.

The new Isis, to which Rudolf Steiner so decisively referred, now starts to recur repeatedly in Zeylmans' lectures—and it is as though the Egypt trip has released something in him.

Is it any surprise, therefore, that immediately on their return van Bemmelen, Herbert Hahn and Zeylmans begin to draft a book on the Egyptian Mysteries?

Since Champollion, a number of outstanding researchers have turned their attention to Egyptian culture. A great deal of material was assembled (Brugsch, Strauss, Budge, Breasted, Moret etc.) Although this material is available, we know only relatively little about the actual content of the Egyptians' religious concepts, and in particular of the deeper purpose of the ancient Mysteries. What is the significance of initiation for Egyptians seeking wisdom? What does the unification of the two lands of Egypt signify? What is the secret of the resurrection of Osiris? Without a comprehensive science of the spirit it is almost impossible to answer these questions. But Dr Rudolf Steiner examined the great epochs of human evolution in relation to one another, pointing to the laws of metamorphosis: just as a plant develops, putting forth one leaf after another, then blossom and fruit, so the cultural epochs develop too. In such a view we catch sight of the unifying direction which renders the various epochs comprehensible to us.

The truth is that all cultural epochs have a particular significance for the overall evolution of humanity. The priests of the ancient Mysteries saw this great direction and sequence before them.

This was Zeylmans' introduction to the planned book, which was to contain a 'series of essays on the real meaning of the Egyptian Mysteries and on the importance of ancient Egyptian culture for our own times.'

Seven authors were prepared to furnish their contributions. Alongside an historical overview, there were to be essays on the *Book of the Dead*, on ancient Egyptian cosmology and religion, initiation practice in the Mysteries, Egyptian teachings of the heavens and stars, and on how the Egyptians experienced death, as well as a study on mummification. Zeylmans planned to write about the myth of Osiris and Isis, and had agreed to contribute an essay on the 'resurrection of the Word'. The book was to conclude with a chapter on the architecture and art forms of the ancient Egyptians.

'Intended as a travel book' is written under the draft plan. And: *'The division of the separate chapters into small sections makes it possible to find a relevant passage easily. The traveller visiting a particular site need only look in the index to find further details about it. The whole in Baedeker format.*

The book never appeared. In the meantime the Anthroposophical Society had been prohibited in Germany—and who would still have been able to publish such a book? But the plan had its value as an impulse: the ideas to be addressed in many of these articles found their way into the culture of the times in the form of courses and lectures.

Immediately on his return Zeylmans gave a series of public lectures on 'Light and dark powers in our culture.' In these he says, among other things:

Our modern times are linked with former cultural epochs, in particular with that of ancient Egypt. The same link arises between man and world—but in another direction, rather as when something is turned inside out the same relationship occurs but in reverse. Modern man lives in matter which it was the Egyptian's task to learn to find. If modern man learns to overcome his intellect, he can liberate himself from materialism. One finds modern mummification in the domain of rigid, intellectual concepts which, like other concepts of our time, find their mirror image in ancient Egyptian culture . . . The human being of our day will need to learn to develop a picture consciousness . . .'

★

Returning from a longer visit to Sicily, Zeylmans wrote the following about his impressions:

One of the nodal points in world history—yes, that really is how one should regard Sicily! So much happened on this island. So much living and suffering! . . . and making others suffer . . .

This is where Odysseus met the beautiful Nausicaa after his shipwreck, as she played on the beach with her fair companions.

Here the Greeks founded flourishing colonies: Syracuse, Agrigente, Selinunte. They raised temples and theatres—which still stand on the coast, most of them in ruins, though here and there parts of them survive undamaged, rising up in yellow-brown stone that shines like gold in the sun.

How this must have looked at the time! A series of golden temples on the spine of a hill, a few hundred metres away from the sea! A deep blue sea, sometimes dark as indigo, almost purple with emerald flecks. And above the clear, transparent blue of the air—which does not seal off the heavens as the mist and clouds do in the West, but opens the heavens instead.

One can imagine the people . . . the priests in the temples, the inhabitants of towns, then the farmers in their vineyards, and the olive pickers . . .

An almost unearthly idyll . . . from a time when man still sensed his divinity on earth, living as man and god simultaneously . . . in beauty and wisdom.

Empedocles lived on Sicily, emanating from here his spiritual light, and testifying to his belief in immortality when he threw himself into Etna.

Plato travelled here and appeared at the court of the tyrant Dionysius of Syracuse . . . Aeschylus—and how many other names could be mentioned from this golden age!

But it all had to decline and fade. The Romans came, then later the Arabs and Normans.

But then, under the great Hohenstaufen, Friedrich II, Barbarossa's nephew, a new golden age flourished. He created an empire which stretched from the Mediterranean to the Baltic sea—but Sicily was where he felt most at home. Here in Palermo, in his palace that was half Moorish and half European, surrounded by blooming lemon and orange trees and almond blossom, he lived and felt very happy indeed in his 'Conca d'oro' or golden shell.

Has the modern age covered much of this up? No, much has remained. It seems as though nature's beauty has preserved much as it was.

There are mighty contrasts: bare, rough cliffs as in Calta Bellotta, where the magic castle of Klingsor, the black magician, stood. And opposite this the most gentle and beautiful nature—flowers in delicate and yet overpowering colours, soft-vaulting hills . . .

And all around the sea, sometimes like a shining silver mirror—or then blue and green, with white foam spraying up against the cliffs . . .

And then, towering over all, Mount Etna! The 'Mongibello', the mountain of mountains . . . enthroned like a mighty ruler over the island, holding dominion over the nations, bearing witness to the all-penetrating power of God. With its snowy peaks this mountain rises up into the heavens. Its broad roots are overgrown by vines and almond trees and vanish into the dark woods of lemon and orange trees with their yellow and golden fruit.

It gazes down from its heavenly heights on the human race. It watches nations arise and fade away. It sees their love, their suffering, their battles and struggles.

And then suddenly it awakes from eternal stillness, breaks out in thunder and destruction. Its mighty earthquakes shatter towns . . . and then things fall quiet again. Eternal repose returns.

Etna has always given me pause for thought. So much beauty and grandeur alongside such a powerful destructive urge—unsettling. Good and evil, light and darkness—so close together. Unsettling when it stands there before you like an archetypal image, thousands of metres high, reaching down from the heavens to the earth, when God reveals the extent of his glory and awfulness at once.

★

Willem Zeylmans can experience everything around him in the depths of his soul. What does he tell us about the world of colours?

There are only a few people who are aware that they are surrounded by colours the whole day long, from the moment of awaking to falling asleep. The human soul perceives, mostly unconsciously, an endless number of colours, nuances and shades. The whole visible world reveals itself to us in colours.

Anyone willing to take the trouble to list the various colours, nuances and shades which surround him at any one moment in nature or in his home, would be surprised by their enormous number.

It is still more interesting to observe not only the colours as they reveal themselves at any one time but also how they change through the course of the day. Every painter knows how a few clouds or a different angle of the sun can wholly alter the colours and relationships of light in a landscape. But even someone who does not paint can notice this. Anyone who is attentive will see how colours continually change, whether outside in nature or in the home.

This points to two peculiarities in the relationship of colour to the human soul: firstly to the all-pervading presence of colours, and secondly to their flux and change. This latter quality is particularly significant, for if one speaks of colour as such, as it reveals itself to the soul, then one can say that the colours appear each morning together with the light, and fade away again in the evening as the light fades. Naturally the colour-bearing substances with their chemical properties remain there in the darkness, but the colours themselves are not seen until certain conditions of light reveal them again. In other words, colour as a phenomenon is born with the light and fades as dark comes. Such an observation may seem obvious, but discovering this can be an important experience for the soul.

Then one recognizes, in fact, something of the delicacy and subtlety of colours, and also of their fluidity, fleetingness and transience.

This description is the beginning of an article which Zeylmans wrote in 1934 for the periodical *De Verfkroniek* (Colour chronicle), the in-house magazine of the society of Dutch varnish and paint manufacturers and retailers. This fairly detailed article on 'The significance of colours for the soul' makes a strange impression sandwiched between technical articles and dry trade statistics. Zeylmans' lectures to Dutch architects on colour psychology and Goethean colour theory had drawn the attention of a broader circle of professional people, and thus he had been asked to write this article. In it he describes the importance and correctness of Goethe's colour theory and depicts how it was not until the twentieth century that 'colours once more entered cultural life, after the grey and colourless nineteenth century'. It was, he said, as though a new element had been born in our culture—in painting, architecture and interior design something of a revolution had occurred in this respect. But people still worked too instinctively out of their sense of colours; and now the 'language of colour' should also be consciously recognized, so that the laws underlying the relationship of colours to the human soul could be investigated and used to good purpose. Colours, he wrote, have a social task—in schools and homes, but also in the realm of health-care and medicine. *One could apply the effects of colours consciously to the human soul.*

Zeylmans had often met people in Holland who were more than just superficially interested in colours. From the many conversations that had arisen, a small circle of specialists had formed who had a warm interest in the potentials of colour for modern culture. Eventually this 'colour commission', as it called itself, became the Society for Practical Colour Psychology which presented itself for the first time in the spring of 1936 at a very well-attended public evening in The Hague.

The ten or so founders, who together formed the executive committee of this society, were very different from each other in character and profession. There was the painter Heyenbrock, director of a 'museum of work', then the architects De Wijs (civil engineer for the town of Enschede) and Auke de Komter, who had founded a museum of architecture. Also Ida Falckenburg, an interior designer with very left-wing ideals, Frans ter Gast, a set-designer who had made a name for himself with a shadow-theatre, and Willem Sandberg, a graphic designer who had also just begun work as curator of the Stedelijk Museum. There were also a few more technically-orientated people, such as the science photographer Tirion, and Rijgersberg, who played an active organizational role in the whole enterprise—he worked for a paint factory and was very knowledgeable about colour shades. Finally there was the engineer de Lange and the psychologist Ovink.

Zeylmans, as chairman of this society, stood up on the very first evening and delivered a lecture on 'Foundations of a colour psychology', giving an overview of the aims of the new group: study of colour psychology in the broadest sense, in particular with the purpose of finding practical applications in industry, art and science. The aim was also to promote knowledge and use of colour under the motto: '*More* and *better* colours in daily life!'

In the four years of its existence the society was able to realize some of its far-reaching aims: a journal called 'Colour' was published and conferences on colour were held, where people from many walks of life gave lectures. Two carpet factories took advice from the society for their range, and for years one of them appended to its pattern-book a small 'colour handbook' which the society had written (see appendix).

From the field of industry came questions about the best colour for lighting in the work place; and textile factories sought help in the naming of their many 'brown shades', which were very fashionable at the time, taking advice too on the best colour combinations. Some paint and varnish producers also collaborated with the 'Society for colours'.

It soon became apparent that there was room for great ideals to be realized in the field of practical colour application. For instance people were seeking to standardize colour names. The librarian Rijgersberg collected a small specialist library consisting of books from all over the world, so that members could access a great deal of information on the still very new field of colour research. The first research experiments were also started.

In London there had already been a British Colour Council in existence for some time. Zeylmans and Ovink travelled to England and acquired sole marketing rights to a series of specialist journals and so-called 'colour-cards' that were, for instance, much in demand with Dutch flower growers, so that they could standardize names for their new flower varieties.

Among architects at that time there was a movement trying to increase the use of colour in architecture. In October 1936 Zeylmans gave a talk to the Dutch Society for Promoting Architecture, among the finest and most mature expressions of his views on colour. The lecture appeared as a pamphlet, together with the discussion which took place after his talk. From this one can discern the quality that made discussions after Zeylmans' lectures so absorbing: the quick-witted presence of mind and instructive way in which he often replied to questions when an audience had become involved in what he was saying. It seems as if, in these discussions, decisive human contacts were sometimes born.

Willem Zeylmans van Emmichoven, 1936

The lecture was called 'Colour and soul'; and in it Zeylmans deals at length with what he refers to as the modernity of Goethe's colour theory, as well as describing the results of his own colour experiments in Leipzig in 1920.

'Human beings have a dormant sense of colours. Through Goethe's method one can gain a conscious and living relationship to the world of colours. The sense of colours needs to be awoken—and it is possible to practise this!' This, in summary, is the rough content of his concluding words.

Ovink, who had joined the group somewhat later, and replaced Rijgersberg as secretary of the society, told forty years later how he had experienced Zeylmans in the executive committee meetings of the time:

'He was a born chairman and mediator between opposite views. We were a society of very different types of people, but executive committee meetings were always amusing and gripping—partly because of his humour, which always had a refreshing and releasing effect. Zeylmans' great energy made him the right leader of such a society. He never appeared doctrinaire though, but had a very practical approach to everything. It won't be possible to write the history of Dutch culture without including the figure of Zeylmans: he had a decisive effect and gave many impulses to people in many fields.' This, more or less, is a summary of Ovink's words.

The last we hear of the 'Society for colours' is in September 1940, in a set of minutes. The war had broken over Holland and some of the executive committee members vanished and joined the underground. The theme of 'colour' was no longer of prime importance compared with the great dangers that now surfaced.

After the Second World War Rijgersberg managed to found a new 'Society for colours', but Zeylmans was no longer involved, for his tasks had now moved to the international, global sphere. Rijgersberg had much success with a colour handbook which was reprinted many times. Nowadays there is still a small active society in the Netherlands; and at the respected Leidse Onderwijs Instellingen institute (The largest Dutch distance-learning organization), one can pursue an extensive course on colour theory.

But for Zeylmans a path of development had come to fruition that had begun, one could say, at the age of two, when he sat under the kitchen table and gazed out at the sunlight until it hurt his eyes. And at the age of 16, when he entered the Rijksmuseum in Amsterdam for the first time, his awareness of colour in art was kindled, and through this he got to know

Heemskerck. Subsequently he pursued a scientific understanding of the world of colours through his doctoral research in Leipzig and Goethe's theory of colours—and came to the idea of the psychological effect of colours. In 1928 he began to see the world of colours as 'therapeutic', as he initiated a new form of treatment using the different colours of patients' rooms. Every illness disturbs the organic equilibrium of the body, and thus also our connection with the soul and spirit. Alongside medical treatment, artistic therapy that calls on a patient's own inner activity can contribute to harmonization of organ functions. Painting with water colours has a dynamic particularly suited for this. For the so-called 'cold' illnesses (such as cancer, rheumatism and depressions) patients need to be encouraged to use the active colours. For inflammatory processes or manic conditions passive colours are appropriate. Heart and asthma patients, with rhythmic system disorders, gain particular benefit from green.

One can therefore say that colours started to be used 'practically' in 1936, through the work of the 'Society for colours'.

In 1940 Zeylmans wrote an article for a small periodical produced by the actor Max Gümbel-Seiling, which I print here to conclude this theme.

Willem Zeylmans (left) and Hans Grelinger, Stakenberg Camp, near Harderwijk, 1930

Willem Zeylmans (left), Eugen Kolisko and Herbert Hahn, Stakenberg

Willem Zeylmans (left) and Pieter de Haan, around 1929

(left to right) Grete Kirchner-Bockholt, Erich Kirchner, Willem Zeylmans, en route to South Africa, 1961

How does the soul live in the world of colours?

'The colours are the deeds of light—its deeds and sufferings'. These words of Goethe are not to be viewed primarily as poetic or symbolic but above all as scientific and real. We have countless opportunities to perceive their reality as long as we are prepared to see the 'mystery made manifest'.

Without light there is no colour. Colour was born in and through light. But without darkness no colour can exist either. As light increases and intensifies, colours grow pale like the stars as the sun rises. One can show this experimentally by putting a number of strong colours on a sheet of paper and illuminating them with a light that grows continually stronger. The colours grow more and more pale, and finally become invisible. Every painter knows that the colours of flowers and vegetation, of woods and fields, are not at their most beautiful in harsh sunlight. A moderate light, that is, the right mixture of light and darkness, gives the colours their full depth. Thus colours are related to shade, which also forms between light and darkness.

A certain relationship between light and dark is necessary for colours to arise: the creative deed of the light and the suffering opposition of darkness which catches up and works upon the light—'deeds and sufferings'.

Colours belong to a sphere that lies between two other spheres. They unfold in this intermediary sphere; and in such a way that yellow forms close to the light and blue close to darkness, as Goethe describes in his colour theory. Yellow and blue are to be seen as the coloured representatives of light and dark. In green the equilibrium is attained between these two spheres.

Opposite green stands crimson. Goethe describes this colour as the true red, as a colour missing from the normal spectrum but which occupies the midpoint in the so-called 'reversed spectrum'. The normal spectrum, as you know, forms when a ray of light passes through a narrow aperture and is then directed through a prism. The reversed spectrum occurs when there is a thin rod in place of the aperture, on the two sides of which light is cast. In this case the spectrum is not, as in the first model, red, orange, yellow, green, blue, indigo, violet; but: yellow, orange, red, crimson, violet, indigo, blue.

This crimson is the truly active principle in the world of colour. It creates the intensification—what Goethe calls 'heightening' from yellow to orange and orange-red on the one hand; and from blue to blue-violet (indigo) on the other hand. In both cases the effect and strength of the colours becomes more intense.

The human soul, too, which perceives and experiences the colours, occupies a sphere between two others: just as the colours are born between light and dark, so is the soul between spirit and body.

From its pre-birth state, the soul descends to earth. Whereas it previously lived in the pure light of spirit, it now enters the dark shelter of the body formed on earth. Consciousness awakens through opposition and unfolds in the soul as inner light. As the soul awakens more and more, it experiences thousands upon thousands of feelings in the world. The realm of grey tones that stretches between white and black is just as much part of the soul as the realm of colours. But to it belong also tones and sounds, fragrances, forms, the gradations from hard to soft, from rough to smooth, and many other sensations and feelings too.

The world of the soul is the world of qualities, of categories. Thus the soul is inwardly connected with colours—yes, perhaps most closely connected with them because they surround us all day long. Our link with colours and tones is actually a deeper one, because our experience of them takes greater hold of our being. But the all-embracing presence of colours throughout the day leads to a more permanent, lasting effect.

The human soul connects with its surroundings and withdraws again, like the rhythm of breathing. The body's respiratory process, with its in- and out-streaming of breath, is only the outer image of forces working deep within the soul. The soul has an inner urge to reunite with the world, with the whole cosmos out of which it was born. But such a reunion is only possible after death. That is why, after every encounter with the manifestations of the world, the soul returns to its shelter, the body. This process continues endlessly: a mighty breathing of the soul that links and then sunders man and world.

So the soul also breathes colours, thereby entering into the spaces and realms of the cosmos. Through colours it enters the universe and leaves it again in the same way. Blue is the colour of the sky's dome arching over us and delineating the boundaries of space. From the blue of the sky golden sunlight radiates through the world. In the dark of night this blue is deep and unfathomable; but the sparkling, shimmering, yellowish, yellow-red and green-yellow stars penetrate it with their thousands of rays.

In golden daylight all the things of the world are revealed: stones, crystals, plants and animals, human beings—all creation—in an endless variety of colours and colour-tones. The sunlight renders them visible for us and brings them close to us.

Where things almost vanish at the horizon we see them in a blue or violet haze. We can see this phenomenon most clearly with the mountains which—great and mighty—can still be seen from far away. But small objects also take on a blue or violet tone when the density of the atmosphere distances them from us. Thus, in perceiving a bluish or violet colour the soul goes out into the world, while things with yellow and red-yellow colours themselves approach the soul. Blue goes away from us, yellow comes towards us.

But in green we experience equilibrium, a pause between in- and out-breathing.

In crimson too the breathing soul pauses for a moment – but now full of expectation and activity.

The soul moves in the world of colours, inwardly related to their nature and manifestation.

★

The book Willem Zeylmans wrote at the age of forty-six was called *De menselijke ziel*★. In the midst of a large amount of work he took six weeks off in the spring of 1939, and wrote three-quarters of it without pause. Then he went with his wife for a few days to the small holiday resort of Ruurloo, where they looked through what he had written, and took walks through the 'eternal woods'.

This book, which he thought his best, was not written at home but while staying with the Wertheym Aymès family in Hilversum. (It seems he needed a change of location in order to write: part of his book about Rudolf Steiner was written in Rotterdam, *Hygiene of the soul* was written while staying with friends in Warmond, and he dictated *The Foundation Stone* in Stuttgart.)

He had a special connection with Hilversum—after all it was here that he had been given the gift of money for his Rudolf Steiner Clinic in The Hague.

Until about 1930 Susanne Bouricius had always invited him to give series of lectures at her house, and later on there was an active anthroposophical 'Groot Gooise' group in this area. From 1936 Zeylmans regularly travelled to the Wertheyms to give lectures. (Later on this family brought the Christian Community priest Cornelis Los to Hilversum, to give their children religion lessons.) Here, in this centre of radio, Zeylmans also gave many broadcasts, and university courses as well.

In 1938 the Wertheyms invited the whole Zeylmans family to go to the Riviera with them for six weeks. Initially it was chiefly Marcel Wertheym who was interested in anthroposophy. Her husband Clement, though, started to show more interest when Zeylmans gave a course on *The Chymical Wedding of Christian Rosenkreutz* in his house.

Later the fate of the Wertheym family took a tragic turn: Marcel, who was Jewish, died in the Theresienstadt concentration camp. From this period came deeply moving reports of her selfless efforts on behalf of her fellow prisoners, whom she comforted and cared for; and of the pure inner light which her soul radiated in the midst of that hell on earth. After

★No English translation available. Hereafter referred to as: 'The human soul'.

the war Clement Wertheym threw himself with great passion into studying the symbolism of Hieronymus Bosch, with particular focus on initiation, and wrote two richly illustrated books on this.

As their guest Zeylmans, as we have said, wrote his book 'The human soul'. Do these facts not have something remarkable to tell us? Later Hilversum appears in his appointments book on one more occasion: on 21 February 1940 he gave his talk on 'Our nation's spiritual task'. He gave his final lecture here, on the Foundation Stone, on 22 February 1941—in the midst of war.

This book, subtitled 'Introduction to knowledge of the nature, activity and development of the soul', was Zeylmans' first and only book on the nature of the human soul. He had, it is true, given a series of lectures as early as 1927 on 'the human soul in sleeping, dreaming and waking', and published an article on psychoanalysis in 1928; and in 1933 he spoke of the dream-forming powers of the soul. But we only find a fuller treatment of this theme when he came to write his lecture plans in 1936 for an introductory series of lectures at the newly opened 'school for spiritual science', entitled 'The human being as body, soul and spirit' (4 lectures).

In the following year, immediately on his return from Sicily, he gave a longer course on the *Chymical Wedding of Christian Rosenkreutz*. Of this mysterious book he once said:

. . . The 'chymical wedding' was the soul's connection with divine forces at work in nature. In the phenomena of living, vegetative nature macrocosmic creative powers are made manifest. The task which the alchemists set themselves was to become familiar with these forces and inwardly grasp their nature . . .

. . . The alchemists knew that one cannot find spirit in nature unless the powers of the human soul are first purified and transformed. They pursued a path of inner schooling.

Zeylmans had a connection with the realm of psychology through his interest in colours, as expressed for instance in his talk on 'colour and the life of soul' (1936) and his first conversation with Rudolf Steiner, where the following significant words were spoken: 'The astral body swims in the seven visible colours—in the etheric of the five crimson colours lives the ego.' (18 December 1920)

Frits Wilmar wrote a long review of Zeylmans' book:

Rudolf Steiner is, in our century, the researcher who rekindled awareness of the whole human being as body, soul and spirit. He created the basis for this in his book *Theosophy*. Under the title of

'Psychosophia' he gave lectures in 1910 which developed this theme in important ways.* In 1917, in his book *Riddles of the Soul*, Rudolf Steiner outlined a 'threefold human organism'—after inwardly working at this for thirty years, as he says himself. From then on he tirelessly extended this idea to encompass practice in education, medicine and the social realm. The overall concept of the threefold organism was thus thoroughly explored, though only in lectures. One of his pupils, Zeylmans, has now taken up the task of applying these ideas to psychology.

In the modern materialistic age things have reached a point where the realm of soul is regarded only as the expressions of organic matter, without individuality or separate existence, so that only the research methods of experimental science are thought to be acceptable. People have been pursuing a 'psychology without soul'.

After a short period in which the work of Jung, Adler, Stern and others led to a more wholesome and generous view of the human being, the situation has now come to be of grave concern once more (behaviourism etc.). Here, as in other branches of knowledge, a basic problem has been to find an activity 'beyond subject and object', which can identify the true interrelationship of subject and object. This need is particularly urgent in psychology because it seems almost unavoidable to regard the object—in this case the soul—as something that is seen by the subject—the soul of the researcher—as an expressly 'subjective element'.

Only a modern science of *the spirit* can offer a solution. And Rudolf Steiner made it abundantly clear that *thinking* is the soul capacity occupying a place beyond subject and object, and that it is through thinking that things can express their own, true being. With this activity the soul enters the realm of spirit. Knowledge of the soul therefore has its basis in science of the spirit. Trusting in thinking as the 'organ of conceiving' leads psychology along a sure and reliable path of research. On the basis of the two pillars of knowledge—observation and thinking—a true psychology can also be built up.

In his research into the soul Zeylmans, like all other researchers, proceeds from observation. This is fundamentally self-observation, founded on self-awareness or ego-consciousness. By this means, though, the soul can awaken to the spirit, so that the perception of its own being acquires an objective character. This objective character can

* See *A Psychology of Body, Soul and Spirit*, New York 1999.

> be expanded and deepened through the results of observation of other souls.
>
> It is difficult to grasp the *middle* realm as an independent sphere, rather than as an amorphous field of tension between two poles. Zeylmans continually succeeds in placing this experiencing, weaving, waxing middle realm at the outset of all his observations, so that love manifests as its chief element, as a power that really structures and transforms. This textbook could become a book of life for a wide readership.

And, in his afterword to the second German edition, H. Müller-Wiedemann wrote:

> . . . Zeylmans draws the reader into a developmental process within his own soul. It is only in such a process that the soul loses the character of 'object of knowledge'. The phenomena which surface there gain their sense in relation to one's own developing knowledge. The subject—the human soul—takes hold of its own reality.
>
> . . . What people at various times think of their soul is not a matter of thinking 'about the soul' which leaves the latter untouched; instead it is a moral act which determines one's self-esteem and actions in the world. Every psychology therefore also takes up a stance which bears moral obligations; and when this remains obscure or unconscious, it comes to be present as a mere ideological factor because the nature of what psychology wishes to understand remains, as it were, concealed in the cloak of so-called objectivity. It then hides from those who seek to know the reality of the soul the foundation that underpins true knowledge. Zeylmans' work offers stimulus both to readers who have no experience in epistemological or scientific fields, as well as to questioning, critical minds. It guides them on the path innate in every soul: the path to knowledge of the self and world . . .

In the spring of 1941 Zeylmans finished the last quarter of the book, but it could not be published straight away because of the war. A colleague he was friendly with, P. T. Hugenholtz, editor of the *Dutch Journal for Psychology*, published the first five chapters in his magazine between November 1941 and March 1943. Via this journal, therefore, Zeylmans' work on the human soul initially came to the attention of Dutch psychologists and psychiatrists. His friend, the publisher Pieter de Haan, had 30 'war copies' of it printed in 1943. The first proper edition of the book did not appear until 1946, seven years after the first draft.

In his preparatory studies for the book, Zeylmans undertook research into language. If one is aware of this it comes to seem likely that he approached the theme of the human soul from the *sphere of language.* In this connection we can also reflect on what Rudolf Steiner said about the human being's origin in the 'divinely working Word', that is, in the realm of the logos.

Zeylmans often told his friends that he wanted to write a second volume, which would have included, among other things, closer research into the nature of memory. Much else besides, which he developed in hundreds of lectures and many courses after 1945, was intended to provide further material for a continuation of the theme.

Among a wealth of notes he left behind on psychology there is a remark which could have been used as a maxim for this chapter:

But it should be shown that it is so difficult to speak of the soul or describe it because it is still so un-evolved—in comparison for instance to everything of a physical nature. Everything in the soul is so much more fleeting and intangible.

While Zeylmans was staying with the Wertheyms in Hilversum in order to work on 'The human soul', Ingeborg Zeylmans awoke one morning with a fairy-tale-like story in her mind, which I would like to reproduce here as a quiet, mysterious image of the 'reality of the soul'.

There were once a king and a queen who ruled over a great and beautiful land.

They loved one another above everything and people said: 'Things go well in this land because love lives here.' Whatever the king did he discussed it with the queen first, and she lived in him with her whole heart.

One day, after a long, dark night, the king sat on his throne and saw that the place beside him was empty. He sent his servants to ask where the queen was, but all anyone knew was that she had gone off into the wood. The king was filled with rare astonishment and he set to work alone. Towards midday the queen returned and could say nothing except that she had been in the wood.

On the following day the king's servant returned with the news that the queen was playing in the wood with a radiant child. Now the king spoke long and earnestly with the queen and told her of his great pain: why did she leave her place on the throne, why did she leave him alone with his burden of cares? The queen also became very sorrowful and promised to remain at home in future. But the days passed under a cloud and it seemed as if the queen still went to the wood in her thoughts.

Things became unbearable, and in her despair the queen called out: 'In that case the child must simply be destroyed.' First they sent a great lion to the wood. Roaring, he approached the child, who very trustingly laid his small hand on the beast's fur. The lion lay down and peacefully began to lick the child's small foot. Then a dark-hearted man was sent out to kill the child. With sunny radiance the child laid his little hand on the man's heart, and he collapsed, groaning. After this the king and queen sent many men with a great net to catch the child, but he changed his shape into that of a butterfly and flew lightly away through the holes of the mesh.

Then the king said: 'If you love me, go into the wood yourself and kill the child.' The queen set out, and when the child saw her it came towards her rejoicing. Listen, said the queen, there is great suffering awaiting us. And as she told this to the child he began to cry bitter tears. Wherever these tears fell in the wood they remained lying there like great dewdrops, and the most miraculous flowers blossomed from them. Then it seemed to the queen that her heart would break and she returned to the king: 'I cannot do it,' she said, and fell down in a swoon. Then the king conceived a new idea, born from his great love. He himself went into the wood, took the child by the hand and led it with him to the throne. There the child sat down on one of the steps, with folded hands, and beamed like an angel.

The king took the queen in his arms, and their love for one another had grown still greater and deeper. And so they lived happily for a long, long time.

IX. THE WAR YEARS

Just as those with some awareness had foretold the Great War of 1914 as early as the end of the previous century, so it was also possible to foresee the broad outlines of current events from 1919 onwards. The only difference is that in the last few years many thousands of people have consciously experienced things that formerly only very few saw. This fact, though, had no effect on the course of events. People's sense of anxiety, their concern and good will, also in relation to safeguarding world peace, turned out to be too weak in the face of the mighty powers which were at work.

Willem Zeylmans wrote this in September 1939, after the Second World War had already broken out. Despite the thoughts he expresses here, though, he had turned to Queen Wilhelmina of the Netherlands only a few months before, suggesting that she should call a global conference to address broad spiritual, economic and political questions.

This initiative arose in the following way:

In 1938, in *The Times*, Lord Baldwin had published an appeal for the 'spiritual and moral rearmament' of humanity. A few weeks later, after a world war had indeed nearly broken out, this appeal was given public support in a statement by a circle of well-known Dutch politicians. And the Dutch Queen Wilhelmina, in a 'message to the people' on national radio, stood behind this: 'The longing for peace,' she said, 'forms a link between all peoples, but if this peace is to be lasting it must be sustained by the ideas expressed in the appeal for spiritual and moral rearmament; and all of us, whoever we are, can make a personal contribution to the growth and development of this idea by working with our whole hearts at this spiritual and moral rearmament: an inner impulse which also brings about an outer change and leads to honesty, trust and love becoming the guiding force between human beings.'

Shortly after this King Leopold of Belgium paid an official state visit to Holland, and in his after-dinner speech at the royal palace in Amsterdam he made reference to the queen's appeal to the Dutch people; and this in turn led to increasing public discussion of the idea of spiritual and moral rearmament.

In January 1939 Queen Wilhelmina once again made a broadcast to her people. It had turned out, she said, that there were many differences of opinion about this idea of rearmament, and therefore she once more wanted to say how she envisaged it: 'The need for inner renewal, the impetus behind the appeals, compels us to a quite new attitude towards all the sufferings of our times.' She went on to say that a spiritual and moral effort was needed, but that this was useless unless one also practised self-knowledge: one should not close one's eyes to one's own failings and errors. In this long, thought-provoking broadcast she also said, among other things, that a wholly new spiritual and mental attitude was needed to the moral and spiritual problems of our time.

The Dutch queen could give impressive talks, very rich in ideas, and well and clearly expressed. She was an energetic person who sometimes had a greater influence over the governing of her country than one might expect in a modern democracy. She had ruled since she was 18 (1898), and was not yet 60 in 1939. Churchill, with whom she often had to negotiate in London as head of the Dutch government in exile, is supposed to have said that she was the only 'man' in the whole Dutch war cabinet!

This slogan-like phrase of 'spiritual and moral rearmament' soon took wing among large circles of people. The idea, though, did not arise from insight into the true causes of an approaching war, but rather from the hope that 'God can bring peace between conflicting political systems' (as long as we are good human beings . . .).

But despite all the many impotent words, these speeches by Wilhelmina and Leopold did stimulate thought and public discussion. And so it is understandable that a Dutch businessman, Emil Menten,* spontaneously took the initiative to study Wilhelmina's appeal to the people more thoroughly. In the Waldorf School in The Hague he organized a conference with talks and discussions. One of those present was right to remark that there was a difference between the two things mentioned in the appeal—spiritual and moral rearmament: 'These are two streams from the same source, the deep origin of our existence.'

The conclusion of the conference was that: 'The only thing of value for the future is what man attains in the *moral* sphere.'

In following months some participants held further discussions about the *spiritual* aspect of the appeal; and apparently came to the conviction

---

* The banker Emil Menten is among those who supported the Waldorf School in The Hague over many years with generous donations. During the Second World War he organized a fund to give financial support to the resistance movement. In Menten's house in Warmond Zeylmans wrote his book *Hygiene of the Soul*. Dr Menten later actively and energetically supported Zeylmans' efforts in developing a psychology of different nations.

that one should try to respond to the queen's appeal by turning directly to her.

One has to remember that these appeals and the discussions which followed them often appeared for weeks on end in the current events sections of daily newspapers. It was thus a logical step for Menten and his anthroposophical friends to take the initiative in this concrete way. They believed 'that the severe crisis now suffered by a large proportion of humanity has *spiritual* origins'.

In their letter to the queen, therefore, they explained what, in their opinion, could help solve the world crisis. Three versions of the letter are extant: the first draft, conceived by Willem Zeylmans, with a brief concrete proposal to call all the countries involved to a world congress that was to have a threefold character; the second draft, formulated by his friend Philipse, in which one senses a more diplomatic tone, and which emphasizes the world economy; and last the letter's final version, as it was sent to the queen on 12 July 1939, in which the accent is placed on the need for rigorous and scientific knowledge.

It was no illusion to hope that Wilhelmina's idea would be given serious consideration. Zeylmans had had a personal conversation about it some days before with the interior minister Patijn. At this time, too, Menten had a personal acquaintance with the queen, and Philipse was a well-regarded and high-ranking official, and later Dutch ambassador in Washington.

Whether or not there would have been any chance of preventing a world war in July 1939, and whether Queen Wilhelmina would have had the opportunity to act on this initiative, are irrelevant questions—for who can judge such a thing? The letter's three initiators were themselves very dubious about the chances, but: '*There are moments when one should attempt what appears hopeless, times when it is necessary to believe in miracles.*'

A few days before they sent the letter, its composers talked it all through once more; and in the version which was sent, the main political idea is that the national character of Holland was psychologically very well-suited to undertake such an initiative. Unfortunately the insignificant little sentence was added: 'The undersigned are aware that the international position of the Netherlands makes it very difficult to take such an initiative in the political realm.'

And it was this very sentence which, in the foreign minister's reply six weeks later, was cited as grounds for the impossibility of carrying out such a plan.

★

One could feel the catastrophe approaching, but when would war break out? Zeylmans had been silent for ten weeks (while writing his book at the Wertheyms and then taking a break afterwards). Now he seemed to have gathered all his strength.

In the twenty-two months in which he could still work openly and in public, he now gave a wealth of lectures and courses. After collaborating in a summer school in Cambridge in August 1939 (the last time he would be there), he opened the study season of the 'school for spiritual science' in The Hague* with a lecture entitled 'Michael' (15 September 1939). This, besides the many single lectures which, as always, he gave in other towns, was followed by eight public lecture cycles on: 'Questions of our time', including:

The struggle for the true spirit of our times
Man, race and nation
The spiritual language of our nation
Human evolution in East and West
The mystery of the middle realm
Life, death and resurrection
The preparation of Christianity in ancient peoples
The arrival of Christ
Christianity as daily social practice
Observations on human destiny
Combating fear
The moral bases of freedom
The spiritual background to the world crisis
The need for a new spirit consciousness
Rudolf Steiner
Christ in our time
The soul's development after death
Reincarnation
Karma and Christianity
On inner development (given 3 times)

* Together with many friends who, like him, had been expelled from the General Anthroposophical Society, he founded this 'school for spiritual science' in 1936.

By then Zeylmans had become a well-known speaker. His lectures in The Hague took place in public halls and were well attended. Each day the newspaper *Het Vaderland* printed detailed and excellent summaries of the lectures, so that they reached a still wider audience.

On 27 November 1939, after the war between England and Germany had already begun, but while Holland was still neutral, he was suddenly invited to England for a medical consultation. He crossed the channel in a plane painted a blazing orange and was thus able to see his brother and his English friends once more. Strange to say, during this very time Eugen Kolisko—a friend and colleague who was living there—died (on 29 November); and so Zeylmans was able to visit Frau Lili Kolisko one last time, before the invasion of Holland forced a five-year separation.

★

The dramatic year of 1940 was heralded for Ingeborg and Willem Zeylmans by a performance of Bruckner's Eighth Symphony in the holy nights, on 3 January of that year. It was conducted by the then well-known German conductor Karl Schuricht, who regarded Bruckner with religious awe (he even forbade his audiences to clap afterwards!). This conductor came regularly to Holland, also to the Scheveningen assembly rooms concert hall. A friendly relationship had developed between him and Willem Zeylmans when Schuricht went to the Rudolf Steiner Clinic for treatment. In the spring (10 May) the German army invaded Holland. On 15 May the Dutch army capitulated after Queen Wilhelmina and her government had escaped to London in a submarine.

As the confusion of the brief, violent war calmed down, Zeylmans sent the members of the Anthroposophical Society in Holland a letter on 24 May, informing them that the Dutch executive committee 'was of the opinion that the best way forward in the present situation was to regard the society as dissolved':

We hope that this wholly free decision will be understood in the right way—it really only means a short-term disbandment of the organizational side of things. What will keep our inner links to one another strong is our connection with Rudolf Steiner and his life's work. This union is of a purely spiritual kind! It is in the spirit, too, that our trust in humanity's further evolution is rooted, and our sacred will to serve this evolution.

From then on there was no longer an Anthroposophical Society in Holland; and when the Nazi forces prohibited the organization, and wished to confiscate membership cards, archives etc., they found nothing. Anthroposophy had 'gone underground', and was all the more intensively pursued in people's isolated living rooms during the five war years.

But as long as the 'school for spiritual science', the Waldorf School and the Rudolf Steiner Clinic still functioned, anthroposophists were able to meet in those contexts; and so, until the first half of 1941 a wealth of courses continued on karma, study of man, psychology and so forth. Zeylmans was still able to give public lectures on a few occasions, and for the last time on 16 March 1941. In the spring of the same year the 'school for spiritual science' was prohibited, and in July the Waldorf school in The Hague was closed.

In the process of metamorphosis of his biography, the following years were comparable to the forming of seed in a plant: an intense 'contraction' and focusing of his forces. Before we speak of this, though, I would like to mention another letter of his in which, in the summer of 1940, he tried to exert influence on political events in his country.

★

Three well-known Dutchmen from public life founded a political party two-and-a-half months after the occupation of Holland, which they called 'Nederlandse Unie' (Netherlands Union). Within a few weeks hundreds of thousands of Dutch people had joined, and a few months after it was founded there were over half a million members—one of the largest parties that had existed in Holland up to then. The 'appeal to the Dutch people' with which this union addressed the public, called on Dutch people's sense of freedom and need to resist, but also a sense of liberation from traditional, ingrained forms of the old, powerless Dutch politics—'that old roundabout' as the former prime minister Colyn called it. During these first months of German occupation nothing fixed had as yet been set up—and so a certain hope gained ground that something new might come about in Holland's political arena: the illusion of a 'breakthrough'. The Nazi government handled things cunningly (Holland had a Nazi administration in contrast to Belgium, for instance, where there was a military regime): it allowed the 'little nation' to express itself freely first of all, before it began to apply violent and restrictive measures. The Dutch Nazi movement, the NSB, a kind of Quisling party, was much hated by the Dutch; and by joining the Union one could demonstrate one's anti-NSB status.

The appeal by the 'three wise men' was full of ideals and ideas of a new human community based on new social forms and institutions.

And when, at the beginning of August, in a crammed conference hall in The Hague, the appeal was made for the general population to 'share in the creation of new ideas', Zeylmans and his friend van der Toorn sat down together and wrote a lengthy letter to the leadership of the new Union. I mention this here because the Union later exerted influence on the attitudes and also the ideas of hundreds of thousands of Dutch people during the war. Despite the pressure of circumstances its members met together regularly in countless working groups, and the three leaders travelled continuously from one meeting to another, inspiring these gatherings with their fiery idealism. Later these Union circles developed into cells of organized resistance to the 'illegality' of the Nazi occupation. Much was born and developed from these ideas, which after 1945 informed and determined political and social life in Holland.

It is not known whether the three leaders studied the letter from Zeylmans and van der Toorn in the great tumult and chaos of this first founding period of the Netherlands Union—it is not very likely! In brief, concise sentences it speaks of the nature and character of the Dutch people, their sense of freedom and the spirit at work in their language, and contains the proposal for forming a 'core group to study the psychologies of different nations' within the Netherlands Union. Then follow suggestions for a wholly new direction in the realm of education (including education that develops 'Trinitarian reverence'...) and indications of how Christianity is still at the very outset of its deeper evolution, and that new insights are needed.

Zeylmans wrote this section of the letter, while van der Toorn, the former treasurer of the Anthroposophical Society in Holland and later general manager of the Dutch postal service, wrote the second part. (Zeylmans worked with him for years on the executive committee of 'Loverendale', Marie Tak van Poortvliet's biodynamic agricultural project.) Toorn gave a complete description of Steiner's idea of threefold social order, including the need for a new way of organizing the ownership of land and property.

Once the Nazi regime had seen the way the Netherlands Union was developing, it went on the offensive. As early as 1941 the Union became a powerless organization. Yet in the small groups of its 'cadres' thousands of Dutch people had come together, and ideals for structuring the future anew flourished in secret for years. It is therefore understandable that this terrible time of outer trials was also, for many Dutch people, the most spirit-filled, intensive period of their lives. In those war years new forms for a future society based on human dignity and the spirit could have been developed!

*

Before the Nazis seized the Rudolf Steiner Clinic in the spring of 1942, the family had lived there in cramped conditions, spread out through the clinic's various wards and sections. I would like to spend a moment or two looking at our family life in those days. Besides a certain external convenience—for instance, our food came from the central kitchens and the clinic cleaning staff also cleaned for us—there were other typical characteristics in the life of a family with four children in a small, private hospital. The spheres of family and clinic often interpenetrated a great deal. For us children the service-rooms of this imaginatively built clinic made ideal play rooms. In the enormous attic beneath the strange, curving roof many of our games took place. Our most adventurous hidey-holes were in the cellar vaults and the large, beautiful garden. Zeylmans' eldest daughter often helped the nurses, later training as a nurse herself. The eldest son disappeared into the caretaker's workshop for hours and watched him at his work. In the evenings the children ran along the corridor in their pyjamas to say goodnight to their father: in his dark-purple study (which also doubled as a consultation room) there were often guests from foreign lands—Ita Wegman, Eugen Kolisko, Elisabeth Vreede—who greeted the children. Sometimes one of the children was allowed to stay in the room for a while and play on the carpet or go exploring in a deep book-case with its strange compartments, medical instruments and an old peep-show box from Dubrovnik. You could smell father's cigar, listen to English or German being spoken and sometimes also pick up snippets of conversation that were not meant for children's ears.

Ingeborg Zeylmans, the mother of the family, filled family life with an all-permeating yet unobtrusive intensity and domesticity. In one kitchen corner a small kettle boiled, for making a 'kopje tee', and a basket of goodies was passed round as people talked. There were almost always guests, and it was rare for the family to eat lunch alone. To begin with we all ate in the large dining room, but later we took our meals in our own living quarters.

At lunch or after the evening meal family life focused on our flat. Father would begin to tell jokes (which he did very well) and the children also practised telling stories. With the 'battery' of a collection of spice-jars, ginger and English preserves which—since he liked them so much—he always had standing on a small silver tray on the table, he built the most perilously balanced towers. He also held wrestling bouts with us children or practised circus tricks.

When Father was there he was always a friend and playmate to us. When we were still little he could join in with our games in all seriousness, though he never became outwardly 'childish'. At the Dutch festival of St Nicholas he would surprise us with comical dolls, paintings, poems or humorous sketches. We sang St Nicholas songs at full volume while a mysterious, invisible hand distributed 'Pepernoten' (ginger-bread cakes). The Christmas crib he made, with inn, lantern and starry sky, was for years the most wondrous focus of our gaze under the Christmas tree.

Since he was often away on our birthdays and during the school holidays—he sent postcards which we stuck above our beds—we children experienced his homecomings still more intensely. He usually had interesting things to relate and always brought back a small gift from his travels: a toy, a cap, a puppet.

Ingeborg shared in all this in her own special, smiling-serious way—we children never experienced any conflicts between our parents, or emotional moods. Around her was a sphere which is most reminiscent of a sketch by Leonardo da Vinci in London: 'Cartoon for the Virgin with Child and St Anne with John the Baptist'—a quality of devotion and selflessness, but never unaware of what was going on around her. When I think of Ingeborg Zeylmans, her memory is always accompanied by something mysterious. Willem Zeylmans once said of his wife that her 'ego power' was far greater than his. Naturally it was a high point for us when Father was there in the summer holidays. Sometimes we had guests or school friends staying with us, so that the company spending each summer together in the country could grow to be a large one. On one occasion (this was already during the war), it rained for weeks without pause, day and night, and Zeylmans made up humorous 'rain-names' to describe all the many dozens of different varieties of rain: each day we looked out to see what 'kind' of rain was splashing down this time! The rest of the time we spent playing card games, after our daily walk through the woods, while Mother hung the whole house full of all our dripping clothes—and we looked back on this holiday as one of the best we remembered.

After leaving the Rudolf Steiner Clinic, Zeylmans found lodgings with his family in a part of town that belonged to the Scheveningen fortress—a part of the Germans' 'Atlantic Wall' fortifications. He also continued practising as a psychiatrist there.

The family now entered a phase of family life that it had not previously experienced: we were 'on our own'. The older children were 19 and 15 at the time (the daughter later moved away to Amsterdam to do her nursing training); the two youngest children were 12.

Life in this 'fortress' was a strange war experience: all the people living there were gradually evacuated until only the doctors and their families remained.

When the children came home from school or returned from town, having successfully got past the check-points, they rode their bikes through the deserted Scheveningen streets in whose ghostly, empty blocks of flats only rats were living. Finally Zeylmans was evacuated too and found a flat in the middle of The Hague where the family lived for the last part of the war.

★

The Second World War also brought inexpressible suffering to Holland. Thousands of people were tortured and murdered. Tens of thousands died from poverty and hunger; hundreds of thousands vanished and never returned, including many Dutch Jews and emigrants. Anyone who reads an account of the five years in which German occupation wrought havoc in this small country will be overcome by the unspeakable horror of it.

In March 1941 Zeylmans wrote his last article before the war ended (in *Vrije Opvoedekunst*). There he describes a childhood memory of Rudolf Steiner's: how, as a boy, he always saw the high, snowy mountain peak in his homeland catching the first dawning rays of the new day and passing them on to the valley. 'This,' says Zeylmans, 'is an image of Rudolf Steiner himself: a snow-capped mountain leading the first rays of spirit light down to earth, like the morning greeting of a new age.'

And while his 'school for spiritual science', then the Waldorf school in The Hague, and finally his clinic were all prohibited and the first persecutions of Jews began (deportations started from the middle of 1942) he looks back on twenty-one years' work on behalf of anthroposophy. From his old schedules and diaries he puts together a list of 'important lectures, trips, gatherings and events from the years 1920–1941'. (It is to this that we owe most of the biographical data.) His conclusion was: What an enormous amount of activity by such a small group of people, what efforts have been made! And the result? The Dutch Anthroposophical Society has grown during these twenty years from perhaps three hundred to roughly six hundred members! So one can see that in working for a spiritual ideal one should *never* take too much account of outer success. A motto of William of Orange, or 'William the Silent' is also his: '*Il n'est besoin ni d'espérer pour entreprendre, ni de réussir pour percévérer*': There is no need of hope in order to act, and no need of success in order to persevere.

★

After finishing the last chapter of 'The human soul' in the spring of 1941, he wrote the poem 'Mysteries' (1942). He had conceived of it in three parts: 'Images', 'Being' and 'Word'. The first part (reproduced here together with the prologue) contains images 'of world revelations in space'; the second part was to describe 'world revelations in the stream of time'. He never completed the second and third parts though. Zeylmans duplicated what he wrote, and distributed the modest little volume among his friends. Dr M.P. van Deventer has written an account of this poem and its aims:

> When I took the opportunity in October 1945 to make my first trip [after the war] to Holland, to visit friends there, Willem Zeylmans gave me a copy of his booklet 'Mysteries' and wrote a dedication in it: 'After five long years a happy reunion.' He also described the outer conditions under which it had come about. The Rudolf Steiner Clinic had been closed. To begin with he could still carry on writing in his study. Then the occupying forces requisitioned the furniture. When his writing desk was taken away, he carried on writing on his knees. When the chairs were taken, he sat on the floor, and wrote and wrote... Listening to him, the image of an artist arose, who with the greatest concentration grasps his inspiration in words. The poem—a small epic—sadly remained a fragment only. The author did not think it worthy of printing at the time, and only gave it to a few friends.
>
> Let me say the following about the content: first comes the prologue, a magnificent creation story. The Trinity and all the hierarchies create the world and finally man, a divine creation, formed in God's image as a living, ensouled spirit, dwelling in the 'temple of God'.
>
> Then the whole world of space is described in its pictorial character. Not as *maya*—which would hardly have been a comfort amidst the misery that reigned at the time. No, instead the world with all its beings arises before us, as a reflection of spiritual beings. The author appears deeply imbued with this eternal truth. His description often assumes hymn-like character. When he speaks of the powers of the heights, the depths and the surrounding world, one senses the active impulse of Rudolf Steiner's Foundation Stone

Meditation. The call: 'Practise spirit recollection!' also leads, after all, into mysteries of world space.

Passages on the youth and maiden, who behold in one another a vision of world soul and world spirit, form a climax to this poem.

It often sounds like a fairy-tale, because it seems to be so far removed from contemporary reality. But perhaps only apparently so. Much slumbers in the depths of human souls which is only covered by a thin veil. This is the 'soul-sensing' that in our time is to come to consciousness.

In ancient times other states of consciousness existed. Rudolf Steiner describes them in connection with the myth of Isis and Osiris, in his lecture of 5 January 1918, stressing that knowledge of these older states of awareness is necessary because they show the way for what needs to develop anew. In ancient Egypt, in the time of Osiris, experience of puberty was quite different from what it later became. At the age of nine or ten, a boy would perceive etheric light forms in the air through the clairvoyant power still existing then. After puberty he sensed these within his own soul. Not only the voice changed but also the life of thinking. He then felt within him what had previously been without. Girls perceived something similar, but also more inward imaginations. After puberty the image of the human being arose in them. Both sexes knew that inside them something was coming to birth that world space had made fruitful within them.

Rudolf Steiner calls this the more concrete shape of the Isis-Osiris myth: 'World wisdom, inasmuch as it is won from the airy sphere, though in organic relation to man's deeper layers', is taken into the soul. Mourning the death of Osiris was connected with the perception that ancient imaginations were no longer experienced after soul-life changed at puberty.

Nowadays the processes of puberty have coarsened. But imaginative consciousness must arise in a new way. The wisdom which formerly entered the soul from cosmic space is now extinguished. New imaginations now need to arise in young people. World soul and world spirit can become real experience when the sexes meet.

One can sense that the author has here lifted the veil of a great mystery, and thus brought a healing impulse into the world. (M.P. van Deventer)

Mysteries

'So grasp hold without delay
of holy revealed mystery'

Prologue

'As everything weaves into a whole,
One in the other works and lives!
As heaven's forces rise and fall
and pass each other golden pails!
With wings of fragrant blessing
through earth from heaven passing
through everything harmoniously resounding!'

Elevated high above all Creation are the gods in the world of spirit. They serve the Father God, the Son God and the Spirit God, the almightiest holy Being of the Trinity, that stands at the primal beginning of eternity. Out of their deep-concealed being, out of their manifestation, out of their manifest working once sprang the whole world of being, the Creation, everything that lives and has its being, which breathes and suffers as it breathes, and in suffering is in turn liberated through the spirit. Not to be grasped by any human comprehension, encompassing the universe, elevated and mighty, the gods of the first hierarchy stand veiling God's countenance: Seraphim, Cherubim and Thrones. In their light that is unearthly and invisible, in their unbounded sacrifice of love, in the eternal streaming of their life, the almighty Father God is concealed in infinite, active peace.

Their being is creative power!

Out of their radiant light of wisdom, out of their warm radiance of love, out of their active cosmic will came forth all existence—the Creation and every creature. They sacrificed their being so that divine being might dwell in all that was, is and will be. From the sun hidden beings radiate through the whole cosmos, weaving in love and the light of wisdom with inner ardour: the gods of the second hierarchy, Kyriotetes, Dynamis, Exusiai. Through them God's being streams actively forth.

Their being is creative light!

Their wisdom floods through the cosmos as virtue bestowing; their eternal movement ensouls and flows through every being; their mighty will lends creatures form and shape.

Forth from their hidden light
Christ, God's Son,
came to the earth,
bearing God's love

to human beings
so that they might become
bearers of the 'I'
that acts from love,
that has its being in freedom.

Connected with human souls there live, in the sphere and compass of earth, in the shining of light and colour, the gods of the third hierarchy: Angeloi, Archangeloi, Archai. They bear God's active being into the stream of existence.

Their being is creative soul!

Their breath weaves, ensouled by God's spirit—the Holy Spirit, that strives to fill all. Their active working is born out of the deepest devotion to all that is above them. Thus they reveal God's Creation to the human soul. Through aeons of time the miracle of Creation arose: the sun, stars, planets, the earth—water, air and clouds, and also divine light, and all-permeating warmth, stones, plants, animals. And so arose too, above all, man himself.

In his soul are revealed the miracles of the universe through the gods of the third hierarchy.

In his life stream, as eternal gift of the gods, the beings of the second hierarchy.

In his body work, world-forming, the continuous powers of the gods of the first hierarchy.

Thus the human being is God's creature, created in his image as living, ensouled spirit, dwelling in God's temple.

The Images

'Everything transient is but a likeness'

The human being is surrounded by the mystery of images. Everything that his eye perceives is image, that his ear hears, that is revealed to his soul in taste and fragrance. The cosmos veils itself in images!

What is the origin of these images, what is their being and sense? The creating gods, who bear the will to form man, sacrifice their essence, bestow their love, bestow their wisdom, reveal their being so that man can come into existence. Their being and their love, their wisdom and their essence is thought and borne forth in the world of divine spirits, is felt and suffered, is realized on earth. It is spread forth infinitely, streaming, warming, and manifested as image; as image that, in thousands upon thousands of images, appears in the world—trembling through space in shining radiance.

Stars, sun, planets stand in the heavens as the radiant images of creative forces—images of the Word of God, of divine will.

So earth too, and all its creatures, are an image.

In mountains and valleys and endless plains the earth reveals its countenance. Here steep, rocky cliffs; there rising in waves from the unfathomable waters. Land through which rivers slowly and quietly seek their way. Veined by streams which rush singing from high places and fall headlong down deep ravines. In all waters are mirrored the stars, the blue of the purer regions of air, the passing clouds. And light is reflected everywhere in thousand-fold colours.

Hidden in the deep earth are the rocks, the bearers of starlight. Rubies glow red, like divine fire; sapphires gleam blue as the dome of heaven and air; aquamarines shine like water; and tourmaline, the bearer of love, is purple-red in ethereal green. All of them are images of starlight.

Like rivers turned to stone, veins of shining metal lie quietly in the earth. Noble gold, and silver with its moon-like, reflective shimmer. Trembling Mercury and radiant copper; here fiery iron and glinting tin; there flexible, heavy lead with its dull sheen. All are images of inner forces living in the coloured wanderers, the planets.

On the earth's solid ground flourishes the plant world's delicate green tapestry. Ancient trees raise their mighty trunks high into the air, spreading out their magnificent great crowns into airy spaces. Bushes and herbs are spread over the earth in endless variety, with thousands of different leaves and shapes. In spring and summer the rich colour world of the stars blossoms forth from their inner being. Pure as moonlight on balmy summer nights, red as the love of sunny, summer days, blue as the ether of heaven's wide dome, deep purple as the stillness enthroned in the world high above the stars.

Animals move between the silent, growing plants. Here creeping along the ground, there gliding through water; rising jubilant into the air or hurrying swiftly over meadows; dumb and constrained, singing and fluting, roaring, giving voice to their urges, plaintive, wandering.

All are also an image of urge and desire, of deep instincts springing from wisdom. In them existence finds its certain, ordained course.

And, as Lord of Creation, noble man—the aim of the gods—wanders over the earth.

His upright form is created for freedom, his breathing breast is fashioned to love, his spherical head is prepared for wisdom. His limbs are powerful and at the same time delicate as flowers; his arching foot presses down on the earth as he walks, yet continually raises itself rhythmically again. Concealing the human race's heavenly origin, the hand's very shape is always ready to serve the earth, to create art, to do courageous deeds, to reveal noble gestures. Man's breathing chest is the bearer of his soul, uniting itself in rhythmic alternation with all the ensouled, breathing, sentient beings beneath the blue arch of the heavens. Clear as the light reflected in its receptive organ of weaving thought, rises the forehead. And the face harmoniously heralds the forces dwelling hidden in the deepest depths of the soul. Thus he is an image of the creative gods. Image, too, of the forces which harmoniously manifest in the cosmos. An image of those forces which descend to earth from the heights, which strive upwards from the depths and which come to fulfilment in the spreading compass of the earth.

Man's worldly senses have evolved in twelve ways. He is open to the world soul, that reveals to the senses in light-woven image what lies deeply concealed within it. Light streams through all the senses, spirit light that becomes tone and colour in the soul, fragrance and taste, everything that the feeling soul receives from the world.

So man, the aim of the gods, stands in the midst of those images which together with him form the content of world space. Space arose from cosmic light that was reflected by the gods; wisdom, radiating as gentle virtue, they once radiated back through the cosmos. Woven from light of wisdom, space arose as a broad sphere, all-embracing, all-imbuing, in which the Creator gave all creatures a dwelling place. Just as the human spirit, ensouled, indwells the body's house here on earth, so light lives as being, streaming wisdom into the house of space. In this space stand the colours like still streams of refracted light. They are born out of the struggle between heavenly light and earthly darkness. Thus space became a world in which the images, once woven from light, encounter one another again as image. There man perceives the creatures around him, recognizing the creative will of the gods, their love and wisdom. There man finds his fellow creatures in the image that reveals to him their hidden being, part of which still rests as germ of future potential in the lap of the gods.

Delicate as a pink blossom a child comes into the world, a gentle breath blown from the highest creative power. The eyes, dark blue with purple sheen, still bear the unfathomably far depths of light. But a mighty will for life still fires the delicate organs, unfolding in the breath and then, in the continuing course of the years, breaking through heavenly memory.

Then comes the awakening to the world of beings, of mother and father, of many other people, animals, plants, things—which all manifest as images to which the child must put names, which are once more images in the form of sound. Now one recognition follows on another. The soul woven from cosmic forces rediscovers and recognizes everything that has become world outside it. And the heavenly child becomes an earthly human being.

Of all the souls who cross his earthly path, the youth then recognizes in one the virgin who would reveal the world soul to him in a delicate image of beauty. It is a rediscovery of what lives on in the soul from the primeval past as a sweet dream of lost paradise, of beauty and heavenly light, as the deepest longing. Shining eyes have the clarity and radiance of sapphires standing guard over hidden dreams of heaven. Forms still slumber and the figure's outline is a quietly uttered promise of a future encounter with star forces in which divine beings weave. The voice unfolding tones from depths of soul heralds a heaven in which the self-sacrificing soul loses itself. The image of the world soul awakens in his heart the impulse for deeds and urge for self-denial. Creative will raises him high above all creation. Confused in the fiery furnace of an imprisoned urge, he stammers his deepest secret: to unite himself with the heavenly forces he once had to leave as earth-born being. For the first time he experiences his loneliness as unfulfilled destiny, and his call sounds out: to be redeemed now from banishment.

Of all the souls who cross her life path, the virgin recognizes in one the youth whose strength and will, whose earthly certainty reveal to her the image of the working of world spirit. Rediscovery of that quiet longing for being truly seen and understood, living on in the soul from the primeval past, awakens a shy and gentle urge in her to give her deepest being. But at the same time a mighty will holds her back from revealing her secret to the other, urges her to conceal herself instead still deeper in sheaths of soul. Thus the sweet game and gentle battle of love arises, in urge and counter-urge. It is only a seeming battle that leads to higher union—when she, now blushing, reveals the warm radiance of her soul, encircling her lover. Then the deepest forces which divine will lets live in human beings flow together from the world soul and the earth-directed spirit. Self-creating now out of the unconscious urge for life, as they become one the seed is fertilized and becomes a gateway through which a human soul can once more enter on an earthly path.

As in youthful years a mighty will for life, streaming through the human soul in a fiery river, forms life's path, so in old age the light of consciousness appears which, radiating from spirit, bestowing clarity on the soul, holds sway in the human being. The unconscious urge of love in youthful years now seeks purification through wisdom. The cool light of wisdom of old age becomes inner strength as it mingles with the fire of love.

The life of a child reveals an image that is continually changing, of a prebirth state that strives continually to manifest as the child develops. The old person, in contrast, shows an image of stillness and peace, wishing to take with him only the little that appeared reality to him in this earthly life. An image arises that resembles the noble image of God the Father who, in perfect peace, slumbers in inner stillness within the human being. The deep furrows of the face bear witness to pain that has been purified through suffering undergone in the light of wisdom. The gentle and heavenly radiance of the eyes reveals divine creative will, which consumed with the might of unbounded fire in soul urges and longings until the still light of love could be reborn again from the ashes. The gestures, in which lie mastery and reverence, reveal the purification of fiery desires. Hands which formerly prayed so often in despair, raised in supplication, now find the strength to be raised in blessing.

Then death comes, and as a last image on earth, reveals the hidden being of the human 'I'. Liberated, the soul-spirit lifts away from the earthly body. It rises in the light that imbues and shines through world space. Reborn in the world of spirit, the soul takes the further paths that divine wisdom once preordained for it.

Thus everything which the human eye perceives and human senses experience on earth is image. An image of divine will, divine wisdom and divine love, woven from heavenly light. In eternal alternation the images pass before the soul. The play of light, of colours, of lines, of forms, of tone, of fragrance. A cloth woven of concealed and revealed light, radiating from the divine world. A living image of forces, woven through with the twelve-fold choir of the higher powers of heaven, whose world-creating breath bestows love, light and life.

★

After the first period of the war, outer material conditions became continually more impoverished. In 1943 heating supplies became scarce and there was less and less food available. In 1944, when the large-scale deportations of Jews had come to an end and Dutch men over the age of 18 were sent to work in Germany, most of the Nazis also left the country. From the autumn of 1944 the western Netherlands were sectioned off and those still living there starved out.

In the Zeylmans family, too, the last potato ran out one day and we tried, as so many other people did, to make a kind of flour from tulip bulbs. One winter evening, when even this 'tulip flour' had run out as well, we heard a lorry stop outside and shortly afterwards loud voices were heard: some German soldiers were looking for Doctor Zeylmans' house. After they had found the right house, with the help of some surprised and suspicious neighbours, a great sack of potatoes was unloaded 'on orders of the Harlingen town commandant', a naval officer called Dr Heinze who was an anthroposophical farmer, manager for many years of 'Loverendale'. This gift to Zeylmans and his family was worth more than gold at the time!

There are no notebooks from this period, no schedule diaries and no programmes. But those who experienced it report how, just at this time of deepest outer misery, anthroposophy was learned and practised in the most intensive way. No day passed without a gathering at someone's house. Anthroposophy flourished in people's living rooms—where they prepared for the coming 'liberation' by studying the great ideas and images of a future humanity. Education, medicine, agriculture, eurythmy, threefold social order, Steiner's fundamental works, the new image of man, the laws of karma and reincarnation were studied in the many small

Willem Zeylmans, aged about 62

groups. There were even meditation practice groups where directions for an inner path of development were explored in deeply intimate, shared work over many years.

During these years Zeylmans came to believe that the structure of the Dutch Anthroposophical Society ought to be changed: the 'centralist' form, going back to Steiner's time and focused on the general secretaries of national societies should metamorphose into a 'peripherally' based structure, in which the former general secretaries' role would only be that of 'first among equals'. In future, he thought, the society should be led by a broad circle of responsible members, gathering in representative 'core groups', with a 'day-to-day' executive committee for managing external affairs. In fact this is how the Dutch society later came to be organized.

At Christmas 1944, 21 years after the 1923 Christmas Foundation Meeting, he gave a lecture in which he distinguished four 21-year periods since Steiner's birth (1861–1882, 1882–1902, 1902–1923, 1923–1944). After a striking analogy with the plant, which also develops through four stages (stem, leaf, flower, seed), and a comparison with human evolution, he spoke of the ideal of 'becoming adult' ('only a few of us are . . .'), and of how one might, by living out of the power of the 1923 Christmas 'Foundation Stone', make a true oath and commitment to it at this dark 'cosmic Christmas' time. Only by us 'becoming adult', he said, could our society find a new basis for its future work.

★

The attack on Holland had begun on a beautifully clear day shortly before Whitsun 1940. In the first chapter of his book *Hygiene of the Soul*, Zeylmans relates how a small circle of friends met at his house during these days, and held long, stirring discussions about the war. Together they developed the ideal of a new way of living, of a 'social health' or 'social hygiene' as they called it, which must start with each individual but can only find fulfilment in shared community. Throughout the whole book (which we will speak of in the next chapter) Zeylmans continually refers to exercises aimed at achieving this 'social hygiene' in every situation of life—fear and doubt, nervousness and hatred, confusion and loneliness. He wrote this book during the winter of 1944/45, in the form of transcribed conversations.

After the Canadian army had liberated western Holland from German occupation on 5 May 1945, Zeylmans gave his first public lecture on 19 May—the Saturday before Whitsun. 'Whitsun' was also his theme; and this marked a new phase in Willem Zeylmans' life—one which went hand in hand with the regeneration of the Dutch Anthroposophical Society.

X. NEW BEGINNING

That the sense of sacrifice is the only true basis for healthy community life belongs to the mysteries of the human 'I'. The 'I', the real core of the individual, only reveals its true nature when it sacrifices itself, when it gives itself to humanity in devoted love.

This is why a number of people—not necessarily many to begin with—will need to take this maturity of the ego in hand, with all possible strength and awareness, filling themselves with the power of the Pauline phrase: 'Not I but Christ in me.'

The true, divine 'I' in man is born from Christ; and for this to happen the human ego must die—not once, not a thousand times, but continually, again and again! We need to keep in mind Christ's words to Nicodemus: 'Do you not know that you must be reborn?' This question is inscribed, as a constant reminder and also a continual awakening call, above the gateway through which all must pass who wish to work together to build a new human civilization.

But if a number of people pursue such a path of ego development, then this will have a continually increasing influence on society. You can take this path most surely if you constantly work to school and develop yourself, striving with all earnestness to harmonize and develop your soul forces, practising spiritual exercises, meditation and everything that belongs to this. 'A deeply humble, life-long learning process', as Christian Morgenstern calls it. But you will need to pursue this path in such a way that your being stands wholly in the world, inwardly connecting yourself with everything, both negative and positive, that the world must undergo. You will need to learn continually to deepen your experience of the miseries of humanity, experience them in your own soul with increasing pain and depth. Yes, simply by experiencing these miseries and this distress, the powers will be bestowed on you which you need for your difficult path. 'A deeply humble, life-long learning process': as strange as this may sound to contemporary ears, it is nevertheless the only true and fundamental basis for the social hygiene of the future.

These words, with which Willem Zeylmans ended his book *Hygiene of the Soul* in 1946, can stand as a summation of his own activities after the Second World War. If one wished to portray his biography in the right way then—at least for the period from 1945 to 1953—one would really need to alter one's biographical method, not placing *him* at the centre of the descriptions but rather the whole wealth of spiritual activity that unfolded around him over years. This would completely burst the bounds

Ingeborg Zeylmans, aged about 50

of this biography: one would have to describe his friends and colleagues, the impulses and ideals which now strove to be realized, the life of the Dutch Anthroposophical Society overall, and the threads and links that were woven with England, Germany, Switzerland and Belgium. One would have to describe the great new initiatives—developing a psychology of nations, building up a Centre for Free Spiritual Life, with its daily courses into which much effort was poured for years on end, and much more; but *not* so that it seemed that all this work emanated from him as a great, central source of inspiration, but rather the reverse: showing instead how he lived *in* and *with* all these activities, only coming into his own through them.

One should see his work in connection with the individual personalities with whom he worked, interwoven with their destiny. I know how easily this view could be misunderstood, in either one or another direction, and that it will not be possible to do this in all that I now wish to describe. But it is a true view of things, and should not be forgotten as we continue to explore his biography.

Already previously, in the years shortly before the Second World War, Ingeborg Zeylmans had increasingly involved herself in the work of the Dutch Society. After the end of the war she became fully engaged in this, becoming a member of the 'daily committee', and also taking on editorship of the anthroposophical newsletter.

People were later astonished at the self-assured way she worked alongside her husband in the Anthroposophical Society—a testimony to her inner independence.

When the Second World War ended people knew that an old world had also come to an end, and that new forms of living and working would need to be found—the old ways were no use any more. Actual circumstances therefore gave rise to the idea that the foundations of the Dutch Anthroposophical Society were 'based on the free initiatives of members, who have the will for shared endeavour...' It seemed to Zeylmans and his friends that 'it accords with the facts if we place the main emphasis of leading the Society on these collaborating members, in order to ensure that the strengths and intiatives of really active members can come into their own to the greatest possible extent'.

From this period comes a passage which Zeylmans prefaced with the note: 'From the diary of Bender Bole'. (You may remember that he had started to compose his memoirs under this name.) This entry is dated 7 August 1947, and runs:

Saint Francis chose poverty as his bride, and kept faith with her throughout his life. I have always wanted wealth as my bride. Not the wealth of expensive clothes, or magnificent palaces where people are served hand and foot—I realized very early on that such exterior trappings only conceal emptiness. No, the wealth I repeatedly encountered was a virgin, whose smile I discovered in the red hue of a rose, the sky's blue and the ocean's turquoise green. I also met her in my wanderings through the world. She came towards me in an unspoken word, I found her bathing in a clear stream, the sunlight mingling with the golden radiance of her hair. Only seldom did she speak to me, but always she bestowed her smile on me. In dark nights of love she seemed to come very close. From the stars she descended to me, laying her veil fine as breath over my body. When the sufferings of earth threatened to destroy me, she appeared unexpectedly, waved her small hand to me and led my soul to light elves dancing on the flower-strewn meadows.

At last I saw the day of our wedding approach. She came towards me more beautiful than ever, and her smile was sunlight. I stretched out my arms to embrace her. But as I drew her to me, I found only a grey veil in my hands, and no trace of her was to be seen. Since then I have had no beloved . . . on my lonely paths I sometimes meet the bride of Saint Francis. She wears a brown cloak—a lady with quiet eyes. Then she smiles at me and I smile back. But between our two smiles lies a world of loneliness.

Willem Zeylmans himself made no further comment on this text; and so we will simply leave it standing as it is. The only thing I would like to add are the words Ingeborg Zeylmans wrote below it in pencil—two lines, written as though in an oval shape:

See the world
Through Christ's eyes.

★

In his book *Hygiene of the Soul*, Zeylmans described the chief experiences he had gathered during twenty years practice as a pyschologist and psychiatrist. It contains twelve discussions—some of which are conversations between a doctor and various patients, while the others are held in the small group mentioned in the previous chapter.

Among these discussions are two which later became known outside the confines of the book: one on 'Anxiety in the twentieth century', which also appeared in newspapers, for example in Spain. The medicines manufacturer Weleda once distributed it in large numbers to all its clients.

The other deals with marriage. He had many thoughts on this theme and, as is clear from the article, many examples to draw on from his practice. The 'Discussion on marriage' is no doubt one of his most important contributions to the 'social hygiene' field. In it he frequently quotes his wife, Ingeborg Zeylmans; and these passages reveal what was otherwise a more hidden side of her. The rest of the book is also largely autobiographical.

His friend Frits Julius, the well-known Waldorf teacher, once wrote of the longing a reader can feel, when picking up a book, for it to 'address a very deep sense in him of something that only otherwise comes into its own at special, high-points of life'; and if this actually happens it brings a moment of highest fulfilment—we become aware of why we exist. There are, he says, 'parts of this small volume by Dr. Zeylmans which can have this effect to an unusual degree . . .' And no doubt he was also referring here to this 'Discussion on marriage.'

Zeylmans' colleague in Stuttgart, Eberhard Schickler, said of the book: 'It is the very thing it deals with: reading this book *is* to practise soul hygiene. It creates order in our thoughts about problems in life, which we are not all able to conceptualize clearly, but which we all encounter on many occasions. By choosing the form of discussions, the author leaves us quite free to take up these conversations and continue them with others. The health of the soul is also very much a social question. Thus the book appeals to us, in the highest sense, to find our place within the community.'

These two reviewers thus point to the salient aspect of all psychiatric care, for—as Zeylmans once said—'the soul contains *all* bad and *all* good in the world; and everything depends on what side one places oneself!

★

I would now like to try to illuminate briefly a theme that was among Willem Zeylmans' central concerns: the psychology of nations. Let us start with the concept of 'humanity' which he often spoke about.

For Zeylmans the fourfold nature of human beings living on earth was a very important reality. For all difficulties and conflicts in which part of this humanity gets caught up have direct or indirect consequences for the rest of us. And therefore it is necessary to know *'of what this humanity is composed'*, as he once wrote. *'Firstly it is composed of human beings, individual beings who show different stages of education and civilization. Then they are grouped in smaller and larger national groupings, and differentiated into various races.'* All human beings on earth compose humanity, in a purely 'quantitative' sense:

. . . but from a deeper, qualitative perspective, we only come to know humanity by experiencing the 'I' as such, as eternal entelechy. In each and every human being the 'I' works as a continually developing, constantly 'becoming' reality: 'the ego that never is but is always developing'. This ego or 'I' is not bound to race or nationality, but is purely human. Yet it is still more: it rises above the individually human and is in the deepest sense part of all humanity. In other words, in its whole being it is orientated towards the whole of humanity. It bears within itself the possibility of inwardly understanding, embracing and loving humanity.

When, in 1955, after a nine-month tour of the world, Zeylmans was invited to write an article on nations and races, he chose as the starting point for this the first three lectures he had heard Rudolf Steiner give in 1920, from the series: *The Bridge Between Universal Spirituality and the Physical Constitution of Man*. According to Zeylmans these offered a systematic example of a path towards real knowledge of the human being; and *'whoever tries to pursue such a path can come to a deep encounter with the forces determining races and nations'*.

Steiner starts from the four known states in which the human organism manifests: that is, solid, fluid, gaseous and warmth states. He describes these in relation to the life and etheric forces working within them (known as life ether, sound ether, light ether and warmth ether). Only a small proportion of the human organism is solid. More than 80 per cent is fluid. The solid part of the organism is bound to earthly laws. In the fluid organism cosmic, peripheral forces are at work, which stream through the solid organism of the physical body as 'ether body' or 'body of formative forces'. The light-permeated gaseous organism is the bearer of the astral body. There the world of the stars streams in, in a qualitative way. The ego or 'I', our spiritual core, can take hold in the warmth organism.

In relation to this spiritual ladder Rudolf Steiner describes the powers of imagining or conceiving (ether body), of feeling (astral body) and of willing (ego). Step by step he leads us up this ladder, beginning with basic physical conditions, passing through cosmic, planetary and astral conditions and right on up to the highest realms of the creative spirit, where freedom and love appear as cosmic powers . . . In their organic and constitutional divergence, people living on earth can be ascribed to different races and nationalities. In their etheric bodies the sun and planets work in different ways, thus bringing about differences in skin colour, physical build and skull shape.

In this article Zeylmans then goes on to describe the origins and characteristics of the five Root Races as Steiner distinguishes them. Then he says:

The person seeking self-knowledge, who gradually forms a more conscious relationship to his own organ processes, and thus also to the working of etheric forces, will by these means gain access to the other races. He will no longer simply view them 'externally' and experience them as 'alien', but will sense a direct connection with them via his own physical and etheric processes. His own organ processes will become sensory tools by means of which he can sense the inner being of other races. He will discover the other races as latent potential within himself. Because a certain process was not emphasized in him, he was not born into this particular race, but the process is nevertheless present in him too. He bears the seeds of all races within his own organism, in a fluid, streaming way. When we consciously experience this on the path of self-knowledge, the organ processes become organs of perception capable of 'perceiving and understanding the same thing in other races'.

Finally, in this article, Zeylmans discusses the origin of nations and races and concludes with the words:

On the path of self-knowledge, therefore, we come to know the powers of our soul; and the deeper this self-knowledge is, the more we begin to sense our limitations and one-sidedness. This also means, however, that we come to know both the limitations of our own nation and those of others.

We come to see that, at a more advanced stage of self-knowledge, we are directly confronted with the powers determining our race and nation. Rudolf Steiner describes this encounter in his book How to Know Higher Worlds, *in the chapter on 'The Guardian of the Threshold'.*

There he describes how nation and race are then no longer concepts accompanied by feelings and emotions; instead we encounter these spirits when we advance far enough to bear responsibility for what needs to happen within our nation and race. Instead of being unconsciously led into our nation's task, we then take this high task upon ourselves in full consciousness. When we reach this stage the term 'humanity' reveals its true meaning.

Thus a self-knowledge that takes it upon itself to rediscover the races and nations within ourselves can, at the same time, lead to a deeper relationship with the being of Christ, who as the representative of humanity, as the ego of humanity, can be a constant example to us on this path.

Based on these ideas, Zeylmans twice made larger-scale attempts to raise the profile of the psychology of nations so that it could be developed further as a field of study and then applied practically to politics at an international level. The first occasion was after his return from Indonesia in 1933/34, when, with Herbert Hahn and Max Stibbe, he organized study conferences on the psychology of nations. It is significant that he travelled to Germany in January 1933, shortly before the Nazis seized power, and held discussions in Stuttgart on a possible international conference on the psychology of nations. There, on 4 January, he gave a lecture on the East-West problem.

In the summer of 1934, in The Hague, the Centre for the Psychology of Nations was founded, for which Zeylmans also sought the advice of his father-in-law Droogleever Fortuyn. The latter, as mayor of Rotterdam, was a member of the International Chamber of Commerce and also able to make a valuable contribution through his work for the League of Nations. A number of accessible monographs also appeared at this time, on the psychology of different nations.

But since Zeylmans had been expelled from the General Anthroposophical Society, and also because of the rise of the Nazis in Germany, it soon became apparent that there was too narrow a working basis to advance this issue in a practical way. He gave his last talk on this theme during a course in England in August 1935 on 'Spirit of Time and Psychology of Nations'.

The second attempt to create a context for study and practical development of a psychology of nations came in the years 1946–1950.

In a longer article, 'The co-existence of nations', he describes how

> *. . . without doubt, much would be achieved in international understanding, both at conference tables and in daily practice, if those at least who occupy responsible positions had some insight into the psyche of nations, based on a genuine psychology of nations—one which could substantiate all that folk wisdom already knows, while at the same time deepening and broadening it. One could even imagine that in future non-partisan specialists might give advice in the field of national psychology, and that this could be an important aid to making decisions in the international arena. At the moment there is nothing like this. And those who have some understanding of the psychology of nations can clearly see that many situations are dealt with in a way that shows politicians do not have any real insight into the soul structure of different peoples.*

Willem Zeylmans tried three times to gain official recognition for this idea. His first attempt was to make contact with the Royal Institute of International Affairs in London, which enjoyed royal patronage and counted the 'prime ministers of the dominions' among its honorary presidents. This was an institute in which highly regarded and influential people from Great Britain's political and public life were active. Zeylmans wrote to this institute, offering to give a lecture explaining his ideas on the psychology of nations (16 January 1946). He added a memorandum outlining 'a scheme for the foundation of an international institute for folk psychology'. His offer was rejected: this was not regarded as part of the institute's task, he was told, which was, rather, 'the factual study of international problems'.

After the failure of this attempt, Zeylmans turned to an influential foundation in Holland, the 'Prince Bernhard Foundation' (which Prince Bernhard himself had no influence over). After long negotiations he was informed that the 'scientific bases of the institute have not yet reached a stage where general agreement might be attained in a responsible and successful manner'.

Zeylmans undertook his third attempt at the *Rockefeller* Foundation in the USA, for which he had a good letter of introduction. After thorough discussions with representatives of this institute and of the State Department, this request for support was once more turned down.

In his study on Zeylmans and the psychology of nations, A.C. Henny writes that 'it was not sufficiently clear to many people outside anthroposophical circles on what basis the proposed institute would be founded. People understood that it would be based on Rudolf Steiner's ideas, which he had expressed in a number of lectures on the psychology of nations (Oslo 1910, Berlin 1914 and 1917), but they believed this was not sufficient foundation for an institute expected to help create a breakthrough in international relations'.

In the meantime this institute was indeed founded, in Holland in 1947, as the 'International Institute for the Psychology of Nations'. A large number of well-known representatives from the fields of science, banking, industry, trade, and also from local government, the navy, health care and education, formed a supervisory committee. Several gatherings were held, and concrete issues were taken up, including the relationship of European countries to Germany and the psychological relationship between the western world and Russia. A conference also took place on the psychological foundations of Belgian-Dutch cooperation. But within a few years it became apparent that a deeper collaboration leading to real results could not happen within this institute.

In our age the earth has come to be populated by many different races and nations, all of whom are human beings however different they may be. But the real issue is whether we can get to know them all, and above all come to understand them. Are we able to feel connected with the different races, to sense the way in which we are related to the other as an equal being? Do we see the being of the other illuminated by the same light of the spirit, the light of Christ?

The answer to this question is of great importance—even, ultimately, decisive for the future of humanity.

The potential of all humanity has been bestowed on every individual human being. When a human being is born in the full and deepest sense, then the essential core of all humanity is also present in him. Seen in this light, races and peoples appear as groups of human beings who reveal particular aspects of the forces and characteristics that are active in every human being.

If we try to read the archetypal images, then, above and beyond all differences, we will start to see something like a spiritual process of evolution passing from childhood to old age. Such a developmental process has nothing whatever to do with better or worse.

People may tend to see this all as an unreal utopia—an all-too understandable reaction. The arguments against it are numerous. But are we really concerned with arguments here? Isn't it, rather, a question of gaining insights into the reality of the evolutionary process unfolding within humanity, and of trying to participate in this ourselves?

★

In his small volume *Amerika en hat Amerikanisme* ('America and Americanism'), Willem Zeylmans presented a short, vibrant summary of his first two trips through the USA—a loving and yet also highly critical description of the United States, and an example of what he was attempting through the practice of 'a psychology of nations'. This study of less than 50 pages is probably one of the most sober and at the same time profound things he wrote on this theme.

In the chronology (see appendix) are listed the towns where he gave lectures on these trips. From this we can see how he became acquainted with large areas of the USA—first over three, then four months. While there he also met the most interesting Americans, through the usual 'lunch talks', dinner parties and cocktail parties, and used these opportunities to awaken interest in his plans regarding a psychology of nations. Casting a glance at the following list of clubs, institutes, universities and societies to whom he spoke can give us a better impression than travel anecdotes of the kinds of groups he encountered. (I have left out the many lectures and discussions in anthroposophical circles). Sometimes these were small societies, with an audience of only 40 to

60; and sometimes also gatherings attended by between 400 and 600 people:

Women's National Democratic Club, Washington
Institute for Advanced Studies, Princeton
Wilton High Mowing School, Boston
Community House, Buffalo
Thomas School, Gowanda
Western Women's Club, San Francisco (× 2)
World Affairs Council, Sacramento
State Teacher College, San Francisco
San Francisco Women's Legislative Council, San Francisco
University Women's Club, San Diego (Calif.)
Teachers' Association, San Diego (Calif.)
San Diego State College, San Diego (Calif.)
Open Forum Group, San Diego (Calif.)
Teachers' Union, San Diego (Calif.)
University of Cincinnati, Cincinnati
Center for Human Relations Studies, New York
Yale University, New Haven
School of Religion, Howard University, Washington
Teachers' General Meeting, San Diego (Calif.) (× 4)
Unitarian Church, San Diego (Calif.)
Congregational Church, San Diego (Calif.)
Scripps College, Los Angeles
School of Fine Arts, Los Angeles
Californian Color Society, Los Angeles
Monterey Peninsular College, Claremont
American Broadcasting (interview), San Francisco
San Francisco State College, San Francisco
Psychological Association of the University of Cincinnati, Cincinnati
Goethe Society, Washington
George Washington University, Washington
Cooperative Forum (Dutch embassy), Washington

Zeylmans' lectures at the end of 1948 got such a response from students in particular, and at some universities, that he was invited to give a second lecture tour, which took place one year later. On this occasion he also got to know the southern states. Through various friends living in the US, including Dr A. Philipse from the Dutch embassy in Washington, and his friend de Kat Angelino, contact was made with representatives from the State Department, with whom he discussed possibilities for a more thorough-going study of the psychology of nations in the USA. He soon struck up a friendship with Russell Davenport, editor of *Fortune* magazine, who was interested in the psychology of nations, and who introduced him to the Chancellor of the University of Chicago, Dr M. Hutchins. After a lecture at the University of Cincinatti (California), he was asked by one of the professors, George Kisker, to write an article on the theme of 'international tensions', which also appeared in 1951 in an anthology (see bibliography in the appendix). Kisker wanted to found in his faculty an American sister-institute of the Dutch Institute for the Psychology of Nations.

At this university sparks flew several times between Zeylmans and a society of professional psychologists; for instance when, in a discussion on the differences in perception, feeling and will between American and Europeans, he went into more detail on the soul life of a central European. One of the audience interrupted him finally to say: 'But how can such people also be democrats?' To which he calmly replied: 'Why should they be?' After a thunderstruck silence, there followed a profound discussion on the many shades of difference in human soul life, which also made a great impression on Zeylmans himself.

He made many such significant contacts, and for a while he hoped that the Rockefeller Foundation would provide subsidies to support regular and thorough studies on the psychology of nations in the United States. When these were not forthcoming the material basis for further US trips was also lacking, and so he did not return to that country until four years later. Naturally much had changed there in the meantime.

The true spirit of America relates to Americanism as light relates to darkness, as spiritual birth relates to material death. Will the epic of America, perhaps to be written in a few hundred years, speak of the birth and development of a wholly new people—or even of a number of American peoples—who have borne great ideals into humanity and also made them reality, above all in the economic and social realm? Or will this epic tell of the tragic fall of a people that was unable to resist the temptations which arose from technological brilliance and material wealth, so that it forgot its true spiritual teachers?

This decision will depend equally on developments in Europe itself. Americanism is increasingly gaining ground with us too, and here it represents a much greater danger than in America itself. Manifestations of cultural exhaustion have in recent years led to terrible results and aberrations giving rise to world catastrophes. A

PAGE 9
SUNDAY, MARCH 26, 1950
San Francisco Chronicle

DR. F. W. ZEYLMANS
Nations have souls

Psychologist Says Nations Have Souls

Nations have souls and psychologies, just like people.

And, as among people, national character varies from nation to nation.

Dr. F. W. Zeylmans van Emmichoven, Dutch physician, psychologist and educator, believes peace will come to the world only when these national psychologies are understood.

And if they are not understood . . . "it will be impossible to find a way out of the international darkness in which we live."

Dr. Zeylmans, in San Francisco for a series of lectures sponsored by the local Anthroposophical Society, is founder of the Institute of Psychology of Peoples at The Hague which is the world center of research and education on national psychologies.

THE INSTITUTE'S GOAL

Goal of the institute—admittedly well in the future—is an independent board of "the best peoples of all countries, experts who really know about the psychologies of peoples."

This board, Dr. Zeylmans declares, should be asked for advice on international affairs by the political leaders of the various countries.

"But the time is short," he said. "The nations of the world are more advanced technically and economically than they are morally."

The determination of a nation's psychology requires extensive economic and sociological studies of its physical character and social organization.

NATIONAL MORALITY

"These are the environmental factors of national growth," Dr. Zeylman explained.

"The environment acts on the people, but at the same time the inner spirit of the people mold the environment.

"In a country, political life is an expression of spiritual quality or the ideals of the people."

National morality is defined by Dr. Zeylmans as "the growth of inner creative forces" in a nation.

"What you are doing in America," he said, "shows, for instance, that in this country your standard of morality includes the ideal of equality.

U. S. IS 'YOUNG'

"Psychologically, you are a young country. When I come here from Europe, I sometimes feel as if I am 150 years old.

"Because youth loves activity, you want to do things immediately. You are reaching out and experimenting at all times.

"In keeping with your character, you like to make your experiments on a great scale. You are like a child, learning. Watch a child.

"To us in Europe, America gives a feeling of great freshness. It makes us smile, sometimes, out of the 'wisdom' of our much older character.

AMERICAN MORALITY

"Because you are youthful and do things on a big scale, you have stronger differences, stronger antitheses.

"One of America's most pronounced moral attributes is a certain inner kindness, which is very good."

The A-bomb, and now the planned H-bomb, are the results of our youthful drive and energy and our method of doing things in a big way, he said.

"Your high degree of technical development is the result of your character," he explained.

LIKE CHILDREN

"But, morally—ah, all of us are like children playing with dynamite.

"That is the problem facing us, the problem of the Twentieth Century."

Dr. Zeylmans' lectures for the San Francisco Anthroposophical Society are free to the public, and are held at the Western Women's Club. He will speak there Tuesday night on "Psychological Relations Between Europe and America," and on Wednesday night on "The Psychology of Fear."

new spirit will have to spring up in European countries, elevating national forces to a higher level, and enabling every nation and people to experience its rebirth.

There was a premonition of such a development after both the First and Second World War. But it turned out that there was not enough strength for people to liberate themselves from continually recurring political and economic predicaments.

Nevertheless it will be vitally necessary, before the end of this century, to create a community of nations at a higher spiritual level, so that people can approach solutions to our current economic, political and cultural problems out of genuine insights into man's deeper being.

The sense that we together form a single humanity, belong to one humanity, lives to a large extent in Americans, even if often in rather primitive form . . .

A deep impression was made on me by something an older American said. I was giving a lecture on the psychology of nations in which I tried to depict the spirituality of different peoples, and he said, in full seriousness: 'Christ is the spirit leading the American people.'

One may be shocked to hear such a thing and recall at the same time all the negative forces also at work in that nation. Yet such a statement should be seen against the background of a mighty struggle of which many in America are aware—a struggle which has already begun to some extent, but which will increasingly unfold in the most powerful way: the struggle between Christian and anti-Christian forces.

If European nations recognize the true spirit of America and try to work accordingly, they can develop hand in hand with this people. But if they fail to see through Americanism, wishing only to profit from it, then they will not only drastically undermine their own countries through the trap of illusory affluence, but will also ill-serve America.

There may well be significance in the fact that Zeylmans' text on America and Americanism, from which the above passage is quoted, never appeared in English-speaking countries, although an English translation was available in manuscript.

★

Before his departure for the USA in January 1950, Willem Zeylmans had invited his anthroposophical friends to Holland to participate in discussions on the themes which were to be aired during that year. He was suddenly taken ill though (he often got sudden and violent migraines), and so had to cancel this gathering. But on 28 February, from New York, he wrote a letter to his friends expressing the things he had wanted to bring up during those discussions, and from this we learn of his intentions:

For me, the idea of threefold structure, both of the human and the social organism, has always been the most central aspect, yes even the epitome of anthroposophy. It is through this idea that real healing of human beings and human society first becomes possible. The arts of education and medicine both have their foundation in this. Only by this means can the social question be led towards reality.

The spiritual edifice of the 1923 Christmas Foundation Meeting was erected upon a foundation stone that bears threefold nature within it, both in intimate human terms and also in the universal sense of spiritual hierarchies—both exoteric and esoteric—and thus provides the archetypal image for a new world order.

Since 1923 people have spoken about these things many times in our Society. The Goethe anniversary year of 1949 brought us more than ever before to awareness of the enormous breadth and scope of Goethe's idea of polarity. The idea of threefold structure that appears in Rudolf Steiner as a mature fruit is already present in Goethe in seed-form.

Through living intensively with Goethe's ideas, particularly those on the metamorphosis of plants, animals and the human being, the threefold idea arose in my mind more brightly and powerfully.

. . . At our last Christmas celebration I spoke about Goethe and Novalis. This was an urgent and inner need that grew ever stronger the more I studied Goethe. It was as though the life of Goethe, as a man, as a spiritual man of earth, summoned up the figure of Novalis more and more, as one coming from the universe: the figure of the spiritual man of heaven. Here too there was a polarity—one of day and night, of radiant day sunlight and quietly gleaming midnight sunlight—of hard-won and manifest Christianity.

Rudolf Steiner lived with both figures more intensively than almost anyone else had ever done before. For him they were two different paths to the spirit: the path to conscious, systematic knowledge of nature and the world, of phenomena, archetypal phenomena and ideas—and the path of magical idealism streaming in from the cosmos.

It seems to me that it would be good to let Novalis live amongst us during the next few years, more strongly than this has happened so far, for many souls who seek a path to anthroposophy will find Novalis a more direct and clearer way-sign. Many too, perhaps, will only really see the path of true Goetheanism when this is illuminated by the light which Novalis' spiritual being shines upon it. These are the themes I wanted to address in my introduction.

⋆

'What is more wonderful than gold?' asked the king. 'Light,' replied the snake. 'What is more refreshing than light?' asked the former. 'Conversation,' replied the latter.

These famous words from Goethe's *Fairy-tale of the Green Snake and the Beautiful Lily* could serve as a motto for the series of conferences which took place as part of the initiative group described hereafter by Dr van Deventer, of which the theme was 'The continued effect of the Christmas Foundation Meeting' (the conference in Dornach at Christmas 1923, when, in the presence of about 700–800 people, Rudolf Steiner laid the 'foundation' for the new Anthroposophical Society). These conferences took place each summer, from 1949 onwards, often in The Hague. Each year a few hundred participants were invited from many different countries to devote themselves to this theme for about a week.

I mention these gatherings here because they had widespread influence and, for many (especially young) people, represented a profound encounter with the 'Foundation Stone' of the Anthroposophical Society. A participant once wrote about them:

> The Hague has built a palace for peace. Repeatedly in the last decades people have come together here who sought mutual understanding; and what they thought they had obtained was trumpeted abroad by the world press. When we held our conference here we sat in the great hall of the Rudolf Steiner School without microphones or any press representatives; and the forum where we held our discussions was of a different kind. For the millions of those who have died, who reside in the environs of the earth, for the guiding spirits of those still alive who seek mutual understanding, there is no need for the communication channels of radio and press . . .
>
> There may have been many different moods alive in the inner landscapes of these 350 souls, but one in particular was present in all: a morning mood, with transparent sky, fresh air, clear waters and ships raising their sails for unhindered voyages. Floods and wrecks may have lain behind us, but today no one was paying these any attention. And we all had the sense that the landscape of Holland, spreading around our four walls, that the soil on which our hall stood, could not have been better chosen. It seemed as though the task of the centre had been taken on at this place and at this hour, a task which means health in the deepest sense. For the folk soul of Holland too has experienced the grace of healing at this mid-point in the century. Wounds of the past decade are healing over, and the power of forgiveness is spreading over old pains. Among us were friends from nine nations, the former allies as well as enemies of the land; and though pupils of Rudolf Steiner had never adhered to these alliances and enmities, it was nevertheless

> symbolic that the language of the European centre could be the natural and self-evident conference language . . .
>
> Through the breaks and pauses intentionally left in the course of each day wove threads of destiny, long-spun and newly formed, as they did too in the midst of general discussions. It was noticeable that what one person said caused a number of others to mount the podium, just as the spirituality of one people enhanced and augmented that of another. Destiny had been mounting up in the long years of inner and outer hindrance, and now came flooding over, into its own. Young friends, above all, reacted as though at a given sign the moment those older ones spoke to whom Rudolf Steiner had especially entrusted the concerns of youth . . .
>
> What had been worked over in the depths now pushed forth to all horizons as we shook hands in farewell. It was no longer necessary to reaffirm to each other that there were more tasks waiting between heaven and earth than all Rudolf Steiner's pupils put together could deal with.

If the many different contributions from participants threatened to produce a kind of disparate turmoil, Zeylmans led these conferences in a way which always enabled unity to resurface. He managed this through his summaries, in which all felt they had been given a place. He had the ability to form a shared picture in which everyone felt represented.

This regularly recurring international exchange of views, in which severe spiritual struggles were sometimes waged, began to produce some fruit from the seed planted twenty years before at the Stakenberg Camp—now made more inward, profound and mature. Many participants owed decisive impulses on behalf of anthroposophy to these conferences.

The following was written after one such conference:

Conversation

A word begins. And many words resound.
One gives, from others it is taken.
The bowl of wine passes around the circle—
Is passed from human spirit to spirit.

It never empties, even if hands tremble.
The wine tastes sweet and does not become bitter.
Yes, something takes care that no single drop
Of the world's fear falls into our vessel.

If life's hardships sometimes open wounds,
These find healing from a wiser utterance.
Meeting blesses him who, seeking, asks.
Here nothing is lost that anybody speaks.

A seed springs up and grows within the heart
Of many—rises, spreads out like a tree.
Humanity's dream is ripening in its leaves...
We speak a prayer to the highest gods.

★

After the end of the Second World War, Zeylmans developed ideas for restructuring the General Anthroposophical Society. Dr M.P. van Deventer experienced his initiatives at close hand, and in the following passage describes what came of them:

> In 1948 Zeylmans developed an important initiative. He sought ways of integrating the work of the Anthroposophical Society and of linking up once more with the Goetheanum at Dornach. The world situation had completely changed after the war, and this required new ideas and a new approach to tasks both in our own country and also throughout the whole Society.
>
> Zeylmans believed that wholesale renewal was necessary, one so thoroughgoing that for a while he even thought of trying to find a different name for anthroposophy. But at his wife's urging he gave up this plan.
>
> When the Dutch Society was refounded in 1945, he tried to bring about renewal by starting from actual conditions among the membership at the time; and he hoped that a similar renewal would also take place in the whole Society. Only then would it make sense to reunite all the different groups. His initiative extended to calling a conference of representative members from different countries, in order to discuss these issues.
>
> At the same time Emil Bock in Germany took up a similar initiative, which started with his first visit to England after the war, in the summer of 1947. There he found that 'the West is calling out for a Michaelic life of spirit'. In order to meet this need before the mid-century had passed, he strove to create an 'initiative-strong spiritual alliance between anthroposophical groups in England, Holland and Germany'. At the same time he believed that, given the world situation, the divisions that had arisen within the anthroposophical movement could no longer be

allowed to persist, and that the German friends could offer 'comradely help' which would help the English and Dutch Societies to link up with the Goetheanum once more.

Thus Emil Bock formed the plan of a 'Friendship Conference', in which about fifteen friends should meet in order to discuss the spiritual situation in the world and the measures that needed to be taken. There were therefore two similar initiatives. It was decided to take up Bock's plan, with the aim of holding a conference in England. However, at the instigation of Zeylmans and Karl König, a conference location close to the Goetheanum was chosen instead.

In June 1948 a first gathering was held, at Arlesheim in a hall belonging to Weleda. Fourteen participants were there—representative members from Germany, Holland and England, and a representative from the USA who happened to be in Dornach at the time. I was also invited to attend in order to represent the colleagues and friends of Ita Wegman.

On the first three days we worked together at the karma lectures given by Steiner in Arnhem in 1924. Subsequently the individual participants reported in detail on the work done since 1935 in each of their fields, so that a comprehensive common awareness arose. Over the next days several additional people from Dornach were invited to join, in order to inform us about the current situation of the General Anthroposophical Society; and during the last day and a half the Goetheanum executive committee (*Vorstand*) took part as well. Though there was not yet a gathering at the 'highest level', the will was clearly expressed to begin 'lower-level' collaborative work between the different groups in individual countries. Then, as Zeylmans expressed it, unification with the Goetheanum would be a 'five-minute matter'.

In December 1948 a further conference was held, with a somewhat different composition of people. Discussions were difficult since some had not attended the gathering in the summer. In the midst of this came the news of Marie Steiner's death. Naturally people were distracted by this and the discussions led nowhere.*

So in 1948 the original initiative had to be put on hold, but it carried on in other guises. On New Year's Eve 1948 Zeylmans gave an

* During the following summer a further conference took place in Dornach, with other, additional people involved—but this had no specific result. Not until 1960 was it possible for the Dutch Society to re-amalgamate with the General Anthroposophical Society, following many years' collaboration at a 'lower level'.

important lecture in Arlesheim on the Christmas Foundation Meeting and the Foundation Stone verses. The next day conversations took place amongst a number of those who had attended it, including many friends from other countries. Zeylmans, who was deeply disappointed by the failure of the previous conference, suggested in these discussions that we—those of us who were sitting there on 1 January—should carry on talking with one another in the following days. This proposal was taken up enthusiastically, and, still moved by Zeylmans' New Year's Eve lecture, Werner Pache suggested the theme of the 'Ongoing effect of the Christmas Foundation Meeting'.

In a small group of about fifteen people—chiefly doctors and curative educationalists—we worked together for three days. Initially we turned our attention to questions about 'the spiritual guidance of humanity'. Through all the discussions we subsequently held every year, the theme of the 'ongoing effect of the Christmas Foundation Meeting' ran like a uniting thread. Each New Year's Eve Zeylmans spoke in a larger circle on this theme, which became the very content of his life. And in subsequent discussions in this so-called 'January circle' we worked further at this theme. This group, though much enlarged, also for a while supported many of Zeylmans' international summer conference initiatives in Holland. Thus the impulse of the Christmas Foundation Meeting rekindled in increasing numbers of souls, and continued to exert a fruitful effect in the whole Anthroposophical Society. A last initiative led, in 1953, to a public 'Europe Conference' in The Hague, attended by about 1,200 people.

Over the years the January circle expanded greatly. It was part of Zeylmans' idea that involving younger friends would enable the impulses of the Christmas Foundation Meeting to pass over to the next generation and continue to work through to the end of the century. Thus the 'impulse of renewal' lived on in altered form.

★

Shortly before Willem Zeylmans ended his second trip through the United States and began his voyage home, his friend Pieter de Haan wrote him a letter from Holland which included the following passage:

> A short while ago, in our initiative group, we had a full and thorough discussion about our Dutch Society. We looked back to the time before it was founded (1923), when we were more inclined towards a general society for free spiritual life, or something similar, so that we

could encompass much broader circles. This need, even its necessity, repeatedly resurfaces. How exactly we should do this remains the big question; but from all sides we are seeing that we will have to arrive at something else, another impulse, alongside our Dutch Society. (5 May 1950)

Zeylmans also wanted to found something along these lines, in the same way that he had already started a 'School for spiritual science' with his friends, in The Hague in 1936.

After his return from the USA further discussions took place; and in July 1951 an announcement appeared that a Centre for Free Spiritual Life had been founded:

This founding is to be seen as an initiative of the undersigned, who was moved to take this step after discussions with a few active members of our Dutch Anthroposophical Society. In the last few years it has become increasingly apparent that anthroposophically orientated spiritual science is meeting with interest in wider circles, outside our Society, and that new and valuable contacts are continually being formed—often with individuals holding influential positions in social and cultural realms. One of the aims of this centre will be to cultivate such contacts and bring them to conscious fruition. In addition, because of the fact that the School of Spiritual Science founded by Rudolf Steiner at the Christmas Foundation Meeting has not as yet been able to develop as intended, some areas of work (sections) of anthroposophy have been left to their own devices. The Centre hopes to be able to have a structuring and activating influence here, at least within our own country. All will be regarded as colleagues at this Centre who seek such work, established on a real basis. People will gather on a certain day each month, the issues dealt with there will be published, and everyone who feels drawn to participate may consider himself invited.

This announcement was signed by Willem Zeylmans. A simple sheet was appended announcing two courses: H.D. van Goudoever on Rudolf Steiner's *Philosophy of Freedom*, and Zeylmans on 'Man and world'. These courses took place each morning.

In the following year the Centre for Free Spiritual Life already had a small newsletter and the morning courses had expanded to three: alongside van Goudoever and Zeylmans the doctor and sociologist Professor Bernard Lievegoed also held a course on 'The new image of man in relation to the development of the embryo'. Over the next three years the most interesting articles appeared in the newsletter, mainly written by teachers from the fast developing Centre. One also finds there several summaries by Zeylmans of lectures he had given.

As the years went by the activities of the Centre increased, spreading to other towns, and were eventually supported by a very respectable number of teachers. (Apart from those already mentioned, the following also participated over the course of the years: Max Stibbe, Jan van Wettum, T. Tymstra, E. Knottenbelt, W. Stigter, M. Laffrée, L. Mees, A. Soesman, W. Veltman, E. Landweer and many others.) The need arose, in fact, to coordinate the ever increasing number of courses, lectures, therapy working groups etc. in a loose affiliation. First efforts to set up professional trainings also gained a more substantial form as a result (for Waldorf teachers, eurythmists, art therapists etc.). The teachers on these many courses, often burdened almost to the limits of their strength, were now to meet regularly and exchange experiences *'in order to get to know the deepest impulses of other teachers; they should encounter each other in their true spiritual will, so as to be able to work in future out of inner unity or harmony'*, as Zeylmans wrote in 1955. He hoped to achieve a spiritual coordination by these means: *'In all our work, after all, anthroposophy is always the mother-ground; and it is one of the most surprising experiences to see how different people draw strength from this anthroposophy (which is the same for all and yet is experienced quite differently in each individual instance).'*

Underlying this Centre for Free Spiritual Life was the fundamental idea of Rudolf Steiner's School of Spiritual Science: renewing education through the impulses of a new Mystery knowledge. *'Ultimately it is a question of the general inner education of human beings as a basis for their esoteric, meditative development, and also as a basis for their possible professional training along anthroposophical lines.'* (Zeylmans, October 1955)

The Centre developed very quickly in the following years, and increasingly came to emphasize social aspects. Not only teaching and learning took place there, but practical, artistic and social activities were also practised:

The intention is not to teach anthroposophy in as comprehensive a way as possible, but the participants can get actively involved themselves by practising capacities of the soul and spirit rather than of reason alone—through confronting issues which live within the human being, connected with his relationship to the world, the earth, the cosmos and to life after death. The aim is to undergo inner experiences which enable the pupil to awaken spiritually and morally to higher, more universal conditions. (Zeylmans, 1959)

The former dwelling in The Hague where these and many other activities took place became too small, and eventually a grand house on Riouwstraat was bought, which in the following years was gradually enlarged with extensions and a new building.

Together with the Centre's 12 to 15 teachers, Zeylmans worked for years to advance these spiritual science studies, and also himself held two or three courses each day (psychosophy, inner development, theosophy, soul development through life and death, occult science, human consciousness etc.).

My work here requires a certain completion or a conclusion with a particular goal in view. That will be our so-called 'Free School' of which the psychology faculty is only the beginning, he writes in a letter of December 1956. *We will have to work hard for about another five years to render the true plan visible, and to gain enough weight in the world. That's why I will tour the world as little as possible next year.*

The number of participants grew rapidly. In the last years he sometimes had between eighty and a hundred people attending his courses each day. But the number of students pursuing professional trainings still remained small. 'The numbers are still low' it says in an annual review, 'but we can comfort ourselves with the thought that seventeen years after it was founded, Leiden University still only had eleven students!'

★

In an earlier chapter of this biography I described how it was Willem Zeylmans' destiny always to 'speak to a full house', if one can put it like this, for once, in such general and simple terms. There is no room in a biography even to begin to characterize the two thousand or so lectures he gave during the forty years of his anthroposophical activity—nor would there be any point in this, since the bulk of this work, deriving from Rudolf Steiner's spiritual science (Zeylmans never left his listeners in any doubt about this) was formed for direct, oral communication. The effectiveness of his descriptions was no doubt particularly due to his personal study and work on anthroposophical themes and content. From the 600 to 800 sets of lecture notes that have survived, from a few (incomplete) recordings, from several dozen stenographic transcripts, and above all from the many newspaper reviews of his talks, we can repeatedly see how Zeylmans made anthroposophy *concrete* for his listeners. All this took place in the light of an inner stance—that had become something like a life maxim for Zeylmans—which Rudolf Steiner had expressed to anthroposophists in The Hague in November 1923: 'Try to grow together with the world! That will be the best and the most important "programme" for you to follow. That is something that cannot be fixed in statutes; but it is something which we should be able to kindle in our hearts like a flame!' Zeylmans' lectures were delivered out of the current situation of people's lives and of human society.

At Whitsun 1952 Zeylmans was invited to Berlin, to a conference dedicated to the theme of 'The human soul in the spiritual struggles of today'. The following sentence was printed on the front page of the programme:

> In view of the social perplexity of our times, we feel obliged to use this event to point to the paths which Dr Rudolf Steiner developed and opened up.

A translation of the thoroughly prepared programme is reproduced here. Zeylmans had often spoken in Berlin before—between 1929 and 1932 especially, he had experienced important things there. He later recalled:

For me the enthusiasm was unforgettable with which Werner Pache had prepared the large-scale lectures in the 'Herrenhaus'. In doing so he had put himself entirely at the service of an idea of Ita Wegman's, introducing a social hygiene impulse into the decadence and spiritual confusion of the Berlin of those years. The response was enormous: three days before the conference began the thousand or so tickets were already sold out. One kept seeing Pache's radiant face—on the steps of the Herrenhaus, amidst the streaming crowds—he had thought of everything, taken care of every detail.

So now, in 1952, the same Werner Pache, together with Franz Löffler, had organized this first large-scale conference after the Second World War. For Zeylmans, as he writes, it was *'one of the most moving conferences I ever experienced, particularly because of the involvement of people from the Eastern Zone [of Germany].'*

The conference was held under the auspices of the anthroposophical conference committee in Berlin, a working group that came together for this task, composed of people who spent their daily professional lives involved with the results of anthroposophical research, such as anthroposophical curative educators and doctors, Waldorf teachers, priests of the Christian Community, eurythmists and painters. The concerns of the

Time	Friday, 30 May	Saturday, 31 May	Whitsunday, 1 June	Whit Monday, 2 June
10.00–11.00	———	B. Lievegoed, MD, Holland The personality between environment and heredity	Franz, Löffler, Berlin Social hopes of the present day	G. Bockholt-Kirchner, MD, Switzerland Illness and healing as destiny factors
17.00–18.30	———	Mr F. Geuter, England Education towards selflessness	Festive Whitsun addresses: Voices for the spiritual task of Central Europe	B. Lievegoed, MD, Holland Anthroposophical insights into illnesses of our time. Overcoming modern psychism
19.30–21.00	Welcome Dr Zeylmans v. Emmichhoven, Holland The Whitsun message in our time	Werner Pache, Switzerland Development hindrances and soul development in childhood	School for the art of eurythmy, Berlin EURYTHMY Cecilia Hall, Wilmersdorf, Nikolsburger Platz	Dr Zeylmans v. Emmichhoven, Holland The path of schooling of the soul towards spirit A social need of our times

conference were specifically related to contemporary problems of social pedagogy, and consciously directed at the public. Invitations went mainly to members of social and social pedagogy professions (paediatricians, psychiatrists, psychotherapists, teachers, college lecturers etc.) and to the relevant council departments of West Berlin. Each of the morning lectures were attended by between 400 and 500 people, while the evening events held in the student quarters (at the Steinplatz, Charlottenburg area of Berlin), were swamped with audiences of 750 or so. Many participants came into closer touch with anthroposophy for the first time as a result of the conference. The numerous entries in the 'interested' lists, and the surprisingly high sales of books confirm that wider circles of the public felt addressed . . .

One of the characteristic phenomena especially apparent in Berlin was the emphasis placed on the need and duty for Central Europe finally to become aware of its true mission between East and West: 'Europe as centre of the world can only survive if it can reintegrate human thinking, feeling and actions into a sustaining world order. The new path of knowledge, which our times require, is anthroposophy . . .'

At the very time the conference was being held as an attempt 'to acknowledge the spiritual task of Central Europe', Berlin's external isolation advanced still further: the authorities in the Eastern bloc stipulated that visas were now required for those travelling to the Eastern Zone, which was more or less the same as a travel embargo. As German workers and police felled trees to blockade access routes to West Berlin, people at the conference, in lectures and discussions, were working hard to formulate healing ideas to help East and West find common ground. Although people from the East were suddenly faced with problems of movement and travel, far more of them attended than one could have expected. And especially those who came from eastern Germany experienced the image which Dr Zeylmans gave in his introductory lecture, and which was felt to sum up this Berlin Whitsun conference, as a joyful confirmation of their own, hard-won and long-suffering experiences: This Whitsun spirit is what can give rise to a new world. Only a few people may be prepared for this, but one should not believe that it is therefore impossible for a new world to arise. If a small lamp is placed into a huge, dark hall, then the whole hall is focused on this one, small light.

⋆

After working for years to foster understanding for, and practical application of a psychology of nations, and having experienced how loving devotion to the folk souls and an intensive, conscious involvement with the being and working of folk spirits was not taken up outside anthroposophical circles, Zeylmans made one last attempt to gain understanding for the spirit of Europe.

Europas Aufgabe im gegenwärtigen Weltgeschehen ('Europe's place in the contemporary world') was the title of a small volume published in 1953 by Herbert Hillringhaus, chief editor of the journal *Die Kommenden.* It contained folk psychology studies by six anthroposophical authors: 'The physiognomy of Europe' (Stibbe), 'Basic features of European history from a national psychology perspective' (Mändl), 'The spirit of Europe as reflected in language' (Hahn), 'Europe between East and West' (Zeylmans), 'Europe between past and future' (Henny), and 'The hope of Europe' (Hillringhaus). This small volume conveys a vivid impression of the ideas and ideals that lived in anthroposophical circles at the time, which people hoped would reach those individuals whose prominent positions gave them the task of deciding on the future of a European community. Two years previously the European Coal and Steel Community had been founded; and the tendencies in western Europe to reach closer international accord as a defence against eastern Europe stimulated these authors to offer the idea of a *threefold* Europe. Zeylmans writes of this:

The number of people enthusiastically setting to work to bring about a rebirth of Europe is not small. They are striving for political unity based on federalism, and for economic consolidation through the forming of international communities. But at the same time we must acknowledge that such essentially valuable efforts are continually hampered, threatened and pushed into a sphere of unfreedom by the military aims and purposes which dictate everything.

The question arises as to whether we should not attempt to found such a European community on a deeper basis, whether we should not first of all try to understand Europe's special position between a western, American world and an eastern, Asiatic one. It is possible, surely, that Europe is now approaching its own true birth as a community; and that only out of the current distress and pressures of its position between the two great power blocs may consciousness awaken enabling Europe itself, through its own insight and will, to establish a true community of peoples.

At the outset of such an attempt, however, we would first need to work towards an understanding of the essential nature of such an European community.

For this purpose a 'Europe Conference' was called in the summer of 1953 in The Hague. Great efforts were put into its preparation in various countries by all who were able to participate. It took place in The Hague under the conference title of: The Birth of Europe—a Spiritual Question. Over a thousand people took part in this week-long conference, and one can understand how great were the hopes of those involved that this gathering would meet with some response in the public domain. In his opening address, which he began in Dutch, continued in English and then concluded in German, Zeylmans said, among other things:

We can regard Europe as a central realm of the earth, whose peoples we need to characterize according to their various soul types. Europe forms, in fact, the midpoint between eastern and western humanity, and has the particular task of manifesting the 'I', as the spirit centre of the individual, in a many-faceted totality of soul forces. It was important that since the fifteenth century all peoples of Europe have come into contact with one another, and have developed in mutual cultural influence. We do not wish to speak of Europe in terms of a national-international federation, as often happens, nor promote some new European patriotism. But we wish to help a Europe to arise that is an intrinsic part of evolving humanity . . .

Novalis coined a phrase that can serve as a motto for our conference: 'Humanity is the higher purpose of our earth . . . the eye which it raises to heaven.'

We hope to touch on something of the higher purpose of humanity in this conference . . .

A wealth of talks, study and discussion groups and seminars on all relevant areas and issues connected with this theme were offered to participants—a wealth that was later printed in summaries. The problem was approached from three angles in particular, based on the human being: his relationship to nature, to his fellow men and to his own country and other countries.

In the text referred to above, Zeylmans summarized the issue as follows:

From such characterizations it is now clear how unique Europe's situation is. The soul structure of European peoples makes it possible for them to participate actively in both polarities of East and West. The western European world is in some respects close to the American, western world—the English language has even come to dominate North America, although the Americans are also continually modifying this language out of their own folk strength. The more earthly orientation of the western European approach to life also appears as a bridge to the further West. On the other side, Russia forms a fluid transition to Asia. The mystic and religious character particularly prevalent in all Russian literature of the pre-Bolshevik period is deeply related to the spirit of the East. It is beyond the scope of these observations to examine here the extent to which this basic Russian tone has been altered by Bolshevism.

Europe as a whole therefore lives in strongly polar contrasts, which can nevertheless be united within the life of soul. But Europe will always need to seek the centre, seek balance. It is the task of Europe both to understand and admire ancient spiritual culture and the life of mind, as well as get to grips with a rationalist and technological approach to life. It can both grasp man's higher being in the spirit and also value the individual in his social aspect. The will to relieve suffering lives there; but at the same time it can see this suffering as a positive thing too. Europe is obliged to fight continually to unite apparently irreconcilable opposites of spiritual truth and outer reality.

The real task of Europe for the future of all humanity forms itself from such knowledge. Especially in Europe people will be able to understand that we can only comprehend man's being by observing him in his totality of body, soul and spirit.

Today humanity is trying to be born. This is apparent in every sphere. Both through the fact that commerce and technology encompass the whole earth, con-

necting all parts of the globe, but also unfortunately in the expansion of local wars into world wars.

But if mankind also wishes to attain soul-spiritual and moral unity, then it will only achieve this by developing deeper understanding for the differences between peoples of the East, West and Centre. Europe's task will be of the very greatest importance in these efforts. When it learns to see itself as a centre, it will be able to form a soul bridge upon which East and West can meet.

Since the time of this 'Europe Conference' the political situation has changed: the polarization of East and West seems to have been pushed into the background by the splits and confrontations between 'North' and 'South' ('rich' and 'poor').

The question of a Europe that takes up its task in a spiritual sense has remained unanswered. What seems clear, though, is that influential Europeans have not yet taken any account of anthroposophical ideas. One might also ask, perhaps, whether there is enough understanding in anthroposophical circles of the problems politicians and economists face in regard to Europe.

★

Already during the war years (in about 1942), Zeylmans began an intensive study of the so-called 'Christmas Foundation Meeting' of 1923–24, at which the Anthroposophical Society was newly founded. Steiner summed up this re-founding in a meditative verse, the Foundation Stone. Just as one lays a foundation stone for a new building or house, as a celebratory and conscious expression of the will to build, so he composed this verse as a foundation for the new Society—which was thus to be a dwelling or habitation for something. If one then asks what was intended to live within it, one may perhaps answer: a spiritual being, who can only work where people gather together as a community—in this case, the Being of Anthroposophy. Rudolf Steiner expressed this by saying that this Foundation Stone was laid in the hearts of the anthroposophists present.

One year previously, on 5 November 1922 in The Hague, Rudolf Steiner had already hinted at why he wished to re-found the Anthroposophical Society: 'You can,' he said, 'have all sorts of peripheral activities, Waldorf Schools etc., but all these things will be without strength and foundation if the centre is lacking.' But for this centre the 'right heart' was missing. Whoever expresses knowledge gained through spiritual science 'without being aware of the responsibility they bear, wreaks havoc in the world... Nowadays we are faced with the need to make the Society an active being at work in the world... The moment the Dornach centre falls apart, everything else will collapse too...'

At the founding of the Dutch Society (18 November 1923), he stated this once more: 'You see, it is like this: all these efforts (clinic, Waldorf School, eurythmy, speech formation etc.) cannot exist without the central striving at their heart: the anthroposophical movement itself. All these activities and efforts derive from, and must be nourished by, the anthroposophical movement itself.' And this movement, he said, must have its centre and heart in the new General Anthroposophical Society and the School of Spiritual Science at Dornach. That was the reason Rudolf Steiner took such extraordinary pains to strengthen this new Society.

In the years after Rudolf Steiner's death, Zeylmans experienced this centre passing through severe conflicts and shocks. In this 'active being at work in the world' which Rudolf Steiner had wished the Society to be, terrible internal conflicts and battles raged. For Zeylmans this was initially incomprehensible. He felt, as he once said, struck dumb by this, and affected in his inmost core. Why did this 'being' have to suffer like this?

The reader may recall the mood of soul which filled Zeylmans in 1931, when the ideal of a general, internationally active Anthroposophical Society could not be realized—a mood of despair and pain. He was released from this state by a phrase that struck him suddenly like illumination and resounded in him as inspiration: *Through suffering BEING is born.* This mysterious maxim accompanied him through the decades; also when the General Anthroposophical Society, from which he had been expelled in 1935, later had to undergo still further trials of destiny. At the laying of the Foundation Stone of this Society in 1923, Rudolf Steiner had created a vessel or 'body' for the being Anthroposophia, which was intended to enable it to work in the world. Could it not be that such a 'vessel' must also undergo suffering, even death, in order to attain a new stage of existence? But where could the General Anthroposophical Society rediscover its archetypal form, the deepest foundation of its existence? In the 'Foundation Stone'! Rudolf Steiner had described this at the 1923 Christmas Foundation Meeting—by saying that the 'rhythms' of this Foundation Stone would be kept alive and cultivated in human hearts.

Now Zeylmans began, first in a very small way and then among growing groups of people, and ultimately across the whole globe, to bear this ideal of the future into the present. First there was a study group of like-minded friends who together undertook regular intensive studies in Arlesheim (Switzerland), which one of the friends referred to as 'the continued working of the Christmas Foundation Meeting.' M.P. Deventer reported on these meetings at some length.

Some years later Zeylmans once more began to give a series of Christmas lectures on this theme in The Hague—which continued without interruption from then on. He gave the first of these in 1952, on the three alchemical processes (Salt, Mercury and Sulphur) in relation to the Foundation Stone. At Christmas the following year he drew attention to the fact that, during the 1923 Foundation Meeting, Rudolf Steiner had presented these verses in seven different, shortened versions: 'We find the right approach to such verses, that have been called forth and heard from the World Word, if we structure them in our own souls in such a way that they cannot leave us. And they will be able to form themselves in this way if you first raise from what has thus resounded the aspects which rhythm can give you.' (Steiner) For those present Rudolf Steiner had at the time written part of the verse on the board each day, over one week; and each time he had written a different version, so that finally seven different 'rhythms' arose.

'Now let us inscribe into the soul the inner rhythm which can bring home to us the fact that these very words resound as though out of world rhythm.' (28 December) '... If I write down these rhythms for you as harmony, this is because they really contain an image of star constellations...' and: 'This is what rhythms depend on which pass through the world. An original spiritual image lies in such rhythms as I have written down during the last few days in the form of our (Foundation Stone) verses, which are organized in a wholly inner, soul-spiritual way.' (1 January 1924)

It can strike one as strange that Zeylmans was one of the first anthroposophists to draw attention to these 'rhythms', thirty years after Rudolf Steiner had stressed their importance to those present as a summation of a week of spiritual work. They were initially to be found amongst a larger collection of lectures and minutes (1944 edition), and were subsequently published together for the first time in 1955. One can understand that during the trials undergone by the 'headquarters' of the anthroposophical movement, awareness of these things had wholly vanished! But Zeylmans, no doubt like many other participants of the Christmas Foundation Meeting, had copied these rhythms down in his notebook in 1923, and since then meditated on them in quiet, inward reverence:

This Foundation Stone has been a spiritual source for many during the past thirty years, from which they could continually draw new strength. With increasing wonder and reverence they recognized in these verses the inner basis of a truly spiritual community life, and still more than that: the basis of all human and social, communal life in the future.

He wrote these words a few weeks before beginning a voyage round the world on 17 January 1954. This Foundation Stone verse was the most important lecture theme on his trip. He gave many lectures on it, for instance in New York, Washington, Los Angeles, California, Honolulu, New Zealand, Australia, Indonesia, Nairobi, Johannesburg, Durban and Cape Town.

XI. THE REALITY IN WHICH WE LIVE

The problem facing the future will not be the implementation of a welfare state based on western pragmatism or eastern historical materialism. These two directions will undoubtedly play a major role in coming years; the most important question, however, is: What will happen after that? And the answer to that question is dependent exclusively on the thoughts which currently live in human souls as seeds of future attitudes to life. Only living thoughts, penetrated by the will to act and by enthusiasm, will be able to set the future on the right path.

Humanity in the West, the Centre and the East is developing in its trinity of body, soul and spirit. The soul is unfolding fully in human beings living in Europe, the Centre—and there the ego can be born. The more the ego grows, the more it can liberate itself from its shackles and awaken in the spirit, the more will it shed its ego characteristics; it will increasingly become spiritual reality, will become part of general humanity without losing its individuality—indeed, quite the opposite will happen: the ego will become increasingly individually real while at the same time encompassing humanity. In the East, where centuries of spiritual culture still live on in the traditions of Hinduism, Buddhism and Taoism, the image of the human being as a divine being still stands in the foreground. However much the East endeavours to modernize its social life, ancient ideas continue to live in its many millions of people. In the West, we find a young, earth-oriented culture which wants to create paradise on earth . . . The people of Europe are positioned between these two. As inhabitants of the earth they can understand the West, as spiritual beings the East. Thus they can also have a real relationship with the mystery of life and death without fearing death or losing themselves completely in life. Equally, they can understand the relative value of happiness and joy together with the deeper meaning of unhappiness and suffering.

They are capable of understanding all these things. Whether or not they will do so depends on their feelings of responsibility towards humanity. If they develop thoughts and feelings which embrace East and West in empathy and understanding, they lay the foundation for the development of a new will which is directed at humanity as such and on the basis of which a new form of co-existence can arise.

The verse which Rudolf Steiner called 'the Foundation Stone' speaks of humanity as such being born or created out of the divine. When the Father God on high, as it says, creates existence in the world below, this existence is the being of developing humanity. The first hierarchy guides the divine creative powers from on high to down below. What resounds on high is echoed below: 'Ex Deo nascimur' or 'Humanity originates in God'.

The activity of Christ within this developing humanity is described as something that is a blessing to human souls. His will is at work in the cosmic rhythms in which human hearts are also encompassed. One might meditate on how there is a great wave of rhythms across the surface of the earth which contains all the individual human rhythms of heart and lungs. Rudolf Steiner often spoke about the connection between the human heartbeat and the cosmic rhythms of day, lifetime, Platonic year. Although all these blood rhythms show small individual differences, they do all have their origin in the great cosmic rhythm. If in this respect we consider that the heart is the only organ which is truly on earth, then we can really say in respect of this wave which flows across the earth and in which all hearts beat together that we have here a new earth in the making. The earth is dying all about us; it is created anew in human hearts and a start of this newly arising earth is found where, in the harmony of rhythms, the basis for a new humanity is being formed. The will of Christ works all around us: that is to say, in the totality of human beings who populate our earth.

These thoughts probably reflect best something of what Zeylmans brought home from his journey around the world, something which would remain a central theme for him in the remaining seven years of his life.

This journey took him for the third and last time to the United States and then to New Zealand and Australia via Hawaii. After that he travelled through Java and Bali, the Indonesian islands which had made such an impression on him 22 years earlier, and then to India via Sri Lanka. After a prolonged stay in that country, he crossed the Indian Ocean to East Africa, finishing his journey with a working visit to South Africa. Seven years later, in 1961, he would undertake his last journey to South Africa.

The invitation to embark on this round-the-world trip came from two people with whom a friendship had previously developed: Willy Roelvink and her friend Mary Wilbers. These two Dutch women (they were fondly called 'the Aunties' by the Zeylmans) had been friends of Ita Wegman and Lili Vreede and had spent the years of the Second World War in the USA. Associating with these educated and idealistic women, with their outgoing attitude to life, was always stimulating and interesting. They knew America well and had previously accompanied Zeylmans on part of a trip through the United States. In other respects, too, their many travels had given them an international outlook, and they now wanted to give Zeylmans the opportunity to accompany them and get to know Asia and Africa. He accepted this generous gift on condition that he would be permitted to travel on behalf and as an official of the Dutch Anthroposophical Society. Thus the three of them embarked on their almost nine-month-long journey in January 1954, sailing westwards across the Atlantic to New York.

If we want to imagine Willem Zeylmans on this world trip, we must also take account of the underlying theme of the trip, the theme of the lecture he gave wherever he was invited to speak: 'From the Philosophers' Stone to the Foundation Stone' (in the context of the first Goetheanum, Rudolf Steiner and 'the birth of mankind'). He lectured on it in New York, Washington, Los Angeles and other Californian cities, then in Honolulu, Auckland and Wellington, in Sydney and Jakarta, and finally in Nairobi, Johannesburg, Durban and Cape Town. If no other listeners were present during the trip, the three travel companions simply immersed themselves in the subject on their own, as they did in Bali (on Whitsunday), at the lake in Kandy (Sri Lanka) or at 2000 metres, looking towards cloud-covered Mount Everest from the Nepal border. But wherever an audience came to hear him speak, many people—in distant countries—heard of the 'Foundation Stone' for the first time through his lectures. When a few years later his book appeared, they were able to see how his forward-looking thinking on the subject had developed. John Davy translated the book for the English-speaking world in 1963.

After his seven-week tour through the United States (largely in California), where apart from his lectures he was also asked for medical consultations and worked with education study groups on several occasions, he landed with his companions in Honolulu in mid-March. This is where, as he wrote home to say, he felt the journey really started.

Among the anthroposophists living there (the 'most westerly' ones in the world!) he met interested hosts for whom he was not only asked to give lectures but who took him on several excursions in his three weeks there to see the sights of these wonderfully beautiful islands with their mighty volcanoes. This made possible for him an encounter with the ancient culture of the islands which had been destroyed by the arrival of 'white' Christians in the nineteenth century. In several conversations, including one with the director of the anthropological Bishop Museum, he heard about the roots of this ancient Hawaiian civilization. Then there was a visit to Jolani Luahine and her 72-year-old 'Aunt Anne', the last of the hula dancers. For a whole morning the two women gave a demonstration of their dances in the ancient ritual form as they had been practised only at the royal court, one-and-a-half centuries earlier. All the sadness of things past came to life in these moving conversations. Sadness also because the two women had sought in vain for many years for a successor to preserve the dances. The guests had already said their farewells when Jolani came running after them and modestly requested that they send her regards to the Queen of the Netherlands . . . Zeylmans was curiously touched when he became acquainted with some anthroposophical business people in these same weeks who repeatedly invited him for talks about the East-West question and wanted to discuss with him the cultural task of Hawaii in the Pacific region; two of them were Chinese in origin. He was also interviewed on radio with detailed questions about the 'European Conference' in The Hague the previous year. Thus he encountered here the remains of a civilization which had already disappeared, alongside an active interest for future tasks. Taking leave from the old and young friends he had made here was a very painful experience for him.

From Tuesday 6 April to Thursday 8 April they crossed the Pacific Ocean in an ocean clipper, simultaneously crossing the international date-line. As a result, 7 April 1954 is missing from his travel journal (and his biography!). After a short stay on Fiji, they reached New Zealand—'home of the Kiwi'—ten days before Easter. 'The England of the southern hemisphere' was his first surprised reaction as he entered the old fashioned, English-style hotel. Over a period of three weeks he travelled all over North Island and immersed himself in Maori culture. During a demonstration of ancient war dances, in which the men repeatedly stick out their tongues, he made a note of the differences to Hawaiian Hula dances: *'Rigid look, bent knees on which they beat the rhythm—songs and dances more earth-bound, many "e" sounds (Mars) and elbows. No Venus element and water here as in Hawaii.'*

Shortly afterwards he visited a Maori village neat Roturna and fell into conversation with the chief, an elderly Maori woman called Rangi who told the traveller a great deal about their ancient customs and religious background and then showed him her little house which had been furnished like a museum. This village lies near an area of geysers which spurt sulphuric steam out of the ground.

Everything boils and hisses here. Sometimes a jet of water will spurt four metres into the air. Sulphur steam hangs over the whole area. There are 'boiling pots' everywhere—small cooking places in the ground where the Maoris cook their meals, or larger holes where they do their washing. The largest ones they use for bathing after adding cold water. A charming impression: a basin full of babies with their black frizzy hair and sparkling eyes, sitting there for hours.

The intensive contact with Mrs Rangi spurred him on to close observation of the characteristics of this people, whose group-soul qualities he experienced as huge, black birds rather like an emu or ostrich—'human-bird-like beings'.

The Waitomo cave, a limestone cave where millions of glow worms cling to the ceiling, was among the experiences which made a deep impression on him. Visitors silently glide along the water in the darkness in small boats with the green-blue lights of the tiny animals shimmering above them like the starry heavens. While in New Zealand he also had meetings with anthroposophical study groups and significant encounters, including the occasion when he gave Easter lectures in Auckland.

Among his major impressions of Australia was its landscape with eucalyptus trees. To his great surprise he discovered that there were hundreds of species, of which some grow as high as 130 metres. He was full of enthusiasm for the exceedingly beautiful landscape which he saw on long excursions, accompanied by his hosts in Sydney. In the Zoo, he studied the strange animals from close at hand: the aquarium particularly fascinated him, with its fantastically-coloured small fish, the octopuses 'as if created by Hieronymous Bosch', the man-eating shark and the stingray, a two-metre long flat-fish moving through the aquarium with huge, veil-like movements.

It was a great disappointment to him that he was not able to meet the original inhabitants of Australia, the Aborigines, who lived in distant and very isolated parts of the huge continent. To make up for it, he had meetings with the anthropologist Professor Elkin, who told him much about the religion and culture of this ancient people.

Here, too, Zeylmans addressed anthroposophists and gave a lecture on 'Psychology as a way to inner development' at the Sydney Women's Club which was attended, much to the surprise of the organizers, by a great number of people: the destiny of 'full lecture halls' caught up with him here, too.

Having spent three weeks in Australia, the travellers flew on to Jakarta on 21 May. His renewed encounter with Java (and later Bali) must have had a spiritual significance for Zeylmans which is not easy to describe. In 1932 he had become well acquainted with and grown fond of large parts of the country. Now he encountered it once again in many excursions, tours and, above all, meetings. The first time he had become acquainted with Indonesia as a Dutch colony—now, after the Japanese reign of terror, it had been a sovereign state for about five years. What had changed? *'Everything has become more eastern,'* he noted. *'The last shimmer of an oriental fairy-tale?'*

Once again he climbed the Borobudur Temple and even flew a wide arc over it in a small plane. Once again he had profound experiences in Indonesia: the botanic gardens of Bogor, the funeral procession of a Balinese prince, visits to ancient temples in the mighty tropical forests, religious dances and a 'Wajang' performance, again at night, with dream-like gamelan music.

Here no watery-type movement; the gestures originate in the light-permeated air element—slow, sometimes fast as well, but always formed down to the last detail. One can see the laws of the astral body working right down into the physical organism. Everything is a gesture, an expression of cosmic-astral laws which affect the organism through light and air. Not just the dances, but the Wajang puppets display this strange image of a being which only expresses a divine or demonic element—while the body has been reduced to a minimum.

The Dutch people who received him and organized excursions for him (only one anthroposophist lived in Indonesia at the time) also brought him into contact with Indonesians. Thus he met the young, modern Manku Negoro VIII of Solo with his family and his old friend from student days, Sumitro, who gave him a vivid picture of the new revolutionary government. On Bali he experienced the Festival of the Holy Kris (a dagger):

In the evening, at the small temple near the hotel, the celebration begins with prayer and sacrifice alternating with ritual dances: two old women stand with bowls of smouldering incense, others run about, dozens of girls fetch new offerings—the large gamelan orchestra plays. Everything, by the way, is very homely and in confusion, men, women, children, eating, smoking, smiling. No one 'watches' the dance but all are involved—an image of how religion should be part of life! But then consciously! No black suits and solemn Sunday expressions, but nature and spirit in natural relationship. The students in Bali, however, with their white shirts and white trousers are already observing it all 'from outside'—it no longer means anything to them . . .

Zeylmans entered into a whole new mood during these weeks in Java and Bali. He looked for the essence in the here-and-now—are the ancient gods silent? What is the attitude of a modern, young generation towards the mighty past full of beauty and religion? What does it seek in the future? After a lecture in Bogor, an Indonesian student and well-known poet approached him: 'Dr Zeylmans, do people in Europe actually see us as we are? Do people *want* to see us at all? Do people understand what is going on here? Do people understand that Sartre and Camus are much more important for our young students than anything that comes from the past?' They had a profound conversation and Zeylmans later notes:

When faced with such a question, one notices how difficult it is for us Europeans to gain a real insight into this 'awakening' of the East. Indeed, it is particularly difficult for us because we feel all too strongly that we have failed to produce a spiritual atmosphere in which this awakening can take place fruitfully and beneficially.

Modern life—is that really what is new? When one of his friends, a university professor in Jakarta, organized a reception for him with the president of the republic, Sukarno, he declined—he would only have had to prolong his visit by five days—and continued his journey with his companions to Colombo.

After a lengthier journey by ship and a five day visit to Sri Lanka—where, among other things, they visited the temple with a holy tooth of the Buddha, and the botanical gardens (one of the 'seven wonders of the world')—the travellers landed in Madras on 21 June to acquaint themselves with India in the following seven weeks. It was to be the highlight of the world trip: Madras, Calcutta, Darjeeling, Benares, Shrinagar, Bombay were the main stops on the visit.

When one sees the endless, bare plains surrounding Madras where, if it rains, rice is meant to grow, one can understand Nehru's main concern: how are these 500 million Indians to be fed? On the arid sandy plains, dried out like cocoa powder, buffalo and goats nibble at bits of dry stubble—dark Indians, dressed in nothing but a white head-cloth, collect water from deep wells—a very impressive image, but also one to put you in a sombre mood . . . Arranging meetings is difficult here. The efficient, western mental attitude of rapidly tackling a matter and 'speedily' bringing it to conclusion should be completely abandoned here. It is, after all, not immediately obvious that an eastern person answers your question with 'yes' simply because, first, he does not want to be impolite and, second, he has no idea what you are talking about.

The hotel in which they lived was built, according to tradition, in the place where 2000 years before the birth of Christ one of the most ancient cities of India from the time of the Vedas is said to have stood. It is said to have been swallowed by the sea; and here and there one can still see depictions of it in ancient temples. Infinite riches of ancient culture were revealed to Zeylmans.

The land where the Apostle Thomas journeyed, and of which Marco Polo told. We drove through Adyar, the famous headquarters of the Theosophical Society, with its mighty complex of buildings in magnificent parks. Visited Kanchipuram, the 'golden city', one of the seven holy sites. Saw huge processional vehicles . . . Trip to Mahabalipuram with the seven pagodas, rock temples with mysterious images . . .

In the evening, they attended a performance of a mythological drama in the open-air theatre.

In about 50 changing scenes of most colourful imagination ('mixture of Shakespearean folk theatre and 1880-style opera') Shiva travels through the air accompanied by butterfly-winged beings, rising amidst coloured spheres—a fascinating and brilliant performance given wholly by boys and men . . . Calcutta, with its seven million inhabitants (the fourth-largest city in the world), was very impressive; but even more so it aroused pity. The streets are full, over-full, with trams, buses, cars, heavily over-loaded handcarts pulled by coolies at a trot, rickshaws, etc. In the midst of all this, large grey cows move about—impressive, solemn, and beautiful—and everything stops or makes way for them. The animals are holy, belong to nobody and are fed by the population. Incidentally, they also help themselves by nibbling at anything edible. And then there are the beggars, deformed and not deformed, women with babies, not their own babies, but babies which, to arouse pity, have been provided by even poorer mothers. One's heart could break.

Chou En-lai, the Chinese prime minister, was visiting India at this time. The newspapers reported the warm reception he was given in Delhi by Prasad and Nehru. A large procession of striking dock workers, dressed in red, was simultaneously marching through the streets of Calcutta.

Now we are sitting here at the foot of the Himalayas, at an altitude of 2000 metres, and have for the last three days been watching the most beautiful and impressive misty landscape there is—constantly changing, at one moment completely closed in, grey and gloomy, then suddenly a fairy-tale performance of majestically moving clouds with blues, pinks and golden-yellows shining through them. Darjeeling is in a wonderful location; in the good season, one can apparently see the snow-covered peaks of the Himalayas—there are about seventy peaks higher than 8000 metres.

We do not see them, but a fantastical Atlantean dream world of misty landscapes . . .

We strolled through the little town with its Tibetan and Nepalese population, the 'hill people' who sometimes resemble the Chinese and sometimes the Eskimos; friendly, very civilized people wearing large chest ornaments.

They are the only guests in the Mount Everest Hotel. While waiting in vain for the banks of mist before their eyes to lift for a moment, they decide to study *The Chymical Wedding of Christian Rosenkreutz* together.

Benares! The oldest city in the world for the ancient Indians, one of the most holy, indeed, the most holy city. It is built in half-moon shape on the banks of the Ganges with more than 1,500 temples, mostly dedicated to the god Shiva. (In the trinity of Brahma—Vishnu—Shiva the latter is probably most similar to the Holy Spirit: the awakener and at the same time destroyer, the inspiration of all that is beautiful and wise, 'Lucifer' in his proper place, seen from a pre-Christian perspective.) There are several paths from the city to the river bank; a number of wide steps and terraces, so-called ghats, more than 5 km long in total, give access to the river Ganges. From sunrise to sunset there is a huge crowd of people milling about: pious Hindus come to bathe in the river before going to the temple to pray. One can also see holy men and merchants who have their wares spread out on mats before them; priests dressed in white reading from the holy Mahabarata or Ramajana to devout listeners, and, above all, the many beggars! Everything lives in the religious sphere. Religion here is practised as part of every-day life. In a certain sense it is the practice of traditions which have become very externalized, are not free from decadence and are commercialized as well, but it is nevertheless a practice which infuses the whole of life. The Ganges is a holy river and those who bathe in it are cleansed, and when the ashes of the dead are scattered on it the soul rises directly to heaven. There are always several fires burning on the ghats in which the deceased, wrapped in white sheets, are cremated. Thousands of pilgrims, it is said up to one million each year, journey to Benares to pray, seek healing, and many also come to die. No one who has seen this can escape the power and majesty of such a religious tradition, however much it may have become externalized.

But this same Benares has a modern university with 8,800 students. On the gables of the buildings there are models of little temples—but that is the only reminder of the religious background here. Teaching is similar to the West, has the same scientific basis, and the present generation is educated there in western style. Our guide proudly points to the College where he himself was educated and speaks with a smile about the superstitions of the population in general, for whom the Ganges is holy. He explains why the priests taught this to the population, namely for practical and hygienic reasons. The view that cows are holy also had such a background; all these things were based on clever, practical considerations without any deeper meaning. But while he is telling us that, all the traffic suddenly stands still on the main thoroughfares because a cow has crossed the road. Thousands of cars, lorries, rickshaws, buses drive along the thoroughfares of the city with its millions of inhabitants and each time all the traffic has to come to a halt because a holy cow crosses the road or stands there to eat some left-over vegetables. Everyone stops or may try to drive around the animal. When the government tried to put an end to this custom some time ago and remove the cows, there were riots among the people. Thus the leaders' modern views and their consequences are in constant collision with the ancient traditions in which the people are immersed.

At the end of July, Zeylmans took a boat trip on the Ganges, which is about 800 metres wide here at this time of the year (in the rainy season this increases to 2.5 kilometres). The river deeply affected him, its source in the Himalayas, originating from heaven, from the feet of Vishnu, through the head of Shiva, over the earth—under the earth. He watched how

. . . the many people at prayer scooped water from the river in their containers and let it flow back again while praying. The cremation of corpses goes on continuously, there are always two or three fires going. An infant who has died is wrapped in sheets, rowed out and lowered into the water weighed down with stones. Nearby, cheerful boys are swimming and diving. (Saints, too, are not cremated but lowered under the water like children under three.) Life and death undivided—a mighty world! The holy Ganges! It is difficult to take leave . . . Towards evening, we see numerous small oil lamps on little boats made of leaves in the light of the setting sun, drifting down river . . .

After a lengthier stay in Delhi, where he met with representatives from the education ministry, he travelled to Kashmir with his companions. *'We spent wonderful days in Shrinagar, the capital here, situated on a river and two lakes. We sailed along the floating gardens in a kind of gondola and across the fairy-tale lotus ponds. Everything here happens on the water.'*

After further excursions through Kashmir and a visit to Martand, a three-thousand-year-old city with a very ancient sun temple, he writes down his final impressions:

The avenues of slim poplars with silver bark (like birches); the chenards (plane trees) with their mighty, incredibly powerful trunks. The lakes, the mountains in the background, some with snow-covered peaks, especially in the evening! The lotus

flowers—a bunch of seven in my hotel room! The floating vegetable gardens—everywhere are marsh marigolds and arrowhead! Apples, peaches, plums, cherries and strawberries (the latter unfortunately just finished!) etc.—Wonderful flight back: dark clouds on the right, clear on the left; in this fashion we fly through the mountains at 1,350 feet.

When Zeylmans later spoke about his travel experiences he finished by telling about his impressions of India. In his notes he writes under *'Social image'*, among other things: *'The dried out rice paddies—the rain. The old and the new. The holy cows. Work or beg? The intellectuals and the people.'* (Then comes a list of people whom he met.) *'Image of the Ganges as an etheric stream, coming from the Himalayas, in which life and death become one through the powers of veneration of those who bathe in it.'* And he compares this stream with another one, the stream of Michaelic forces today ... two streams which cross in our age.

From Bombay, Zeylmans and his friends Roelvink and Wilbers flew to East Africa on 2 August 1954, making a wide arc over the Gulf of Aden, which shimmered under them in the light of the rising sun, and then over southern Ethiopia. Before they landed in Nairobi, Mount Kenya appeared before them, 5000 metres high, with its snow-covered peaks above the clouds; snowy mountains on the equator...

At the airport there was a joyous reunion with his elder brother Peter, who lived there as a businessman, and with the anthroposophical friends who had invited him to lecture. *'A strange feeling to talk German again after such a long time. It feels "like being carried on the wings of the spirit", as one of those present remarked.'*

There were excursions to Uganda; visits to Kampala and Entebbe on Lake Victoria, as well as to the source of the Nile which originates here on the high plateau. They crossed the Rift Valley, the deep east African trench, and travelled southwards to Tanzania and Mount Kilimanjaro, the highest mountain in Africa with its almost 6000-metre-high, eternally snow-covered peaks, at the foot of which the large game reserves are situated. They drove through herds of zebra, saw huge flamingo colonies, gnus, antelopes and gazelles, giraffes and hyenas, a jackal, ostriches and secretary birds, hippopotamuses and monkeys and, finally, two lionesses with their young.

'It is winter here, i.e. bright sunshine during the day, and two blankets at night,' he soberly wrote home. But in Nairobi he made a detailed investigation of the secret cults of the Mau Mau and en route learned to distinguish the various native tribes.

Then, three weeks later, he embarked on an eight-hour flight south to Johannesburg. One of the active anthroposophists in this 'City of Gold' was Guy Wertheym Aymès—a son of the Hilversum family where Zeylmans wrote his book on the human soul in 1939. He had established the Weleda medicines company in South Africa and now organized a wealth of work for Zeylmans with the resident anthroposophists. A never-ending series of speeches, visits, meetings and consultations starts; for the first time since his visit to California, Zeylmans is once again fully occupied with work. In eight days he gives nine lectures, including one on folk, race and the psychology of nations at the University of Pretoria.

In Johannesburg we were able to see miners' dances; they belong to the various Zulu and other tribes. The groups, who appeared one after another, were dancing long before it was their turn. Three strong policemen were meant to prevent them appearing before their turn and had their hands full doing so. But it was almost more difficult to make the ones who were dancing stop again! These movements and leaps are almost incomprehensible to a European—the movements they are able to make seem to defy all the laws of gravity. And not just the movements they can make: their urge to move is almost unstoppable. Later, after the performances had long ended, we still saw individual groups continuing to dance in the lorries which were meant to take them home . . . Thus the typically mercurial characteristics of these tribes is apparent not only in the shape of the skull, the hairline etc., but also in that other archetypal expression of the watery element: motion.

Then Zeylmans continued his journey to Durban and Port Elizabeth (on the east coast).

In Cape Town, he was met by his old friend Chris Wegerif, who, as a young student of architecture, had been involved in organizing the Stakenberg Camp in 1930. This active anthroposophist had him deliver eleven lectures in the eight days before his departure; in addition, Zeylmans had dozens of meetings here which exerted a strong influence. The ladies Roelvink and Wilbers, too, gave lectures and supported the work through many personal contacts.

'Our small conference in Tokay started with 30 and ended with 60 participants. The public lectures were initially attended by 100 people, but numbers grew to such an extent that the hall holding 180 was much too small by the end.'

An enthusiastic Wegerif wrote, shortly after he had accompanied the three visitors on board for their departure: 'Anthroposophy: this term has been made public here for the first time, perhaps still in vague outline but as a serious scientific matter of importance for human development.'

Zeylmans had indeed found people here who wanted 'something new'. As a consequence of this meeting, he responded positively to a second invitation to South Africa seven years later.

'Psychologist Says: Nations have Souls'—with this headline an American newspaper once summarized a lecture given by Zeylmans in the USA on the psychology of nations. There is probably no other subject which he presented to the public so intensively, so frequently, and with such a response, as this one: that nations have souls and *'that it will be impossible to find a way out of the international darkness if that is not recognized.'* A Dutch newspaper once carried the headline: 'Steiner follower says: every person carries all of humanity within himself', above an extract from a lecture in which Zeylmans described how each person can discover that they sometimes react like an Italian, sometimes like a French person, then again like a German or a Briton. This happened completely unconsciously, he said, for the simple reason that each person carries the whole of humanity within him or herself. It was very important to leave all nationalism behind, to experience oneself as part of the whole of humanity and to know that each person carried responsibility for it.

When Zeylmans returned from his world trip he described how a person on a path of development to higher consciousness gains a conscious relationship with his organic processes, thus gaining direct access to the other races through physical and life processes: '*His own organic processes become sensory organs for the inner being of other races . . . He carries the seed of all races in a flexible, flowing way in his own organism.*'

But when one of his closer friends asked him what the deepest impression had been which he had brought home from his world tour, he thought for a moment and then said: *'The suffering of humanity.'*

*

Among the participants in the so-called study group 'for the continuing impulse of the Christmas Foundation Meeting' was an individual (whom we have already briefly mentioned) with whom, over the years, a very fruitful working relationship had arisen. This was the writer Theodora Krück von Poturzyn, who lived in Stuttgart. Together with her Dutch friend Elisabeth Knottenbelt, she had already translated several articles by Zeylmans into German. They got to know each other better when the book *Wir Erlebten Rudolf Steiner* ('We experienced Rudolf Steiner') was published, a collection of reminiscences by fourteen anthroposophists. Dora Krück had taken the initiative to bring out this anthology, and Zeylmans had also been invited to contribute. The book was beset by problems initially, as some of the collaborating authors believed they should act as censors for the others. Thus Frau Krück repeatedly had to mediate between the various people involved, and also asked Zeylmans to make radical changes to his essay at many points. A longer correspondence between them began, during which Dora Krück got to know Zeylmans from a new angle, coming up against the limits of his patience and willingness to compromise. Zeylmans also came to appreciate Dora Krück in a new way, as a skilled, experienced editor where both difficulties of language and principle were concerned. Once work on the anthology was complete, therefore (it was published in 1956), he asked her to help him on his book, *The Foundation Stone.* It was because of her collaboration that this book first appeared in German. The modest little blue volume was published shortly before Christmas 1956; and when he learned that 1600 copies of the first print-run had sold straight away, he was very pleased indeed: *'The numbers show that there are already so many anthroposophists for whom the Foundation Stone means something.'*

Dora Krück had a great gift for forming the texts Zeylmans dictated to her in such a way that his ideas came to full expression. Shortly before his death he dictated two further chapters to her, which were then added to the second edition in 1961. Dora Krück also later translated other books and articles by him; and it is a matter of great regret that Zeylmans did not write more with her help.

In April 1957 he planned to write a book together with ten other anthroposophical authors, edited by Dora Krück, on the heavenly hierarchies. However she immediately saw the difficulties in such an undertaking, and first listened to what the individual authors had to say on the subject. It very soon became obvious that hardly a single one of the invited guests wished to attend the marriage! So the book remained an idea only.

The theme of the heavenly hierarchies was one which preoccupied Zeylmans from an early stage. It could hardly have been otherwise since Rudolf Steiner had invoked the three choirs of the hierarchies in the Foundation Stone. At the age of 35 Zeylmans gave a lecture on this theme at the opening of the new Goetheanum in 1928; and from then on it continually resurfaces in his work until shortly before his death. In his book *The Reality in Which We Live*, he says among other things:

For Dionysus the Areopagite the three times three choirs of the heavenly hierarchies are spiritual realities, just as they were for all initiates of ancient cultures, including those of the Old Testament. Modern man can in general only approach such ideas by regarding them as symbols and viewing them without personal involvement. He naturally has the right to do so, but this does not help him much further.

The plan for the structure of this book also contains the subtitle: 'On the nature and significance of teachings about the hierarchies, with particular reference to Rudolf Steiner's descriptions of the hierarchies.' The content was planned as follows:

Pre-Christian doctrines about the hierarchies, explained through several examples: India, Persia etc., Egyptian-Chaldean teachings about the gods.

Christian doctrines about the hierarchies: Dionysus the Areopagite—the problem linked with his personality from a historical perspective—Paul—the influence of this teaching on the philosophy of the Church Fathers up to Scotus Erigena—the school of Chartres—Scotus Erigena, the scholastics, Thomas Aquinas—the renaissance, Pico della Mirandola—how teachings on the hierarchies developed—loss of reality.

Teachings about the hierarchies in Rudolf Steiner's anthroposophy: The path of research. The stages: Imagination—Inspiration—Intuition—descriptions in *Occult Science*—descriptions in the lecture cycles on the hierarchies—description from the evolutionary perspective—life after death, in relation to the hierarchies—general observations about the importance of this teaching, dealt with objectively like natural forces, at the same time with the deepest reverence. Science and morality become one.

Applications of teachings about the hierarchies to various fields of knowledge: Higher mathematics—physiology, organ functions etc.—psychology.

Simply elaborating the notes and lecture drafts Zeylmans left on the hierarchies would fill a small book. Here I would just like to refer to the chapter on the hierarchies and the essence of the Foundation Stone in his book on the Foundation Stone, and the study on the mysteries of Ephesus and Samothrace, the categories of Aristotle and the Foundation Stone verse, in which he deals with the hierarchies in relation, among other things, to the tree of Sephirot. But what underpinned the plan for an anthology on the hierarchies, which very few were probably aware of at

Comburg 12. April 1959

Kategorien und Hierarchien

Zur Einleitung eine Erzählung: Iwan Mestrovic – der Priester –

Hierarchien < Symbolik / Rel. phil. Begriffe.

R. Steiner: Die Wirklichkeit.

Geistig Wesenhaft: die Zyklen: unzählige Aspekte.

Aristoteles: ♄ · ☉ ☾ ♁ ---> die Kategorien.

ganz nüchtern: die Welt hier! was, wie, wo, wann u.s.w.

So in unserer Wissenschaft; aber auch in unserer Sprache.

Aber: R. St: eine Weltenschrift, mit Gedanken, statt Buchstaben.

„Tief esoterisch" unzählige Möglichkeiten

Die Frage des Aristoteles: Um uns herum die Wesen, die Einzelwesen. Dieses Wesen oder Substanz tritt in die Erscheinung. Wie verwirklicht sich das Wesen in der Erscheinung? „Das Wahrhaft-Wirkliche; das durch seine Form in sich bestimmte Einzelding" (Windelband).

„Ein sich verwirklichen", ein Prozess also, keine Fixation. Dadurch die Möglichkeit Organismen, die Seele, die Tätigkeit des Menschen zu verstehen.

„Das Wesen entwickelt sich und verwirklicht sich in den einzelnen Bestimmungen, die teils seine Zustände, teils seine Beziehungen sind."

Diese Erscheinungsweisen ~~der Substanz~~ heissen Kategorien.

Wesen, Substanz, Sein als die Kategorie.

Dazu kommen: Quantität, Qualität, Relation, Räumliche Zeitliche Bestimmung, Sich befinden, Tun, Leiden, sich verhalten.

Eine gewisse Gruppierung versuchen.

Als Ausgangspunkt die Seele, oder: das Ich in der Seele.

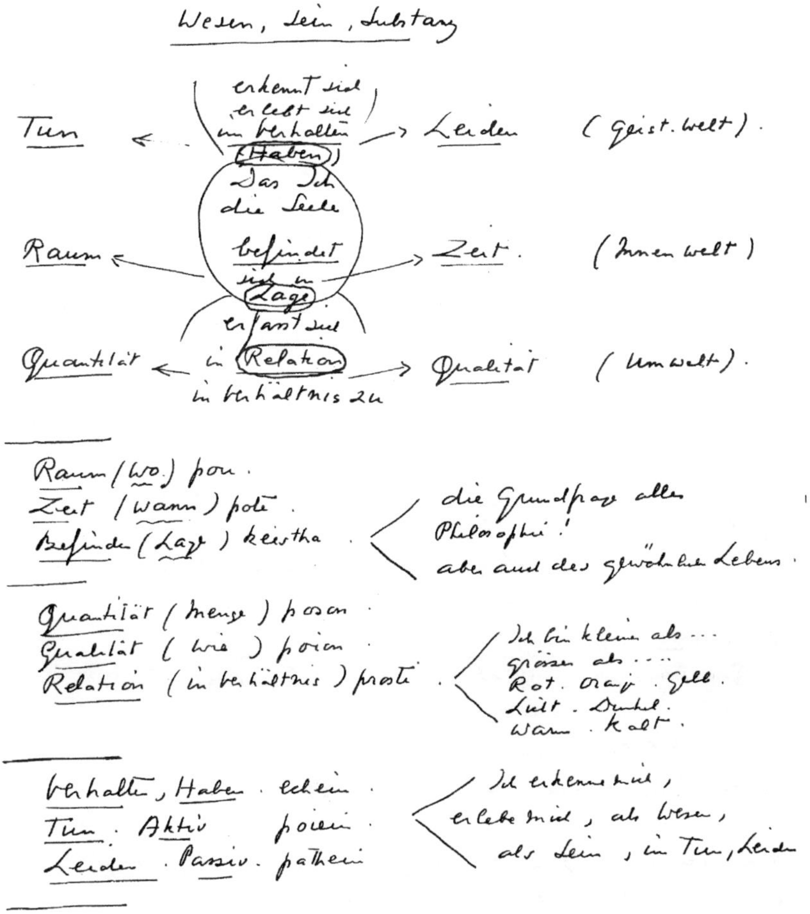
Wesen, Sein, Substanz
erkennt sich
erlebt sich
im Verhalten
(Haben)
Tun
Leiden
(geist. Welt).
Das Ich
die Seele
befindet
sich in
Lage
Raum
Zeit.
(Innenwelt)
erfaßt sich
in Relation
in Verhältnis zu
Quantität
Qualität
(Umwelt).
Raum (Wo.) pou.
Zeit (Wann) pote.
Befinden (Lage) keistha.
die Grundfrage aller Philosophie! aber auch des gewöhnlichen Lebens.
Quantität (Menge) poson.
Qualität (wie) poion.
Relation (in Verhältnis) pros ti.
Ich bin kleiner als ...
grösser als ...
Rot. Orange. Gelb.
Licht. Dunkel.
Warm. Kalt.
Verhalten, Haben. echein.
Tun. Aktiv poiein.
Leiden. Passiv. pathein
Ich erkenne mich, erlebe mich, als Wesen, als Sein, im Tun, Leiden

= Nun die Hierarchien. Eigentlich kein Schema möglich. Alles wie ein Weben.

„Wie alles sich zum Ganzen webt!
Eins in dem andern wirkt und lebt!
Wie Himmelskräfte auf und nieder steigen
Und sich die goldnen Eimer reichen!"

S. Ch. Thr. Lasset aus den Höhen erklingen, was in den Tiefen das Echo findet
Kyr. Dyn. Ex. Lasset vom Osten befeuern, was durch den Westen sich gestaltet.
Ar. Ar. Ang. Lasset aus den Tiefen erbitten, was in den Höhen erhöret wird –

– Dazu noch die verschiedenen Qualitäten, Stufen. (Vater, Sohn, Hlg. Geist)

Throne	Seraphim	Cherubim
Tun	Haben	Leiden
Exusiai	Dynamis	Kyriotetes
Raum	Lage	Zeit
Archai	Archangeloi	Angeloi
Quantität	Relation	Qualität

– Wo: Wesen, Sein, Substanz?
Die Frage etwas später beantworten.

Dynamis: Geister der Bewegung. Zentral, in der Mitte.
Die Lehre als Bewegend. Lage ist immer wechselnd,
Ein – Aus; Oben – Unten; Vorne – Hinten u.s.w.
Vorher – Nachher. —

Formgeister: Begegnung der zwei Räume! ♀

Exusiai: Raum. ☉ Kyr. → Archangeloi. Aufgestiegen durch ☾ u. ♁ z. Exusiai ×

Kyriotetes: Zeit. ♄ Archai, durch ☉ ☾ ♁ zu Kyriotetes. Das Wesen der Zeit (Pflanze, Tier, Mensch).

Angeloi. Qualität. In der Qualität begegnet der Mensch ein Engelwesen. (Licht, Farbe, Ton ---) Sinneswahrnehmung

Archangeloi. Relation. Erkennendes Verhalten. Denken

(Wie stehen die Farben zu Licht u. Finsternis?)

Archai. Quantität. Urbeginne: die Zahlen.

Seraphim. Haben das Antlitz der Gottheit, der Trinität. Aus Ihrem Verhalten entsteht die Welt. Liebesfeuer.

Cherubim. Leiden. Geister der Harmonie!

„Wiederfinden": Und er sprach das Wort: Es werde!

Da erklang ein schmerzlich Ach
Als das All mit Machtgebärde
In die Wirklichkeiten brach".

Throne. Tun.

Wo: Wesen, Sein, Substanz?

Die alles durchdringende Totalität der Trinität.

Oben: am Anfang? Unten: Sub-stanz?

Vater – Sohn – Hlg. Geist

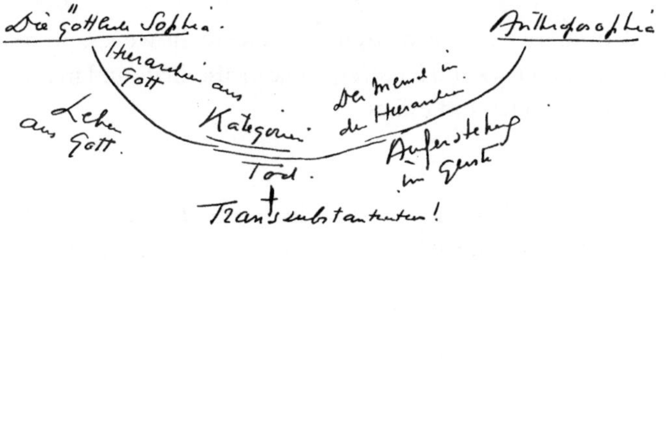

the time, was his *motive* for the book: to create a work for those not yet born, like a welcome greeting and way-finder for a generation of souls who will only feel at home on earth when they learn of the forces through which their human nature has been formed.

This unrealized book on the hierarchies does not stand alone: Zeylmans had other ideas for books which never came to fruition. In becoming aware of these we can form some idea of the sorts of things he was pondering, the initiatives which lived in him. Thus the reader will recall that in 1937 he had also planned a kind of anthology on Egypt. A second part to 'The human soul' was announced (1961), for which much material is still extant. In this list too belongs a study on 'Rudolf Steiner and the psychology of nations', which he wanted to write in 1955 with Dora Krück's help. If we add, finally, his planned autobiography (which he imagined as a 'book of encounters') we can form a picture of what his total œuvre would have looked like if he had completed everything he intended. (In the list below the books not written are in brackets and italics.)

'The effect of colours on the feelings' (1923)
'Rudolf Steiner' (1932)
'Development and spiritual conflict' (1935)
(*Egypt—anthology, 1937*)
'The human soul, part I' (1939)
'Hygiene of the Soul' (1946)
(*Rudolf Steiner and the psychology of nations, 1955*)
(*The hierarchies—anthology, 1957*)
'The Foundation Stone' (1956)
'The Reality in Which We Live' (1959)
(*The human soul, part II*)
(*Book of encounters, an autobiography*)*

The foundations for these unwritten works were, however, presented in a large number of courses and lectures, and can also be found in many long-since forgotten articles and essays.

*

Willem Zeylmans called the last book he wrote *The Reality in Which We Live*. He wrote it in the winter of 1958/59, as a summary of the last courses he gave at the Centre for Free Spiritual Life on the central place

* For a list of English translations, see Bibliography, page 281.

which the event of Golgotha has in human evolution, and at the same time as an introduction to Rudolf Steiner's anthroposophy. The title of the book already contains the whole theme. Søren Kierkegaard had struggled with the concept of 'reality', and in his 1849 sketch entitled 'Situation' described what would happen if a famous theologian mounted the pulpit one Sunday and declared that:

> 'Preaching in these surroundings is *not* Christianity—Christianity can only be preached in reality! And now I transform this space, this house into reality... I am now in your power... This is an attack on the whole church and the whole "decent" congregation. Christ was not a "decent man" who preached, in a decent church to decent people, that truth suffers—it was a *reality* that people spat on him!' At this the whole church would be filled with commotion, all would call out: 'Away with him, out of the church!' But he would respond in a thundering voice: 'You see! Now it is true—now I am preaching Christianity!'

In Zeylmans' library there was a copy of Hohlenberg's book on Kierkegaard, in which this passage was underlined. But he would have attached even more importance to what he heard as a young doctor, when Rudolf Steiner was lecturing in Stuttgart:

> Reality is something that comes to us through perception and knowledge. Reality is not something we must seek. Reality is something we create, in which we participate creatively. And the secret of the human being consists of the fact that, when he is born, a world surrounds him which is not full reality; and that he is born so that he may bring to what appears to him in outer sense phenomena something that only arises in his inner life. The process of perception and knowledge is something man must elevate himself to, so that reality is sustained in his world.

Seen in this light the first sentence of Zeylmans' book can give us particular pause for thought. It runs: *'At a particular stage of my development I came to the knowledge that Christ is the reality in which we live.'* As Margarete Hauschka once wrote:

> The whole work which follows this sentence continually broadens and enlarges its basis; and without demonstrating proof—for the recognition of this truth must be the wholly free deed of each individual human being—we are led through the history of the facts about Christ, and through everything both before and afterwards that is linked to

them, so that the way is opened for this recognition. Appeal is made to those forces which we can and must use to understand the world and also the mystery of the earth—the forces of common sense.

I have taken up this book at various different points in my life, and only now that I am old do I recognize the many layers in this mature work. Only now does it open its depths to me and show its true nature; for one first needs much life experience before the phrase: 'Think of *what*, but think still more of *how*' can come to be uppermost in the soul . . .

Rudolf Steiner expected his pupils to take up the treasures of the spirit through his words, but then also unite their own souls with these treasures, so that what he gave could be reborn out of the 'I', and passed on in 'individualized' form. This has a much deeper effect than the merely literary, and also reminds one of the first dissemination of Christianity 2000 years ago. Such an effect, entering deeper layers of the soul, also emanated from the lectures which Dr Zeylmans gave all over the world, and which were not forgotten; for wisdom reborn through the 'I' is sustained by love . . .

This book therefore has a great task in the future. Its mighty content not only conveys, as already mentioned, an astonishing basis of spiritual knowledge, a rock under one's feet, but this knowledge differs from normal intellectual acuity by virtue of the spiritual links that unite everything. One is never simply left with 'all the pieces in one's hand', unable to form them into a whole. One is led by a golden thread, like that of Ariadne, through the labyrinth of human evolution in the broadest sense. All cosmic beings and universal powers involved in this are only described as they appear on the scene in the ongoing drama of prehistory, history itself and then the consequences of the Mystery of Golgotha. This Mystery is reality: the Christ substance in the earth and in the human being is the reality in which we live.

The astronomer Elisabeth Mulder (the first Dutch Waldorf teacher) once said of this book that it reminded her of a phrase by Pascal: 'Je n'ai pas eu le temps d'abréger' ('I had did not have time to shorten this work'). 'Zeylmans,' she said, 'took nearly a whole lifetime to write this book; that is why there is not a word too many in it, and every word absolutely finds its mark.'

And she also said it was a 'typically Dutch book': in its logic, its artistic handling of light and dark, and in the way it wasn't at all 'dressed up'.

★

During their 38-year marriage, Ingeborg and Willem Zeylmans frequently went on longer trips together. They were often in England, twice travelled in Ireland, visited eastern and southern Germany, Paris and southern France, Switzerland and Italy. In 1957 they were invited by the two ladies Roelvink and Wilbers on a six-week trip through Greece—which was to be their last longer holiday together. The chronology in the appendix lists the places where they stopped on the way.

Ingeborg Zeylmans had a very profound experience of this journey, although she was already ill and had recently undergone an operation. The high-point was their visit to Ephesus, where the great marble statue of the goddess Artemis—which probably stood in the famous temple originally—had recently been excavated.

It now stands in the modest museum at Ephesus, between flowering rose and oleander bushes. In the background is a whitewashed wall, above which curves the dome of the heavens. The figure, three metres high, is of white marble. The face still bears the spiritualized features of very ancient Greek statues. Upon the fairly broad head sits a crown—that strange construction which people usually call a 'mural crown'. Around the throat is a kind of collar descending to the chest, on which various different human forms are depicted. Below this is the upper body with the many breasts, as in other famous Artemis statues. Trunk and legs form a closed pillar on which one can see animal forms, some of them winged, mostly arranged in groups of three. They are chiefly lions, cows, goats and bees—symbols of life and fertility. Although not undamaged, the statue makes an overwhelming impression.

They also visited Samothrace, where landing was a risky and exciting undertaking.

Samothrace was also one of the most ancient Mystery sites. Here, according to legend, Poseidon had observed the course of the Trojan War from the peak of Phengari, the 1900-metre-high mountain dedicated to the moon. Samothrace is a mountainous island in the northern Aegean, still partly covered in thick oak woods, with crevasses and earthquake-shattered terrain. It is not easy to reach, due to sudden violent storms. The ancient Greeks believed it to be a place where nature demons worked with great violence and power.

In the thick woods of those times people worshipped the sacred Cabiri, the great and mighty gods! Strange gods whose names have come down to us from an unknown, prehistoric language: Axieros, Axiokersos, Axiokersa. There was also a fourth, called Cadmillos, who was less prominent or apparent. The 'Great Mother' was also worshipped there, probably the most ancient goddess of all, older than

Demeter, perhaps related to Thea or Cybele. There were also other gods and goddesses, such as Aphrodite Cerynthia, depicted with three breasts, and the two Dioscuri who protected seafarers in storms.

As long ago as 1932, Ita Wegman had written to him about this landscape:

> I'm sorry I can't tell you about my trip in person. But you may be pleased to hear that I was in Samothrace, in Ephesus, and that I passed through Macedonia; then from Athens visited all the Mystery sites, such as Eleusis, ancient Corinth, Mycenae, Argos, Epidaurus, the Mystery sites of Asclepius and Delphi. And through Rudolf Steiner's teachings it was possible to make very clear distinctions between the different kinds of Mysteries, and find some things that offered solutions to some unanswered question. For me, the finest experience was to let the landscape of each Mystery site work on me in such a way that one could recall that Aristotle, Plato, Alexander had seen the same landscape and found great joy in its beauty. Thus the present started to fall away, and one could live completely into ancient times, could experience Ptolemy's enthusiasm for the great Cabiri spirits, to which he gave expression in his Ptolemy temple, whose foundations and pillars still lie around, as well as in the Arsineium.
>
> And it made a strange impression on me to read, in Greek, on a great gable stone, the clear words: 'Here Ptolemy and Veronica honour the great Cabiri.'

In her matter-of-fact way Ingeborg Zeylmans wrote to her elderly mother in The Hague:

> From Mycenae one sails to Delos in a motor- and sail-sloop. That is really a wonderful journey, lasting about an hour. You sit on simple wooden boards and get sprayed by waves from all sides. The islands stick up like great beings out of the deep blue sea. A wonderful world, which at night-time sometimes seems to engulf you completely. Wind, air, water, rocks—everything streams and flows around you. The sea can be very tempestuous. A Greek girl tells us that a three-hour trip to another island can sometimes take three days. At such times the sea is so wild and foaming that one can do nothing but wait and take care that the boat doesn't capsize! On our way back the wind suddenly blew up, and the helmsman had great difficulty in holding a straight course. It was suddenly easy to imagine Odysseus' journey. The cliffs are almost completely bare, with only a little green here and there: fig-trees,

flowering oleanders, dark red corn poppies, and a kind of candle-flower: tall and yellow but with velvet-grey leaves. The grey donkeys are also part of this landscape—you see them everywhere. Did I tell you that we went up Patmos on the backs of little donkeys like these? That was part of the trip. I was rather anxious to start with, for these animals do what they like: suddenly rush up a flight of steps or amble close to a chasm. After 20 minutes we came to a Greek monastery at the top. It was Ascension Day, and a special service was held in a small, dark, square little church, everything decorated and the floor strewn with chamomile flowers—a wonderful scent. Four priests were celebrating the mass, and each time a voice came from a different direction, then a small door opened and closed again. The Greek Catholic priests all have dark beards, a broad, black cloak and a four-cornered hat on their heads. In Patmos there is a famous old monastery where only 30 monks live, but with a training seminary for 250 students. We have already seen many Greek Catholic priests and visited their monasteries, but this Greek Orthodox Catholicism makes a quite different impression on me than does Roman Catholicism. Fiery and vital—when you see the priests here walking they look like dancers—no comparison with *our* parish priests! Whether they are pleasant to talk to I don't know. They certainly didn't look simple to me! We have taken many photos and will tell you all about the various sites when we return. There is a grotto on Delos in which Apollo is said to have been born, from the same period as Mycenae (1400 BC). This epoch is for me perhaps the most impressive of all. There too we climbed up high and stayed for quite a while. In the grotto the light is dim and some plants are growing. I briefly did some eurythmy there—that seemed fitting for Apollo. It was hard to leave Mycenae yesterday. The ship slowly sailed away over the mirror-smooth sea, and from the distance we saw only the fading shapes of something rising out of the sea. I can imagine one could become very attached to these islands, and that they might become like home.

This trip to Greece gave Zeylmans the inspiration for an in-depth study of the ten Aristotelian categories, which he linked, among other things, to a spiritual figure who meant much to him, and to whom we will therefore briefly turn our attention. This was Raimundus Lullus, the zealous missionary of Majorca.

Ramón Lull was a mystic, philosopher and preacher against the Arabs. He lived from 1232 to 1315. Majorca's 'greatest son' is mentioned in all tourist brochures about the island. This figure interested me as early as 1924, when Rudolf Steiner spoke of him. After initially living the life of a young nobleman (with all that went with it), he withdrew to the mountain of Randa near Palma after seeing five visions of the Crucified One. There he had many inspirations and wrote countless books. The best known is his Ars Magna, *a kind of revelation of the Logos, arranged under many systematic headings. The* Ars Magna *exerted a powerful influence on medieval thinking. Reading it now, it all seems rather abstract. Many later alchemists and philosophers were influenced by the* Ars Magna, *such as Agrippa of Nettesheim, Giordano Bruno and Nicolaus Cusanus. For Majorca he is more of a mystic and missionary. Majorca was in the hands of the Arabs from the eighth to the thirteenth century, when James the Conqueror made it part of Catalonia and then 'christianized' it. One of the first to receive property on the island was the father of Ramón Lull.*

Raimundus Lullus, about whom Rudolf Steiner spoke in a lecture for the workmen (10 May 1924) was said to be the first to try to express the relationship of God to man in a number of divine qualities, inspired by the tree of Sephiroth. He drew up an Ars Magna *or* Ars Universalis, *in which sixteen different divine qualities are arranged around a certain sound (A = God), in groups of four, for example:*

Kindness, greatness, eternity, power,
Wisdom, will, virtue, truth
Honour, perfection, justice, benevolence
Mercy, devotion, mastery, patience.

Although this seems rather random, on closer scrutiny one can understand what is meant. The intention, in fact, was to meditate on such a schema, quality by quality; and to do this in relation to another schema, in which another sound (e.g. S) would be surrounded by three soul qualities or seven virtues and an equal number of vices.

As great as this striving was, (Raimundus Lullus intended to demonstrate the irrefutable truth of Christianity in this way, and thus convince Jews and Arabs through logic) one can't help seeing a kind of powerlessness or even tragedy in it. Spiritual realities are no longer perceived in their full dimensions, and the concepts at this early stage of thinking consciousness are still insufficiently developed. This is the same period at which the great scholastics, especially Thomas Aquinas, were struggling to christianize thinking.

Among the many works that Ramón Lull wrote, his novel *Blanquerna* became very famous. One of its chapters is called 'The book of lovers and beloveds'. Ramón Lull himself describes how he came to write this:

> As Blanquerna cried and prayed and raised himself to God with the utmost power of his soul, he was so overwhelmed by reverence and fervour that he saw that the power of love has no limits, when the lover loves his beloved beyond all measure. And in this way he conceived the idea of writing down the book of lovers and beloveds, in which the lover is a devout Christian and the beloved is God.

Lullus was called the 'pearl fisher of his own soul'; and one can see that he was a very poetic pearl fisher, when one reads, in the 365 'conversations between the lover and the beloved':

> The lover spoke to the beloved: 'You who fill the sun with radiance, fill my soul with love.' The beloved replied: 'Without love's fulfilment your eyes would not be streaming with tears, nor would you have come to this place to see the one who loves you.' (6)
>
> The birds sang to greet the dawn, and the beloved awoke, who is the dawn itself. The birds finished their song, and in the rosy dawn the lover died for his beloved. (26)
>
> The birds sang in the beloved's garden. The lover came and said to the birds: Even if we do not understand each other's language, we understand one another through love; for in your song my eyes see the beloved. (27)
>
> The individual and the community met and became one, so that friendship and good will would exist between the lovers and the beloved. (44)
>
> The heart of the lover raised itself to the heights of the beloved, so that it was not hindered from love in the depths of this world. And when it had reached the beloved it looked at him with bliss and joy; but the beloved led it back to this world, so that it could look upon him in grief and longing. (56)
>
> People asked the lover: 'What wealth have you?' He replied: 'The poverty which I bear for my beloved.'—'And wherein lies your peace?'—'In the restlessness which love gives me.'—'And who is your physician?'—'The trust I have in my beloved.'—'And who is your teacher?'—'The signs and witness which the creatures give of my beloved.' (57)
>
> Love illumined the veil of clouds that had come between the lover and the beloved, and made it as bright as the moon at night, the evening star

> at twilight, the sun at midday and the understanding in the will. And through this shining cloud the lover and the beloved spoke to one another. (123)

> Love is a mixture of bravery, fear and passion; love is ultimate will and longing for the beloved; love is what kills the lover when he hears someone singing of the beauties of his beloved; and love is what contains my death and what my will renews itself in each day. (171)

★

Shortly after their return from Greece, Ingeborg Zeylmans had to undergo a second operation. This was the beginning of a period of illness from which she would not recover. Outwardly she now had to withdraw more and more from her work for the Anthroposophical Society, in whose daily executive committee she had been active since the end of the war. But from her sickbed she took great interest in everything relating to this small but extremely active community of people. She had the remarkable habit of regularly scrutinizing the list of members, rather as a gardener occasionally stops at his flowerbeds to see how his plants are doing. In those days there were fewer than a thousand people on this list, but she knew all of them and took the destinies of many of them to heart. She also always got someone to read out the amount of contributions which had been paid in to the 'eurythmy fund' she had started, like a housewife who carefully manages her household allowance. Behind these seemingly small external matters stood the most brightly shining ideal of her life—the development of eurythmy.

She had studied eurythmy in 1920 and 1921 with Annemarie Donath at the Goetheanum. In the early period in Holland she established eurythmy courses in large cities—for instance in state schools—with her friend Paula Hoorweg among others (who became the first eurythmy teacher at the Waldorf School in The Hague). After taking a training course in eurythmy therapy at Arlesheim, she practised this with patients at the Rudolf Steiner Clinic in Scheveningen. When the Dutch Anthroposophical Society split apart in 1935, collaborative work on promoting eurythmy collapsed. After 1945 this state of affairs continued for a while, until, as time went by, personal links began to form between members of the Anthroposophical Society in Holland and the Dutch Section of the General Anthroposophical Society. This latter group, which we have not yet had space to discuss, included a number of important eurythmy artists; and Ingeborg Zeylmans found it very painful to be prevented by the conflicts in the Society from working with these artists for years on end. 'One cannot force these things—they often have to wait for favourable human constellations', she wrote. In 1953 such a constellation arose through practical collaboration with Astrid von Wageningen and Willy Woldijk. These three eurythmists decided to form a Dutch Eurythmy Foundation. This collaboration advanced eurythmy in Holland in a wonderful way. Everyone retained the freedom to practise eurythmy in the way they wished, but there was now an organizational and financial basis for collaboration between the two groups. The two anthroposophical societies in Holland, on the other hand, took another seven years to re-amalgamate. In the shared practice of eurythmy many old wounds began to heal, which had arisen through differences of conviction and knots of destiny.

While Willem Zeylmans was in America in 1950, his wife stayed for a long time in Ascona. Here she collaborated with, among others, the eurythmist Nora von Baditz, thus getting to know this remarkable and brilliant individual better.

> I have much contact with her as always. With all her peculiarities she knows how to get one to enter the etheric world in two or three eurythmy movements. At the moment I am working at a Persian poem (light-dark) in eurythmy, and every comment she makes absolutely hits the nail on the head. She really is an 'A1' teacher!

When the opportunity arose in 1951 to bring Nora von Baditz over to Holland, Ingeborg Zeylmans started a special financial campaign to support this through her Foundation, and so the work of this dynamic pioneer gave eurythmy in Holland a further stimulus.

When Ingeborg Zeylmans became ill, she also had to give up editing the anthroposophical newsletter. The way she had nurtured and 'brought up' this much-loved child of hers for years revealed a side of her that otherwise remained more concealed. The newsletter of any association needs to be like an organ, through which a community of people can perceive itself. Properly developing such a periodical requires considerable input and effort. Her secret in doing this was the selflessness with which she devoted herself to this task, together with her friend Mieke Lagewaard. In the large sitting room of the Scheveningen house, where most of her activities for the Anthroposophical Society took place, the dining table was full of proofs of the new issue on certain days each month. Both women then composed and rearranged, pasted and cut up the journal again, re-pasted it and added things. In between she continued to manage the household, cooked, received guests and offered them tea or coffee. Above all she conducted innumerable telephone conversations. Strangely, though, there was never a sense of hectic rush, and she did not appear to be organizing things particularly: everything just ran like a living, busy household. When everything was ready she got on her bicycle to take the proofs to the printers herself, often staying away for hours in order to correct the little mistakes and typos that always seemed to creep in. Under her care this newsletter flourished.

In earlier years, in Milan, she had once gone to see the 'Last Supper' by Leonardo da Vinci (doubtless before it was restored), and later reported how long it had taken her to begin to perceive the painting amidst the almost indecipherable mass of spots and surfaces; but that it then began, more and more, to reveal its whole heavenly beauty and mysterious power. Perhaps this is also a picture of the way many people saw Ingeborg Zeylmans herself. It was not always easy to see her deeper being amidst her friendly simplicity. She also never did anything to draw attention to herself, but put her will into things and into the tasks around her. She referred to her own input at meetings and Society gatherings as 'perspectives from the living room'. Her friend Elisabeth Knottenbelt wrote of this after her death:

> She could not have described it better; for isn't the wonderful thing about the living room that, concealed within everyday family life, children's souls are formed there for their whole future life? In her sober and simple way she laid seeds in our souls.

In his first letter to her Willem Zeylmans had written: '*Your dancing simply unfolded like simple, clear, eternal truth amidst the mysterious darkness in which human souls live.*' At that time she was no more than sixteen years old. But it was no different when she was sixty—this mood permeated all her daily life. Just as people in very ancient times performed services in the temples, she occupied herself with the daily routine. It is likely that her husband was also greatly indebted to her, at decisive moments of his life, for her reasonable and down-to-earth approach. He hints at this in his 'Conversations on the health of the soul', when he describes his ideal marriage:

When a man and wife suit each other well, this contrasting approach to life can be very productive. For instance, if the man is occupied with something as a scientist or artist—let us say, if he is working at new ideas or working on a new type of painting, and shows the drafts or preliminary sketches to his wife, or discusses them with her, then his wife's opinion can be very important to him, even if she isn't particularly knowledgeable or expert in the field. Why? Because in many cases she has the ability to understand the importance of the new approach in a direct way, or rather to sense and intuit it.

A man who is really deeply connected with his wife—and in this case it does not even have to be his own wife but can also be a good female friend—will place great importance on a feeling judgement of this kind. I have even known various instances of artists and other creative people who rely solely on the judgement of their wife or female friend. If they are halfway sensible, of course, they will also listen to the views and criticisms of experts—but they could actually make such criticisms themselves. What a woman says, on the other hand, comes from a quite different world, one that is not so rooted in the earthly and transient world of appearances, but which has something of the eternity in which things originated in their archetypal, inmost being.

From the time when Ingeborg Zeylmans fell ill comes the reminiscence of a female friend, who looked after her in the country for a while:

> I still have a strong memory of her combination of physical frailty and quiet inner fire. Years earlier, when I attended the first course at the Centre for Free Spiritual Life, Dr Zeylmans described Michelangelo's 'David' so vividly, as the first 'no-sayer', to illustrate the consciousness soul. Later, when I was nursing Ingeborg, I experienced her very much as a 'yes-sayer'—this unexpressed but self-evident 'yes' to everything that she knew, deep in herself, was fast approaching.

At the time of her illness and death, a friend of Zeylmans, the navy doctor Buining, was studying cancer, and in a longer study explored what he saw as the sacrifice someone makes when they suffer this illness. He distinguished three categories of illness and tried to link these with the three hierarchies:

> If one tries honestly to be aware of what is happening in tumour processes, it is difficult to avoid seeing that something mighty is occurring: it is as though a giant were clearing a path for himself with cosmic force. Could this not be the anatomical result of a purification process in the will life of all humanity? And so I ask myself: Do we not see before us the sacrifice that so many people are making, in order to allow cosmic will to be born within humanity? Or, if one prefers: to bring this will into harmony with human capacities? There is no other process of illness in which the physical organism is so completely sacrificed as it is here.

Ingeborg Zeylmans died on 21 January 1960. She herself had chosen the music for her funeral: Bach's *Geistiges Lied* ('Spiritual song'):

My heart rise up with joy,
And see what now takes place
How, after such suffering
There comes so great a light!

My saviour was laid in
The place they bear us to,
When from us our spirit
Departs for heaven's door.

How deep a connection of destiny there may be between two people is perhaps shown by a dream which Willem Zeylmans had as a young student (in 1915 or thereabouts), and which was found among his papers after his death:

I was in a great building, decorated all over with marble and many coloured stones. I was walking about searching for the 'eternal truth'. Climbing up a yellow stone staircase I came to a wall and then had to retrace my steps downwards again; then I came to a small room with a fountain of green stone—but I knew that I ought not to be there. I was in a great hurry. There were also other people wandering about in the building, searching. At last, after descending some stairs, I entered a white marble chapel. In the middle of it was a rotating disc of white marble on which stood many golden signs. This had to be the place I was seeking. I began to look for the one right symbol. Then a girl approached, wearing a close-fitting, green-grey gown. She had black hair and was beautiful in an unadorned and simple way. She asked me: Shall we go on searching together? She sat down beside me, and together we examined the disc. Finally we saw a place where two small golden circles stood beside each other, from which rays went forth. In one circle stood a large G, for Golgotha; in the other there was only an unknown symbol. We did not know which one of these two we should take. Then there came a tall young man with a dark and beautiful face and thick black hair. He wore a brown cloak. He told us we were very close, that we had almost found it. Then we went away, arm in arm, and walked happily through the garden around the building. We were so happy because, once we had found it, we were to marry, and also become teachers in that building, like the young man.

XII. COULD IT NOT BE . . . ?

On the last page of Willem Zeylmans' schedule diary, which was found after his death, he had written a short verse that runs as follows:

> Who's an apprentice?
> Everyone.
> Who's a journeyman?
> One who has some skill.
> Who's a master?
> One who created anew.

Anyone who surveys the life of Willem Zeylmans will, I believe, have no doubt about whom he regarded as 'master': surely one alone, Rudolf Steiner. I believe that he saw himself as 'journeyman', and therefore carried this verse with him to remind himself of the difference between the two. This is a necessary self-knowledge for someone who is admired by others, to whom many listen and who 'has some skill'. But the verse also shows what unites master and journeyman: they are both also 'apprentices'—like everyone. It can move and even shock one to see the many small pieces of paper on which he wrote notes, during the last year of his life, for every little talk or press conference, for every lecture, every radio interview about the life and work of Rudolf Steiner (1961 was the hundredth anniversary of Steiner's birth), even though he had already spoken about this 'master' hundreds of times during the previous four decades.

Zeylmans' last article (in German) perhaps tells us even more about this. It is entitled 'Rudolf Steiner and the future community of man'. The essay is based on a lecture which he gave in The Hague on 27 February 1961, Rudolf Steiner's hundredth birthday, where he said: *'I believe that it is important to make a memorial celebration such as this into a matter of the deepest self-reflection.'*

In the article he writes, among other things:

One of the most striking aspects of Rudolf Steiner's personality was his capacity to unite human souls. Whenever he entered a full hall, many experienced this as though a spiritual light suddenly began to shine, encompassing all those present.

We know that he regarded the development of a sense of community as one of the most important tasks of anthroposophical group meetings and gatherings. Since we live in an age of inner isolation, in which antipathy and sympathy, judgement and condemnation hold sway, it is of great importance that groups of people should practise overcoming and transforming these forces out of a higher consciousness.

As early as 1915 (on 15 June) Rudolf Steiner spoke about this at the inauguration of an anthroposophical group in Düsseldorf. There are three great human qualities, he says, which will only come to full fruition when the Spirit Self develops in the coming age, but which we need to prepare in the present: a brotherly social community, in which we feel the suffering of others as our own; the experience of complete freedom of thinking and religious conviction; and the practice of a science which is wholly orientated towards spiritual science and based upon it.

Then Zeylmans describes how Rudolf Steiner repeatedly appealed to the deeper forces *'which slumber in the depths of the human being and which are capable of truly uniting people when we . . . awaken through the soul and spirit of the other.'* And he goes on:

The Anthroposophical Society is intended to be an association of people who wish to cultivate individual soul life and the soul life of the human community, on the basis of a true knowledge and perception of the spiritual world . . .

When we read in the address given at the 1923 Foundation Stone meeting: 'And the right soil into which we must today lay the foundation stone, the right soil is provided by our hearts, in their harmonious collaboration, in their good, love-permeated will to carry anthroposophical striving through the world in shared endeavour', then it is clear that an appeal is being made to the deepest forces which still slumber in our souls—forces such as engaged interest and love for the being of another person, even when this other seems alien and perhaps unappealing to us.

There is often no lack of striving for 'knowledge' in our circles. But what 'quality' do our thoughts have? Again, in a lecture in Stuttgart, his first there after the burning of the Goetheanum, Rudolf Steiner said: 'Ideas are, for anthroposophy, the vessels carved from love, into which the true essence of the human being is drawn from spiritual worlds in a spiritual way. The light of true humanity, cloaked in lovingly formed thoughts, should illuminate anthroposophy. And knowledge is only the form in which, through human beings, the opportunity is given for the true spirit to gather and focus in human thoughts, out of the far expanses of the cosmos, so that, from the human heart, it can shine through human thoughts. And because anthroposophy can only be truly grasped by love, it creates love when people grasp it in its true sense and being.'

The three ideals which Rudolf Steiner described in Düsseldorf were, according to Zeylmans, further developed in very concrete form in the 'Foundation Stone' meditation:

'Practise spirit remembering' not only means that we learn how 'our own "I" is part of God's "I" '—no, out of cosmic heights we hear resound: 'From the divine, humanity takes its existence', the humanity together with which we must come to a brotherly, social community. Thus 'Practise spirit reflection' is a path of schooling for meeting the being of Christ, the cosmic ego, the 'I' of humanity, to which in the far-distant future all human beings can find their free relationship. The third task set us, 'Practise spirit vision', is ultimately the path from natural science to spiritual science, from anthropology to anthroposophy.

In this (only partially quoted) essay, therefore, Zeylmans described these three exercises as the social tasks of every 'apprentice' of anthroposophy.

This is probably the right place to mention that, in April 1960, at an annual general meeting in Dornach, Switzerland, Zeylmans announced the re-affiliation of the Dutch Society to the General Anthroposophical Society. The road leading to this involved many extensive discussions and difficult negotiations, which had to be conducted with patience, tact and discipline.

If we are ready—says the official letter of September 1959—*to reintegrate with the General Anthroposophical Society, this is because we believe that time is pressing, and that we ought at least to make our contribution to building up a General Anthroposophical Society which deserves the name 'General' because it includes all who see themselves as honest pupils of Rudolf Steiner.*

Here it says 'because time is pressing'. In his address in the Goetheanum on Easter Saturday, 16 April 1960, Zeylmans puts it a little differently by saying: *'And if people should ask us why we are reintegrating with the General Anthroposophical Society, we can only give one reply: because we WISH AND HAVE THE WILL TO!'*

In Cairo (in September 1961, shortly before he died) he reportedly addressed this theme in yet another way. He replied to friends who asked him about the reasons for this re-affiliation, that it had come about 'for Rudolf Steiner's sake'. Thus we have three motives for a deed which ended decades of tragic separation: firstly because *'time is pressing'*; then *'for Rudolf Steiner's sake'*; and thirdly *'because we WISH AND HAVE THE WILL TO!'* The whole human being is contained in these three!

Mankind is progressing in its evolution. The forces which must lead to this further evolution, which need to build a new social structure, cannot be drawn from the past. 'The only justified revolution,' Rudolf Steiner once said, 'is that from passive to active thinking' . . . It was always my deepest longing to help to bring about such a 'revolution': to transform what exists without denying it, or at least without fleeing from it—affirming the world as it is and also acknowledging it, but at the same time working for renewal through the spirit; helping, out of a thinking imbued with love and will, to bring about an 'ascending metamorphosis' of our whole social existence . . .

In anthroposophy one can find a mighty stream of resurrection forces that overcome the death forces threatening our civilization. It contains the seed of new mysteries which give man the inner and outer opportunity to unite with the world. These mysteries are intrinsically social—they do not try to lead man to higher knowledge as a separate individual, but show paths towards comprehensive social renewal . . .

The path of the individual leads through great loneliness; but it is in this very loneliness that people seek each other. In the broad scope of the world situation in which we live together nowadays, the dire needs and misery of the human race can become fully apparent. These hardships are in the first place of an inner, spiritual kind. Only by developing a new and fully conscious relationship to the earthly and cosmic totality in which we live can we help to overcome this misery and hardship. The world can become a temple to us, which we can enter with new spiritual forces, in deep connection with our fellow human beings, building a social approach to our lives, a social practice, which is rooted in the spirit.

When we turn our attention to the last years of Willem Zeylmans' life, the period from which these words come, we can become aware how surely he trod this path of the 'new mysteries' right to the end of his life.

As a youth he had called out: *'Love is the mightiest, most inward, most powerful, deepest revelation of God's spirit in human souls! Can there be anything else in the world?'* In later years he suffered renunciation, poverty and inner death with such sovereignty that his wife warned him with words that sound like a 'manifest secret': 'See the world through Christ's eyes.' And in one of his last diaries there is an entry (on 7 January 1959), sandwiched between lots of different meetings, appointments and flight departure dates, which runs: *'Could it not be that the force of resurrection is actually the starting point for everything? That everything proceeds from it?'* He, who had thought so much about the Christ mystery, must suddenly have been struck by a quite new perception of this in the last years of his life. Thus one can see the period which concluded the life of this 'pioneer of anthroposophy' also as a beginning, even in its outer events. It is from this perspective that I would like to describe the last months of his life.

After the death of his wife Zeylmans received more lecture invitations than ever. In April 1960 we find him in Dornach and Stuttgart, in May in Ascona and Arlesheim, straight afterwards in Göteborg and Stockholm; then in Odense (Denmark) in June, and in London in July—each time giving lectures, courses or attending conferences. After a holiday in Engadine (Fextal) he goes to Dornach in August, and to Belgium in September. Over the winter there are large numbers of courses and lectures in Holland; and, as had almost become 'tradition', he gives a New Year lecture in the Ita Wegman Clinic at Arlesheim, on the Foundation Stone. A few days later he travels to Ascona and Lugano, before getting back to his regular work in Holland. On 5 April 1961 he goes to Majorca for ten days, and returns via Arlesheim. At the beginning of May he is in Stuttgart, where, among other things, he gives a lecture at the Liederhalle (concert hall) entitled 'The reality in which we live', as he does again shortly afterwards in Nuremberg. In the middle of the month he is back in Dornach for a Whitsun conference, and in England by the end of May. In June he is invited on a trip to Italy and Sicily by his friends Lili and Pieter de Haan (Domodossola, Siena, Naples, Sorento, Salerno, Paestum, Palermo, Monreale, Agrigento, Syracuse, Taormina). In July he once more takes part in a conference in Dornach, then visits Antwerp; and August brings a large public conference in The Hague, in celebration of Rudolf Steiner's hundredth birthday. After this he sets out on his last trip, flying via Zurich and Rome. On 7 September 1961 he lands in Cairo, just as the sun is setting over the desert. *'Arrived safely'* he notes in his pocket diary.

The following day he is invited on a wonderful trip to Sakkarah and Memphis, and sees the pyramids and the Sphinx again, for the first time in 26 years. The next day, when he returns from the museum in Cairo to his hotel, he finds his passport is missing—the proof of his outward existence! It is Saturday afternoon—and what no one believes possible happens: within four hours he gets a new passport with the help of the Egyptian police and the Dutch embassy, with all the travel visas he needs; and shortly after midnight flies off in the crowded BOAC plane, on the eight-and-a-half hour trip from Cairo to Nairobi.

*

Zeylmans only stayed three days in Nairobi. He met up with some anthroposophical friends there, who invited him for trips to wildlife reserves in the Rift Valley, the Flamingo Lake and the great bird reserve. Vivid memories of his visit seven years previously (on his world trip) accompanied the beginning of these last ten weeks of his life.

In Salisbury intensive work awaited him. The anthroposophists active there had arranged a meeting with the education inspector, he gave a lecture to students at the Rhodesian University on Waldorf Education, two lectures at the Women's Club on Rudolf Steiner and on nations and races, and a talk to the National Affairs Association on the same theme. Then he spoke four times for the Anthroposophical Society (about the Foundation Stone, karma and reincarnation) and on 16 September was taken on an expedition into the country's interior. The following day they visited the Zambesi river and the Victoria Falls, and standing *'at the place where Dr Livingston had once stopped on his voyage of discovery'*, he was deeply moved to see the great rainbows shining in heavenly beauty.

At the same time that Zeylmans set off on the flight to Johannesburg five days later, a man died in Africa who, in quite different dimensions and also in a quite different way from Willem Zeylmans, had also made great efforts to promote peace and understanding among different peoples and races, and devoted himself to the cause of humanity's future. This was Dag Hammarskjöld, the famous general secretary of the United Nations. On this day he was also at the African equator, on a flight over Rhodesia, and crashed (or was murdered). It is strange to think how close these two men came at this point: one in Ndola, the other in Salisbury.

★

When Willem Zeylmans visited South Africa in 1961, the anthroposophical work there was still in its infancy. But in only a few years settlements had grown up in various places and new impulses were starting to flourish. This work had begun with the founding of a home for children in need of special care in Hermanus, east of Cape Town, at a place where there had formerly been a Christian missionary leper colony. In the following years, in Johannesburg, Cape Town and then in Port Elizabeth, also on the east coast, further institutes were opened, as well as a branch of Weleda, a Waldorf School and a kindergarten. In 1958 an Anthroposophical Society in South Africa had been founded, inspired not least by Zeylmans' first visit in 1954. Dr Karl König, the great curative educationalist and founder of the Camphill movement, had just paid a productive visit to South Africa. And now, six months later, Zeylmans arrived. Erich and Grete Kirchner-Bockholt travelled with him, and this fortunate constellation gave Weleda and the medical work new stimulus.

One of the first lectures he was asked to give after arriving in Johannesburg was a talk to the Philosophical Society at Pretoria University, on 'Race relations in the light of a new knowledge of man'—probably the most topical theme in the country at the time! With great calm and composure Zeylmans told a packed hall that he wished to leave political considerations to one side, addressing the theme from a philosophical and psychological point of view. A recording of this lecture (in Dutch) has been preserved and conveys a very immediate impression of his rich imagery and multi-perspective approach. Unfortunately the end of the talk is missing, so that one can only conclude how he finished it from listening to the rest: probably a description of Rudolf Steiner's threefold social organism—a basis for society's future structure which would, if realized in South Africa, be able to avert much damage and misery!

For the next few days Elisabeth Wertheym had invited him on a round trip through the famous Paul Krüger Park, where he once more gained a powerful impression of the South African wilderness and its animals. 'Dr Zeylmans', she said, 'was always cheerful, even when there were no animals to be seen; and he continually made jokes, even about spiritual matters, so that we sometimes thought we ought to censure his impertinence.' After returning to Johannesburg he spent some time with the Wertheym family; and one afternoon, as the young wife records, 'he came to speak with me as I was cleaning the car and wished to talk about death. At the end of his "lecture" as he called it, I asked him whether he really thought that the moment of our death was predestined. He replied: "Yes, absolutely predestined, unless there are very unusual circumstances, for instance when our personal destiny is interwoven with that of a country, such as in a state of political turmoil." He also said: "If you wish to be of use to anthroposophy, then as many of you as possible must prepare yourselves to give lectures. After an initial study of anthroposophy in general—and that doesn't need to take too long—you must specialize in one field. Choose an area in which you would like to immerse yourself thoroughly. Then give yourself a set period—3 to 6 months—during which you prepare a course of 3, 6 or 10 lectures, just as you like. And then you can give *one* lecture. It is not sufficient to prepare a single lecture and then give it immediately. Spend some years concentrating on this one field, so as to build up some kind of real basis."'

In Johannesburg people had organized a great deal for him to do: a radio talk, opening of a kindergarten, two lectures on racial questions at the university. In November it was envisaged that, after his stay in Cape Town, he would return to Johannesburg, where he would give a talk on

Waldorf education in connection with plans to found a Waldorf School there (which later started). In one of his South African lectures Zeylmans gave such a clear and living picture of the ideals underlying the Waldorf School that one of those present, a businessman, stood up afterwards and—as it were pulling out his cheque book—called out: 'We must have such a school! That is what we have been waiting for!'

No one who has been to Cape Town will ever forget the landscape there. Table Mountain rises up 1100 metres in the background, dominating everything. Seen from the West it has the form of a mountain which once soared high into the heavens, of which only the lower part remains—as if its peak has been sliced off by a divine hand, to provide a kind of table for the gods. Between this and the sea, on the western seashore, the town lies spread out; and towards the East, behind mountains, the Indian Ocean begins, while the Atlantic Ocean stretches out towards the West. Former seafarers called this place, which they had to circumnavigate to reach India, the 'Cape of Storms'. According to tradition, Henry the Seafarer, Grand Master of the Order of Christ, baptized it 'Cape of Good Hope' on his quest to find the legendary Prester John.

Zeylmans was taken up this mountain as soon as he arrived in Cape Province on 5 October, and looked out over the sea with Erich and Grete Kirchner:

A remarkable trip through the pass between Oudshoorn and Prince Albert: an ancient formation of bizarre and wild cliffs, like a giant ocean whipped up in a great storm, that suddenly freezes and whose waves crash and break upon one another—remains of the catastrophe of Atlantis. There is more here that reminds one of the most ancient times of earth's evolution . . . afterwards we traversed the wonderful steppe region called Karoo . . .

Here Zeylmans saw a part of the Lemurian sea-floor. Geologically this 'Cape Folds' area is a strange region. Geologists attribute it to the Old Palaeozoic period, with its brown Mediterranean seafloors and strange bush formations.

He was enthralled by this landscape. He kept returning to it in his talks, as though trying to answer an unsolved question.

In Port Elizabeth the anthroposophists, who until then had had little public profile, organized an impressive programme together with their tireless and enthusiastic member Basil Gibaud; and for the last evening published announcements in the local papers that appeared as follows:

YOUR ONLY CHANCE
to hear
DR. ZEYLMANS
VAN EMMICHOVEN
ON
KARMA
(YOUR DESTINY)
REINCARNATION
LIFE AFTER DEATH
AT
ST. JOHN'S GATE
Rink Street
TONIGHT at 8.15
Admission Free
LP70713/20

In fact it wasn't the 'only chance' to hear Zeylmans in Port Elizabeth, for he gave seven lectures there in six days, and the newspaper reported on them under the heading: 'Life after Death lecture in City'—a strange title if one thinks of Zeylmans' subsequent fate, and also of the fact that Basil Gibaud, the enthusiastic organizer of the whole event, died soon afterwards himself!

During these days Africans were alarmed by the volcanic eruption on Tristan da Cunha, a small archipelago in the South Atlantic, during which 292 refugees were rescued by a Dutch freighter. Zeylmans was greatly affected by this.

Zeylmans and his Cape host and friend Chris Wegerif travelled back from Port Elizabeth to Cape Town in 2 days, engrossed in stimulating conversations. Both men were preoccupied with many issues; and as they journeyed through this unspoiled and perhaps most ancient region of the world, their thoughts revolved around one of the newest and youngest 'pioneer movements' in the world, with the question: how can we sow anthroposophy here, so that it grows to be a blessing in this tragically conflict-ridden land?

Before a group of young doctors Zeylmans described the stages of human development: in the first 3 years the child takes hold of space (first year), establishes a relationship to time (second year) and begins to say 'I' (third year). Then he develops through 3 seven-year periods until adulthood; and then, if one looks at the whole course of a life, one can see how we develop *physically* during the first 21 years of life, develop in terms of *soul and emotion* in the following 21 years, and then, up to the age of 63, develop *spiritually: 'After this age, wisdom is gained and he disregards the critical world and may perform some of his greatest work!'*

The Waldorf teachers in Cape Town recalled how he spoke with them about social troubles and problems: 'As master of the golden mean, Dr Zeylmans had developed the Christian capacity to urge people to become clear and tolerant, deep and broad, individual and universal. Not "either—or" and "neither—nor" but a constantly re-acquired "not only—but also" is the foundation of esoteric life.'

He treated the Antroposofiese Verenigung in Suidelike Afrika as a 'purely spiritual family and allowed it to experience how the Foundation Stone had been laid in their hearts too'.

The convincing impression he made in public now gave rise to a warm connection with headmaster Petersen and his junior school for 'coloured boys', and with some of the teachers. Here he was asked to speak about social conflict, doubt and anger, a wholly unexpected request to make of a white European—for among whites and coloureds in the union there was a belief that no one who had not lived there for years could properly judge the unusually complex conditions in the country, and that Europeans would do better to refrain from any opinion.

When Petersen introduced a difficult youngster to him, who, whenever he had completed any schoolwork always carefully crossed it out again, Zeylmans took the boy's head between his hands and bent over him, in silence and the deepest concentration. After spending a few minutes like this, he let him go, after the boy had promised to do better. From that moment on something healed itself in the boy. At one of his first meetings with Rudolf Steiner Zeylmans had asked him what he should do with his strong magnetic capacities. 'Don't pay them any attention,' was the reply—advice which he followed until that moment. But coming into contact with black people in these weeks, such as with this boy, he experienced something that he had sometimes previously felt with people of other races: it suddenly seemed to him as if he became one with the other: melting with the other individual in something like mystical fulfilment.

'Sunshine entered our school,' said Petersen later about Zeylmans' visits—and that might serve as a motto for Zeylmans' whole journey to South

Africa. For does this not express in a single phrase what anthroposophy asks of human beings and what Zeylmans himself said in 1924: *'We should proclaim anthroposophy in the world like a gospel!'*?

Three days before he was due to leave Johannesburg, Zeylmans invited several friends for the evening, to talk with them on a major theme of his life: the new Isis, whom on this evening he described at the foot of the cosmic cross, in the light of a new, future, 'John' Christianity. He saw this as this country's special task.

> We found him in bed as though resting. As usual he had placed a second pillow under his head for his morning meditation: his eyes were closed, his hands folded over his chest. His papers and books lay there in ordered fashion, and he had placed the house key on the table so that it would be found.
>
> The evening before there had been a farewell celebration, brought forward by one day for space reasons. There he gave us his message. He reminded us how much closer one is to friends who have passed over the threshold, since no coarse body prevents them becoming one with us, and how thin the veil is which separates us from the so-called dead. He spoke of how we are really one large family within anthroposophy, whether on this or the other side of the threshold; and of how we can be aware of this fact as long as we are spiritually active in our work with Michael, the great being of spirit with whom we are all united, whatever aspect we may approach him from through our personal karma. And now, in great stillness, he had died on Saturday morning; and we recalled the legend of John the disciple and his message: 'Little children, love one another', whereupon he folded his hands over his breast and died.

In these words his host and friend Chris Wegerif described his passing. And Heinz Maurer added:

> His humorous, light, radiant way of lecturing and conversing, which left you free, could easily awaken the impression—despite the fact that the foreign language set some obstacles in his way now and then—that all this required absolutely no effort on his part. But if one paid attention and really asked him about himself, occasionally one picked up hints that the unexpected number of talks and addresses had cost him great effort.
>
> We, like our friends from overseas, could reproach ourselves for having taxed him too greatly. But everyone who experienced his

warm, light-filled readiness to give without holding back, would probably have done as we did—simply accepted what he offered with great thankfulness, admiration and enthusiasm.

The Dutch visitor, of whom Petersen later said he had brought sunshine into the school, had been invited to a large school celebration at the Athlone High School for Coloureds on 18 November 1961, at ten in the morning. Two hours before this celebration began, Petersen got a call telling him that Dr Zeylmans had just died. The celebration took place nevertheless. Petersen explained to his pupils that, although Dr Zeylmans was not there, he was present nevertheless; and so the dark-skinned children—only hearing of his death at the end of the event—played their music joyfully and devotedly, accompanying his ascent into other realms with music from the heart of Europe.

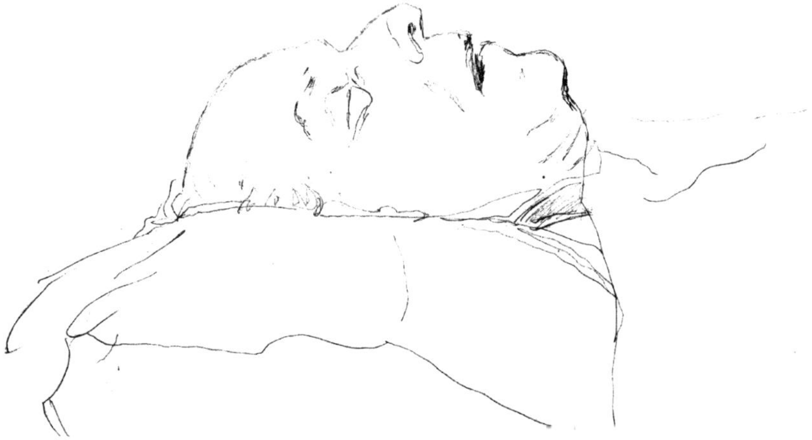

Zeylmans on his death-bed in Cape Town

CONCLUSION

When we flew off to South Africa in November 1961 for Willem Zeylmans' funeral, a sharp, cold wind was blowing at Schiphol. But on landing at Cape Town a day later, the sun there was shining from a clear, blue sky—a warm spring day welcomed us to the southern hemisphere.

The cremation was on Thursday, 23 November, his sixty-eighth birthday. The next afternoon we climbed Table Mountain; and as we looked down from 1100 metres at the town spread out all around the foot of the mountain, we scattered the ashes of his earthly body at the edge of the western cliffs. Shortly afterwards a gentle wind blew up from the Atlantic Ocean, lifting the light dust over the rocks and blowing it back towards the East. And as we were climbing down and looked up one more time, small cloud-heads were forming at that place, rising up and sinking down around the cliffs, as though trying to bear some of his ashes upwards with them.

So the death of this exemplary human being was like his life: an expression of his being right into the outward phenomena. But the exemplary quality in his biography (what Novalis called 'canonical') was no rigid 'destiny' but a wonderfully living, continually fluid strength which led him in the realization of his great ideals—and came to effect within him.

He had chosen as his task the striving for a future that anthroposophy was bringing, and living, into the present. He himself was like a seed laid into the earth. For the earth is not only the site of trials and death's grave, but also the temple where the soul learns to see its divine destiny. Like the Knights Templar in the thirteenth century, who relinquished their own wealth and selflessly took responsibility all over the world for the flourishing of commerce and harvests, for countries and peoples, so Willem Zeylmans took up his task, and that of the Anthroposophical Society, for modern humanity. He did this out of a sense of responsibility for the flourishing of the human soul; and still more, for the very redemption of the soul of humanity. The last words spoken to him by his great teacher were: 'Occupy yourself with the Templars and the Rosicrucians.'

After his death I found in his briefcase a piece of paper on which the following words, apparently by Rudolf Steiner, were written in the

Table Mountain, Cape Town, South Africa

handwriting of his wife Ingeborg. I would like to close his biography with these words:

That is what we must learn in our time: to live out of pure trust, without any security of existence, out of trust in the continually present help of the spiritual world. There is really no other way. Let us educate our will in a fitting way and seek awakening from within, every morning and very night:

O Michael, I commend myself to your protection,
Unite myself with your guidance
Out of my heart's whole strength.
That this day may become an image
Of your destiny-directing will.

APPENDIX

Willem Zeylmans' Doctoral Thesis (1923)

The dissertation 'De werking der Kleuren op het gevoel' (The effect of colours on the feelings) was accepted by Amsterdam University on 25 September 1923. W. de Haan, publishers in Utrecht, brought out the first edition the same year. The theses required in Holland for such a text have also survived, as well as a school exercise book of notes for presenting the dissertation.

W. Zeylmans collected the material for the dissertation from July to mid-December 1920 in Leipzig, in the laboratories of Professor Wundt, which were directed by Professor F. Krüger at the time. In the practical execution of the trials he had help from Professor A. Kirschmann.

In the introduction the author gives an overview of colours, the history of colour research, colours in contemporary painting and the effect of colours on adults and children.

In the following chapter Zeylmans deals with the problem of the quantitative and qualitative view of colours. Against the prevailing scientific view, going back to Newton, he sets a qualitative way of examining colours based on Goethe's colour theory, describing how Rudolf Steiner developed Goethe's ideas further and gave them an epistemological basis.

In chapter 3 an overview of existing literature on the subject is given, and then the author describes his own preparatory colour experiments with school children. At the end of the chapter he briefly characterizes the human soul.

In the next chapter the technique employed in his colour experiments is described.

Then follow the results of the experiments and an analysis of the test subjects' personal impressions. There is also a description of the various nuances of feeling arising in his self-examinations.

In chapter 7 he evaluates the results of the tapping trials, and in the final chapter Zeylmans gives a summary, a critique of the trials and concluding remarks.

A connection is apparent between the three categories of soul life—thinking, feeling and will—and the three areas of the colour spectrum; and it seems that everything in feeling life which tends towards the will side of the soul is enhanced through the warm colours: yellow, orange and red; while the other realm of the soul, related to thinking, forming judgements and also meditative reflection, is more closely connected with the cold side of the colour spectrum, where the blue and purple colours are to be found. The feelings themselves—let us say the uncomplicated feelings—are related to the colours which oscillate between yellow and green and blue.

This conclusion could be deduced in my Leipzig colour trials from the reactions of the test subjects. Thus one can assign the various realms of soul life to particular realms of the colour spectrum!

The most remarkable result, however, was apparent in the case of crimson—the crimson that does not naturally appear in the colour spectrum, but which occupied a very marked place in the trials. Everything that occurred with the three other groups of colours appeared once more with crimson. Thus crimson revealed itself to be a colour which represents a synthesis. All reactions in the spheres of feeling, will and thinking which appeared in the other colours, were brought together once more in crimson! All this is of course only a beginning; and much more and deeper research is still needed.

Willem Zeylmans' Appeal for the Stakenberg Camp (1930)

We direct this appeal to all young people who wish to serve the true spirit of the times. We do not ask whether they belong to a particular group or orientation. In many different groups and orientations people with ideals come together, people who have the will to work for these ideals. All wish to serve humanity. But whoever wishes to serve humanity must know how humanity is best served. He must know the zeitgeist, the spirit of the times which is striving to manifest at a particular time in the hearts and minds of those who wish to help bear responsibility for mankind's further evolution.

Rudolf Steiner spoke of the zeitgeist in all seriousness and reverence—as someone speaks who tries to found mankind's evolutionary path in his own deepest being, with warmth and inwardness; as someone speaks who has endured human suffering. He showed us what kind of time we are living in—an age so heavily burdened by a materialistic world view.

Out of this materialistic world view comes a near-perfect technology—undreamed-of progress in the realms of science, but at the same time a loneliness in human souls, a loss of spirit which leads to despair. But in this loneliness the longing has been born for a time when human beings can once more find their way back to a connection with the spiritual powers who lead mankind clearly and purposefully; a time in which everything that human beings have so far mastered can come to serve a world view formed through spiritual will.

We who heard Rudolf Steiner believe that his words reveal to us the will of this true spirit of the times. We who knew Rudolf Steiner believe that his work opens the way for us to a new, approaching time. He became a teacher and guide for thousands. His guidance respected every belief and conviction. It appeals solely to the human being *who lives within all of us.*

Do we still know what a teacher and guide is, in an age in which hyper-individualism triumphs on the one hand, while on the other hand the concept of collective man extinguishes individual consciousness?

Do we know that it is possible to choose a teacher and guide in freedom, through whose leadership alone we can eventually come to full freedom?

We direct this appeal to all young people, to all who wish to find the human being slumbering in their depths, the human being who is at risk of vanishing in this technological century. Technology does not only hold sway in external life—its numbing and ossifying forces also enter human souls. They mechanize thinking, numb feeling through the rhythms of machines, paralyse the will because they make it mechanical and automatic. But the human soul longs to be redeemed—the true human being is striving to be born.

Natural science tries to understand human nature. But only spiritual science will be able to rediscover the human spirit. Such a spiritual science gave us anthroposophy. It has the precision and the methods of natural science, but leads beyond the limits which confine the latter.

Who was Rudolf Steiner? Many have perhaps never heard his name, many know his name but nothing more, do not know what he did for humanity. One can understand this—our time sees many movements arise and pass away, and there are large numbers who believe they can bring a new and healing teaching to humanity.

One recognizes the tree by its fruits. The interest of those who devote themselves to a new teaching frequently fades fast, when they sense that such teaching does not change the reality of life.

Our time is not satisfied by beautiful teachings. The only valuable ideas are ones which can bring a new and better reality, because they are born out of the leading spirit of the times. Such ideas are also sought by the young people of today, who cannot simply accept the present time and everything which goes with it.

We direct this appeal to all young people.

What do young people wish? What have they always wanted? They want to realize their ideals, they want to change and improve the world. This will is sacred to them.

It has always been thus. But the young people of our times have changed. They still have ideals but they have become critical.

Modern culture has brought with it a great development of consciousness. This consciousness throws a false light on external realities.

Young people today are at the same time old. They take up experiences into their young souls which formerly were gathered over the course of a long life, and have therefore become critical or indifferent. Many who experience the decay and decadence of our time alongside its great achievements feel how the glow of idealism fades from their souls. They comfort themselves with the thought 'that one has to accept the way things are', and that everything is as it 'has to be'. But the part of their souls that remains inconsolable seeks to numb itself in the many diversions and distractions which our times offer. A small number are drawn towards despair or madness—or to crime.

We direct this appeal to all young people. To all who have ideals and all who have lost their ideals. Those who have ideals believe they can change something in the world; those who no longer have any believe the same until the world shows itself to be stronger than they are. For young people the world can be a task or a heavy burden. A task which they seek to fulfil with the deepest seriousness, or a burden which they carry or try to throw off.

We wish to fulfil our task together with all those prepared to put their youthful strength at the service of human evolution; but we also wish to help to lighten the burden of those for whom it is a great difficulty. We are convinced that there is a path which makes both things possible. Rudolf Steiner knew young people's idealism and despair. Perhaps no one ever loved young people as he did.

His was a love which gave vision. From this love sprang understanding. This understanding enabled him to show a path forwards into the future. A path leading to a goal that already lies as a germ of possibility in this path itself. Not an abstract goal, cleverly thought out in the abstract, but a goal that continues to ripen and mature as we develop and evolve.

He was able to show that every human being, born out of the world of spirit, must find his path on earth through many developmental stages; and that his connection with the material world leads him to knowledge of his own inner strength. In former stages of existence he strode easily through life, led by divine powers who ruled his whole being. It was the task of materialism to liberate the human being. But through this liberation he lost his connection with his spiritual origin. The end of the last [nineteenth] century brought a turning point. Now a new power has begun to germinate in the human soul. To all who wish to see it the task presents itself of pursuing the path further. The task of rising from external reality to a new, spirit-permeated reality. The interconnection between earth, man and cosmos can once more be seen by those who wish to follow the path of spiritual science, just as people have for centuries been pursuing the path of natural science. Originally man experienced this interconnection in a dull, dream-like consciousness. Now consciousness has awakened through the encounter with matter. It has awoken and become all-embracing, already at a young age.

What enters this consciousness? An outwardly magnificent world view, which however is inwardly empty because of decay and degeneration in almost all realms of life. Only that? Or also the science of the spirit which can value this world view and at the same time show ways to overcome the decay?

A broader awareness also brings obligations. Do we wish to accept these?

Many complain about the misery of our times. Yet the misery of the times is the misery of human beings. The times take their lead from the human beings who create them. When human beings change so do the times. How can people change? By coming to know their own being—not in abstract, scientific ways, but by penetrating spiritual laws which rule earth, man and cosmos, which form the human being as body, soul and spirit.

The times are changing. What seems to be mere repetition is metamorphosis: ancient truths do not simply resurface in new clothing, but new truths are revealed. The truths which are right for a particular time.

So our time, too, stands at the birth of a revelation of truth which can once more show us where our true place is in the universe. What the past has to teach us about this is vague and confusing, and brings only despair. What the future will teach us depends largely on us ourselves; on our will to recognize the truth of this time; and on our love for this truth.

Whoever wishes to find the paths that lead the human soul towards the future will have to search for these paths; and whoever sees them before him will have to follow them.

Idealism is will directed in such a way that ideas from spiritual worlds can be formed into earthly reality.

A famous man once coined a rather gloomy maxim: the youth of 20 is an idealist, the man of 50 a cynic and the man of 80 a childish old man. The idealism that leads us to cynicism and from there to the weaknesses of old age cannot help us. We wish to develop a different idealism in our souls, one which metamorphoses youthful fire into a radiant light of the spirit that can work creatively and formatively in society and the human world.

Rather than speaking of the spirit let us come to know the spirit in a clear and precise way, as we can through the kind of genuine spiritual science that Rudolf Steiner developed through decades of self-sacrificing work. Let us not speak of the spirit but rather show how, in many different fields, spiritual science leads to results which ought no longer to remain unknown to those who truly wish to serve evolution. Rather than speaking of the spirit let us help the spirit grow within us to a power of will, to a strength for deeds, so that we can become human beings—living, experiencing human beings who create out of the spirit, bringing a new reality to birth.

Do people know that Rudolf Steiner was the founder of the School of Spiritual Science in Dornach, near Basle? That he was the originator of impulses for a new art of education, a new art of medicine? That he laid the foundations for a new science? Do people know of the new paths in drama, fine art, speech formation and eurythmy? Are they aware of the results that have been obtained in these fields? Do people know what insights he offered into man's evolutionary path? What paths he showed to seeking souls? Such souls, who wish to form their own powers and undergo an inner schooling, a path of self-development? Do people know what Rudolf Steiner taught about the nature of religions, of the central place of Christ, the high divine Being, and His relationship to man and the world? And of the relationship of Christ to humanity in the time nearly upon us now? It is our aim to speak of such things. To speak with you about them. To listen to your constructive thoughts that can extend our understanding, to hear your doubts and criticism. We wish to ask you to come to work with us, to live with us for a short while. In this collaborative work, in living together with other young people, the seed can be laid for a new reality. That is why we direct this appeal to all young people. To all of you!

Small Colour Handbook for a Carpet-pattern Book (1939)

The significance of colours for our feeling life is too great to leave radiant and harmonious colours no place in the intimacy of living rooms. The descriptions of various colours which follow here are intentionally brief, and to some extent follow the style of Goethe's chapter on the 'moral effect of colours' in his famous Theory of Colours.

Yellow and its shades (warm yellow and orange yellow)

Yellow is a radiant, cheerful colour, most closely related to sunlight itself. Its general character is: happy, cosy, gently stimulating. A landscape viewed through yellow glass on a gloomy day appears cheerful and warm. 'The eye feels pleasure, the heart expands, the mind is cheered.' (Goethe)

The stimulating character of yellow is the reason why this colour is much used in today's interior designs, particularly in large cities where sunlight often enters a dwelling only sparsely. In artificial light the warm, comforting character of yellow is usually well sustained.

The pronounced character of yellow is only slightly lost when diluted with white, so that its specific effect is retained when applied to large wall surfaces. Yellow is highly recommended for halls, anterooms and living rooms. In darker rooms it has a brightening effect.

The fine character of yellow is lost as soon as it goes in the direction of green (lemon yellow).

Orange and its shades (yellow-orange and red-orange)

In orange the radiant character of yellow is intensified by the warm red. As the most strongly activating colour, red makes yellow more aggressive and effective; yellow, in contrast, with its gentle, light-bearing character, dampens red's flaming passion. Thus a balance arises between light and strength; and orange is capable of awakening a sense of health and well-being. When used in moderation in the home, it introduces an element of warmth and good company. Orange expresses a healthy, strong idealism and stimulates the will. Using it too undiluted would naturally lead to a sense of restlessness. For walls, therefore, we usually strongly recommend adding a good deal of white or grey, which give rise to lovely shades of brown and beige.

Red and its shades (orange-red)

Since red is the strongest and most active colour, it is usually only feasible to apply it in delicate shades of pink and pinkish-red. Intensification of the warmth element that we saw in orange becomes almost unbearably strong with red. Goethe says that children and more primitive peoples especially love this colour, which conveys the greatest possible energy to the human soul. Its tingling, stimulating, animating effect can assume an almost boisterous and exuberant character with a really strong red. By mixing it with a good deal of white or grey, red becomes very pleasant and gentle: its more peaceful aspect appears, in the presence of which the human soul will be glad to open up and expand.

The darker shades of pink and red can also create a pleasant atmosphere. (Here one can recall the upholstery of chairs in concert halls etc.) Red is not generally recommended for the walls of smaller rooms.

Purple

This remarkable colour is very attractive to many people. The warm, stimulating effect of red here encounters cool, receding blue. Contrasting elements achieve a particular effect: activity and calm, sensation and inner stillness! No wonder that this colour has a deep significance for people with a propensity for the mystical.

Blue and its shades (green-blue)

As light is expressed in yellow, so the element of darkness appears in blue. 'In its highest purity', as Goethe says, this colour 'is like a delightful emptiness'. Above all it is the colour which bestows peace and calm. This effect becomes increasingly intense in its darker shades—it can assume a heavy, even melancholy quality. The brighter shades of blue have a pure, delicate and cheerful aspect, without losing its calming effect. Blue especially stimulates our thinking.

This colour is at the cool end of the spectrum. When applied to large surfaces this cool element can have a disturbing and depressing effect. In a spatial sense this colour moves away from us, in contrast to yellow and red. This can make a bright blue room appear larger than the same room painted in a warm colour.

Green with blue-green and yellow-green

Green is the colour of vegetation in nature. It stands between the two opposite poles of yellow and blue and therefore has an inner calm and equilibrium, which exerts a harmonizing effect on the human soul. The active and passive elements—radiating towards us and fading away from us, stimulating and calming—are all balanced in green.

Green is the colour of a stillness which is not uniform, and a lack of movement which is not dead.

Mixed with blue, green can assume a cool character, which even gives a cold and frosty effect when intensified (ice blue). In brighter shades the colour acquires a more friendly character.

Mixed with yellow, green generally makes a cheerful, happy impression (spring mood).

From a Report on Willem Zeylmans' Stay in Cape Town, November 1961

Willem Zeylmans died while staying with Sylvia and Chris Wegerif in Cape Town, on Saturday 18 November 1961. In 1977, Madeleine van Deventer asked Chris Wegerif to write an account of Willem Zeylmans' last days. Wegerif gave Dr van Deventer permission to use the material in any way she liked, so she passed it on to Emanuel Zeylmans. The following is a translation of excerpts from that account.

> Friday 17 November 1961. After breakfast, Sylvia drove into town. In one of the small streets close to home she saw a man and noticed that he was walking with hesitant steps, bent forwards, like someone who has suffered greatly in his life. As she passed him she saw that it was Willem Zeylmans, who thought himself unobserved. A quarter of an hour later he came home—strong, upright and cheerful after his walk. Lunch was as usual: relaxed conversation, interspersed with occasional hints of more serious themes, as was typical of Zeylmans.
>
> After his afternoon rest he received a few friends for personal conversations. Then followed the farewell evening for him in one of the church rooms, which were rented out for such occasions. Fifty to sixty people attended. After a brief introduction, a eurythmy performance was given on the rather primitive little stage, and Zeylmans watched this with rapt attention. This was followed by a cold buffet and much small talk. Zeylmans' humour turned the evening into a really cheerful gathering. We had no idea that we were about to lose someone whom we all admired and had grown so fond of.
>
> The farewell speech Zeylmans gave after this was quite different: with extreme gravity and great emphasis he spoke of the responsibility which we anthroposophists had in this country. It is very difficult to give an account of this talk sixteen years later: I have forgotten much, and may also have added things of my own in the intervening period. I have tried to question other friends who were present, but this has not helped much. The following, therefore, is at best an approximation of the talk he gave.
>
> Zeylmans thanked us for the well-organized evening, which formed a fitting conclusion to the weeks he had spent among us. He thanked the eurythmists and described the attempts, forty years earlier, to introduce eurythmy in Holland, mentioning the efforts of his wife Ingeborg in particular.

He spoke about the importance of persevering with Waldorf education here, also expressing his hope that serious medical work would arise, likewise agriculture and eurythmy. At the same time he paid tribute to the first attempts at developing biodynamic agriculture, which the Wegman family had already made at Stellenbosch.

Then he became more serious still, and (as he had also done in branch evenings) referred to the great importance, alongside maintaining and developing various practical anthroposophical activities so important for this and the coming generation, of beginning to develop an awareness here of [what was needed for] the earth's redemption.

During his travels through this country and its landscape, he said, he had been deeply affected by the special character of the soil and rock formations. This was one of the few parts of the earth which had remained largely untouched by human beings, and which still lay as it had been created by divine powers. He spoke of the intentions holding sway in Creation, that the southern parts of the earth, of Africa, India and also the Persian sub-continent, should extend southwards from the northern earth-mass as pure triangles. Retarding powers had deformed these triangles, and this fact was of particular importance in the case of Africa as counterweight to Europe: the southern point of Africa should really have lain directly opposite the heart of Europe (the Cape Town meridian now passes roughly through Greece and Budapest). If Africa had been a pure triangle, the meridian would have passed directly through the Basle area which, since the early middle ages, had been a centre of mystical culture. Here in Africa, he said, we stand at the foot of the cross.

South Africa had never been a colony, but always the midpoint and focus of contact between West and East, a path to the mysterious kingdom of Prester John.

The southern part of Africa, said Zeylmans, was the oldest, earliest-formed region of the earth, still older than Lemuria. It bears within it the birth mystery of the earth, the direct influence of the Father God. It was also typical that the old Boers did not wish to be subject either to the influence of West or East, and that their strict Calvinism, whatever one thought of it, was wholly founded on the Father principle, and barely mentioned Christ.

South Africa conceals the secret of the earth's birth, and should serve as a link between East and West, but itself remain free. Central Europe has the task, through the working of Christ, the Son, who built His church on the forces of Peter, to continue with the birth of the human soul, in particular through the path of development which Rudolf Steiner made possible in his anthroposophy: the development of the human heart, that teaches us to think of the heart of the cross lying spread over the earth.

Following the end of the dark age and the appearance of Christ in the etheric, southern Africa has the task, now that the time of John has come, to develop the human spirit in freedom: to receive the Holy Spirit that can become active at a time when John follows Peter. It was at the foot of the cross that Christ spoke the words to John: 'See, that is your mother'; and to Mary: 'See, that is your son' (John, 19,26).

Then Zeylmans mentioned the great development undergone by our small Society over the past eight years, linking this growth with the task of the earth's redemption—not only through cultivating the earth itself, though this was also very important, but by developing a new, imaginative thinking that continues the work of Goethe and perceives the spirit in Creation, thus liberating it. This work stands under the protective help of John.

After this Willem Zeylmans spoke about his own departure. He hoped to be able to visit us again; but, very seriously and with a certain joy, he said that if he passed over the threshold before returning, and could no longer be among us in human form, the veil between the 'so-called dead' and the living was so thin that it could be penetrated, and that he would always be among us and could be found by those who sought him.

So the evening ended in a mood of sadness, tinged with joyful hope of being able to find this connection. We were little aware of how difficult it is to penetrate the veil he had spoken of, however thin it might be.

As so often after his lectures, on this occasion too we carried on chatting at home with a few friends. These hours were for us always the most enjoyable of the day. After our day's work, we drank coffee, Willem Zeylmans smoked his small cigar and always started telling humorous anecdotes of his experiences during an eventful life. These evenings sometimes lasted until 2 in the morning; and there was always something memorable woven into them.

On this particular evening Zeylmans was in the best of moods. His anecdotes were sometimes so funny that we almost fell off our chairs with laughter. One of his last stories related to a particular friend of his: she was a 'stoven zetster' (a woman who brought round glowing coals for the wooden foot-warmers in church, called 'Kieken'). In summer she tried to earn a little extra by all sorts of means. She was very clairvoyant, and especially saw the dead who had just left their bodies. One morning she met Willem Zeylmans on the street and said: 'Do you know that the German Kaiser has died?' Zeylmans was astonished. 'Yes,' she said, 'this morning I looked out of the window and saw a fellow walking about outside, dressed in white. I thought "Ah, the milkman has come too early," but then I had another look and saw all his insignia and medals pinned to his chest; and so I saw that it was the German Kaiser in his white uniform. And I thought "Ah, so he has died".' After this and similar anecdotes, Zeylmans leaned back in his chair with a hesitant smile and said: 'Strange that I remember all these things, tonight of all nights.' By now it was 2 in the morning and we went to bed.

The next morning, 18 November, Sylvia heard Zeylmans go to the bathroom at about 6 am (she was not sleeping much at this time). Since it was too early for his coffee, she started reading [Steiner's] lectures 'Man as supersensible being', which we were studying at the time, and did not bring him his coffee until 7.30. He lay on his back, as though sleeping, with folded hands, and she did not want to wake him. But after half an hour she felt unsure, and, going back into his room, saw that he was lying there without moving, and called me. You know the rest.

The above account comes from Wegerif's first letter to Dr van Deventer. A week later he wrote to her again, with the following additional material.

On the evening before the farewell gathering I described, we had a smaller gathering at our house. Willem Zeylmans had asked us to invite a few friends, with whom he wished to speak about the new Isis. These friends should, he said, have a certain knowledge of anthroposophy, and be able to understand German, since he could not speak about this theme in English. If I remember rightly, six friends came on this occasion. Unfortunately I no longer remember what he said, only that his observations concluded with an Imagination of the new Isis which one needed to perceive when meditating on the Christ statue.

It was typical of our situation that he invited my wife Sylvia on the following day—who, because she does not understand German, had not been present—and briefly summarized for her what he had spoken about on the previous evening. The same morning I had a short conversation with him, during which it became clear to me how despondent he actually was, although he never showed this. He said to

> me that he had no idea what further tasks he had . . . several times he said something which revealed that the nights were the best part of the day for him, for then he had a connection with Ingeborg (his wife). It was clear that in this final period he longed to leave the earth, so as to be close to Ingeborg and all the others again, and support them.

I would like to add to these excerpts from Chris Wegerif's letter a few short points. In relation to the new Isis it is worth mentioning that Willem Zeylmans wrote about this in the last chapter of his booklet *The Foundation Stone*, where he refers to Rudolf Steiner's lecture of 6 January 1918.

This may also be the right place to mention a letter which Erna van Deventer, née Wolfram, received from Willem Zeylmans at this time. She made me a copy, and it runs as follows:

> Dear Erna
> To your last letter I can only reply as follows: If there are difficulties in the Anthroposophical Society or in the Christian Community, or among the eurythmists, I have only one piece of advice to give: 'Children, love one another.' Now I'm sure you will think that Willem has grown old and is starting to preach. Yes, I have grown old, and for that very reason I do not know what else to advise. For only when I really love my opponent do I see him in an impersonal and objective way. And this is the only Christian basis for approaching one another. Just believe me! We have known each other long enough, after all. However: not love as sympathy, but love as substance. My warmest greetings to you, your Willem.
> P.S. Africa? There is no work for me in Holland any more. Holland no longer needs me, so I am going to Africa.

I would also like to mention here, in response to questions I have been asked, that Zeylmans' family in Holland decided not to bring his body back to Holland, but to hold the funeral in South Africa. The scattering of the ashes was briefly discussed by those present after the cremation. At their suggestion, Emanuel Zeylmans decided to scatter the ashes from Table Mountain, and this took place the same day.

Among the anecdotes which Willem Zeylmans liked to tell during those evenings at the Wegerif's house, after his lectures, were descriptions from his early youth: how, when a young child, he always imagined himself as a king leading a great army through foreign lands, and fighting battles, as he also describes in the childhood memories of 'Bender Bole'.

My obituary 'Bij de dood van mijn vader' ('On the death of my father'), which I wrote on my return from South Africa for the Dutch newsletter of the Anthroposophical Society in Holland, in December 1961, contains many direct comments by friends in Cape Town, Johannesburg, Hermanus and Durban, which I noted down in the days immediately after the cremation. One of the most noteworthy facts was how cheerful Willem Zeylmans was in these last days in South Africa. He enjoyed joking with everyone, there was much laughter, and he seemed tireless. During these weeks a large number of African friends dreamed about him too. In conversations he also made subtle references to death, and, among other things, said that the place and time of a person's death is most deeply linked with his personality, is an expression of his individuality.

Chronology

1893

23 November: Born in Helmond, Holland (North Brabant province), as second and last child of Pieter Zeylmans van Emmichoven (1861–1945) and Emma Malsch (1864–1929).

1898

14 October: Ingeborg Droogleever Fortuyn born in The Hague, as oldest of three children. Parents: Pieter Droogleever Fortuyn (1868–1938) and Helène Bruinier (1873–1959).

1899

August: Starts school in Helmond.

1909

January: The Zeylmans family moves to Amsterdam. Willem attends secondary school.

Autumn: Willem contracts typhus.

1912

July: Takes his school-leaving exams.

September: Enrols for medical studies at Amsterdam University.

1914

Summer: The Zeylmans family moves to The Hague. Willem continues his medical studies at Leiden University.

November: Military service in Haarlem.

1915

August: First meets Ingeborg Droogleever Fortuyn in Vierhouten. Taken on as 'trainee medical officer'.

1916

September: Meets Jacoba van Heemskerck and Marie Tak van Poortvliet in The Hague.

1917

August: Marie Tak van Poortvliet enables Zeylmans to buy himself out of his contract as a future doctor in the colonies. She finances his further studies.

1918

March: Passes his medical doctor's examination, and then undertakes practicals in various clinics.

Summer: Colour experiments with Jacoba van Heemskerck, with children of the summer guests in Domburg (Walcheren).

September: Meets Ingeborg Droogleever Fortuyn again in Leiden, where she is studying law.

November: Employed as medical officer for refugee aid at the Belgian border in Rozendaal.

15 December: Becomes engaged to Ingeborg Droogleever Fortuyn.

1919

Passes his second-stage medical exam.

1920

12 March: Receives doctorate from Leiden University medical faculty.

June–December: Stays in Leipzig, where he becomes member of the Anthroposophical Society in October.

17–23 December: First meeting with Rudolf Steiner in Dornach (Switzerland), where he attends his lectures *The Bridge Between Universal Spirituality and the Physical Constitution of Man* (GA 202).

1921

January: Employed as a doctor at the state lunatic asylum Maasoord in Poortugaal near Rotterdam. After a few months is promoted to ward doctor for four women's annexes ('my 220 girl-friends').

26 February–2 March: Attends some of Rudolf Steiner's lectures in Holland.

11–18 April: In Dornach, for Rudolf Steiner's second course for doctors and medical students (GA 313).

29 August–8 September: In Stuttgart for the conference 'Cultural perspectives of the anthroposophical movement', where he attends Rudolf Steiner's lectures *Fruits of Anthroposophy* (GA 78).

27 September: Marries Ingeborg Droogleever Fortuyn.

1922

January: First lecture on 'Anthroposophy and Medicine' to students in the De Turk hall at Leiden: the beginning of a career as speaker that spans roughly 2000 lectures up to his death in 1961.

7–13 April: Anthroposophical Science Course in The Hague, with the collaboration of ten Waldorf teachers from Stuttgart. Rudolf Steiner gives six lectures: 'The significance of anthroposophy in the cultural life of today' (GA 82) and the branch lecture: 'The teachings of the Risen One' (GA 211).

26–28 October. In Stuttgart as participant of the 'medical week', where he attends Rudolf Steiner's lectures for doctors (GA 314).

31 October–6 November: Attends Rudolf Steiner's lectures in Holland.

End of November: first child born, Johanna Veronica.

1923

10–17 June: In Dornach for the Delegates Conference. He attends Rudolf Steiner's lecture cycle: 'The history and conditions of the anthroposophical movement in relation to the Anthroposophical Society' (GA 258). (*The Anthroposophic Movement.*)

September: Founding of the Vrije School in The Hague.

September: Master's Degree from Amsterdam University for his study: 'The effect of colours on feeling'.

October: Moves to The Hague and begins his psychiatric practice.

13–19 November: Rudolf Steiner in Holland.

Founding of the 'Anthroposofische Vereniging in Nederland'.
Opening of the Prinsevinkenpark clinic in The Hague.
Rudolf Steiner gives two lectures for doctors, two on education, and the cycle 'An anthroposophical view of man's supersensible being' (GA 231). (*Supersensible Man.*)
Zeylmans becomes General Secretary of the new Society.
23 December–9 January: In Dornach for the Christmas Foundation Meeting to found the General Anthroposophical Society. Attends Rudolf Steiner's lectures 'World history in the light of anthroposophy and as foundation of knowledge of the human spirit' (GA 233) (*World History and the Mysteries in the Light of Anthroposophy*), the course for young doctors (GA 316) and 'Mystery sites of the Middle Ages' (GA 233a).

1924

23–27 May: In Paris, where he attends Rudolf Steiner's lectures and meets Edouard Schuré and Jules Sauerwein.
17–25 July: 'Pedagogical anthroposophical summer conference' in Arnhem, where Rudolf Steiner gives the lecture cycle 'The pedagogical value of knowledge of man and the cultural value of pedagogy' (GA 240).
8–21 September: In Dornach, where Zeylmans experiences Rudolf Steiner's last great lecture cycles:
Course for pastoral medicine (GA 318). (*Pastoral Medicine*)
Course for speech formation and dramatic art (GA 282). (*Speech and Drama*)
Esoteric considerations of karmic relationships (GA 238). (*Karmic Relationships, Vol. IV*)
Last meeting with Rudolf Steiner.

1925

30 March: Rudolf Steiner dies.
November: Beginning of many years' medical work in London.
December: Lectures in Copenhagen, Oslo, Stockholm and Helsingfors (Helsinki).

1926

Lectures in Jena, London and elsewhere.
August: Son born, Johannes Emanuel.
Trips to Weimar and Tintagel.

1927

Lectures in London, Jena, Edinburgh.
Travels through Scotland and Ireland.
November: Laying of the foundation stone for the Rudolf Steiner Clinic at Parklaan in Scheveningen, near The Hague (opens 1928).

1928

Lectures at the World Conference in London, and in Dornach.

1929

Lectures in Berlin, London, Jena, Prague, Brno, Vienna, Pressburg, Linz,

Salzburg, Innsbruck, Gnadenwald, Zagreb, Belgrade, London, Dornach, Berlin, Riga, Reval, Helsingfors, Dorpat, Hamburg, Berlin.

November: Twins born, Swanhilde Elisabeth and Adelbert Johannes.

1930

Lectures in Berlin, Nuremberg, Dornach, Stuttgart, Leipzig, Jena, Edinburgh, Leeds, Berlin, Dornach.

Trip to Italy.

August: The Stakenberg Camp.

1932

June-November: Trip through the Dutch East Indies (Indonesia).

December: His book on Rudolf Steiner is published.

1933

Lectures in Stuttgart, Essen, Bonn, Cologne, Paderborn, Barmen, Bangor, Dornach, and elsewhere.

1935

Expelled from the General Anthroposophical Society in Dornach.

1935–6

December-January: Egypt trip.

1936

Lectures in London, Bangor. Travels though Ireland with his wife.

10 March: Founding of the Institute for Colour Psychology in The Hague.

19 May: Founding of a 'school for spiritual science' in The Hague.

1937

March–April: Travels to Sicily and Italy. Lectures in London and elsewhere.

1938

Trips to Zurich and London. Summer holidays with his family in the South of France.

1939

Lectures in London and Cambridge.

September: Outbreak of the Second World War. Holland remains neutral until 10 May 1940.

1940

Lectures in Belgium.

10 May: The German army attacks Holland and occupies it. Voluntary dissolution of the Anthroposophical Society in the Netherlands on 24 May.

1941

July: The Free Waldorf School in The Hague is prohibited.

November: Last public lectures on anthroposophy.

1942

April: The occupying forces requisition the Rudolf Steiner Clinic.

1943

'The human soul' is printed in an edition of 30 copies.

1945

5 May: End of the Second World War. The Canadian army liberates Holland.

19 May: First lecture after the war: 'Whitsun'.

Christmas: New founding of the Anthroposofische Vereniging in Nederland. Re-opening of the Rudolf Steiner Clinic as a general hospital.

1946

First trips abroad since the war: to Switzerland, Belgium and England.

Hygiene of the soul and *De Menselijke Ziel* (The human soul) are published.

1947

Lectures in London, Antwerp, Mechelen, Brussels, Arlesheim and elsewhere. Founding of the Institute for the Psychology of Nations.

1948

First trip to the USA, with lectures in New York, Washington, Boston, Buffalo, Chicago, Milwaukee, San Francisco and California.

1949

Lectures in Stuttgart, Dornach, Mannheim, London and elsewhere.

1950

Second trip to USA with lectures in New York, Washington, Los Angeles, San Francisco, Chicago, Pittsburg, Cincinnati and elsewhere.

1951

Founding of the Centre for Free Spiritual Life in The Hague. Trips to Majorca, Spain and elsewhere.

1952

Lectures in Freiburg, London, Copenhagen, Stockholm, Helsinki, Järna, Gothenburg, Berlin, Le Havre, Bedford, Antwerp and elsewhere. Holiday trip to Ireland.

1953

Lectures in Basle, London, Stuttgart, Zurich, Berne, Stockholm, Helsinki, Göteborg, Berlin and elsewhere.

August: Europe Conference in The Hague.

1954

Tours the world, through USA, Hawaii, New Zealand, Australia, Indonesia, Ceylon, India, East Africa and South Africa.

1955

Lectures in Arlesheim, Basle, Bochum, Antwerp, Comburg, Stuttgart, Helsinki, Stockholm, Järna.

June–September: Exhaustion and falls ill.

1956

The Foundation Stone is published.

1957

Lectures in Antwerp, Dornach, Berlin, Arlesheim. Trip to Greece (Crete, Knossos, Rhodes, Patmos, Delos, Mycenae, Samothrace, Athens, Eleusis, Ephesus).

1958

Lectures in Arlesheim, Ascona, Antwerp, Göteborg, Oslo, Stockholm, Järna, Odense and elsewhere.

1959

Lectures in Antwerp, Comburg, Stuttgart, Nuremberg, Vienna. Death of his brother Peter Zeylmans. *The Reality in Which We Live* is published.

1960

21 January: Death of Ingeborg Zeylmans. In this year he gives about eighty lectures, in Arlesheim, Göteborg, Stockholm, London, Dornach, Bruges, Antwerp and elsewhere. Re-affiliation of the Dutch Society to the General Anthroposophical Society at Dornach.

1961

Gives about 115 lectures during this year, in Ascona, Stuttgart, Nuremberg, Dornach, London and elsewhere. Last trip to Majorca. Holiday trip to Italy and Sicily.

7 September: Flies to Cairo. Visits Sakkara, Memphis, the pyramids. Flies on to Nairobi.

13 September: Lectures in Salisbury, visits the Victoria Falls.

18 September: Begins his journey through South Africa, giving 54 lectures in various places including Johannesburg, Pretoria, Port Elizabeth and Cape Town, where he dies on Saturday 18 November between 6 and 7 in the morning. The cremation takes place on 23 November, his sixty-eighth birthday. His eldest son scatters his ashes from Table Mountain.

Bibliography

I. Books

De Werking der kleuren op het gevoel ('The effect of colours on the feelings', doctoral thesis), Utrecht 1923.

Rudolf Steiner. In the series *Helden van de Geest, VIII* ('Heroes of the spirit, VIII'), The Hague 1932. Reprinted Zeist 1960. German edition translated from the Dutch by Arnica Esterl, Stuttgart 1960. Offset reprints 1976 and 1977.

Ontwikkeling en Geestesstrijd, The Hague 1935. German: *Entwicklung und Geisteskampf,* translated by Dr Elisabeth Vreede, Stuttgart 1935. English: *Development and Spiritual Conflict,* translated by Matthew Barton (awaiting publication as part of volume 3 of *Who Was Ita Wegman*).

De menselijke ziel, small, war-edition Utrecht 1943. First edition Utrecht 1946, New editions: Zeist 1961 and 1974. German: *Die menschliche Seele* ('The human soul. Introduction to discovering the nature, activity and development of the soul'), translated by M.B.A. Laffrée, Basle 1953. New edition: Stuttgart 1979.

Hygiene van de ziel, Utrecht 1946, 1948. German: *Gespräche über die Hygiene der Seele,* translated into German by M.J.Krück von Poturzyn, Arlesheim 1957, 1979. English: *Hygiene of the Soul* (translator unknown). New York, 1955 (new edition planned).

Amerika en het Amerikanisme, The Hague 1950, 1952. German: *Amerika und der Amerikanismus.* Translated into German by Elisabeth Knottenbelt and M.J. Krück von Poturzyn, Freiburg i. Br., 1954. Spanish: *América y el Americanismo,* translated by Mathilde Kersten Costerus, Montevideo 1962. English translation in manuscript: *America or Americanism* (archive).

Der Grundstein, German version with the collaboration of M.J.Krück von Poturzyn, Stuttgart 1956. Second, enlarged edition, Stuttgart 1961. Further editions 1965, 1971. English: *The Foundation Stone,* translated by John Davy, London 1963. Dutch: *De Grondsteen,* Zeist 1977. (Spanish translation in manuscript form.)

De Werkelijkheid waarin wij leven, Zeist 1959, 1974. German: *Die Wirklichkeit in der wir leben,* translated by Arnica Esterl-Mees, Arlesheim 1959, 1977. Spanish: *La Realidad en que vivimos,* translated by M. Kersten Costerus, Montevideo, 1962. English: *The Reality in Which We Live,* translated from the Dutch by René Querido, East Grinstead (Sussex), 1964.

II. Essays and brochures (English selection)

Of the very large number of articles and essays by Willem Zeylmans, only the following have been published in English:

'Physical and moral hygiene', in: *Anthroposophy*. London 1926, pages 354 ff.

'The human soul in sleeping, dreaming and waking' (lecture to the World

Conference in London on 24 July 1928.) German: 'Die menschliche Seele im Zusammenhang mit Wachen, Träumen und Schlafen', in: *Natura*, 1928–29.

'The Netherlands', in *World Tension. The Psychopathology of International relations.* By 22 leading psychologists and psychiatrists of 20 Nations. Edited by George W. Kisker. Prentice Hall, New York, 1951.

'Rudolf Steiner in Holland', in *Rudolf Steiner, Recollections by some of his pupils.* Translated from the German and edited by A. Freeman and C. Waterman, London 1957.

Numerous essays in Dutch were published between 1922 and 1961 in:

Anthroposophie, maandblad voor sociale, pedagogische en geesteswetenschappelijke vraagstukken. Utrecht 1921 and 1922.

Hollandsch Bijblad van Het Goetheanum, The Hague 1924 to 1927.

Mededelingen (en Berichten voor leden) der Anthroposofische Vereniging in Nederland. The Hague 1927–30, 1931–35, 1935–40, 1945–61.

Ostara, Tijdschrift voor Pedagogie van R. Steiner. The Hague, 1927–1932.

Vrije Opvoedkunst. Sociaal-pedagogisch Tijdschrift. The Hague, 1933–1961.

Brieven over Geesteswetenschap en kunst. Edited by Max Gümbel Seiling. 1940 and 41.

Mededelingen van het Centrum voor Vrij Geestesleven. The Hague, 1952–60.

III. Early works

A brief description of 64 articles, short stories, stage sketches and operettas, dialogues, fairy-tales, prose works and aphorisms which Willem Zeylmans wrote between 1911 and 1919.

Sailors' suffering and joy (October 1911). The dramatic story of Geertje, who loses her husband and son, both sailors, in a boat catastrophe. The description of the sea is striking.

A hurdy-gurdy in a large town (December 1911). A lovely mood description. Rich range of experiences, social empathy. The story is really like a painting.

Re-encounter (Circa 1912). Dramatic description of a young man who, after an unhappy love affair, sees his former beloved again in a spa, together with her fiancé; and later hears the two approaching along the beach. In despair he stares at the sea, where he suddenly has a vision of her face. Fine description of nature.

Re-encounter. Beginning of an unfinished story, similar to the passage in Bender Bole where Christie and Bender see each other again after years and she tells him that she now loves him.

A grave-yard in a lunatic asylum. Brief description of a lunatic asylum's cemetery, written from a philosophical and psychological perspective, with characterizations of two dead people.

Martha. Sketch of a long story involving a nun in a monastery. The same theme is also dealt with in an unfinished poem.

The squirrel. Sad sketch of a trapped squirrel that finally dies.

The artist. Mocking and humorous sketch of a failed artist.

A nation is exterminated. Indignant description of the extermination of the Mohammedans by Ferdinand of Bulgaria. Condemnation of war waged by Christianity.

Modern painting. Brief draft of a longer essay. Great acknowledgement of Cézanne. Written in lively style, like a review.

Sculpture at the four-year exhibition. Review of an exhibition.

Tommy. Tragic sketch of an orphan boy. He lies in a sick-bed and has no one to love him. The story ends without resolution. Caringly written.

The drinker. Naturalistic sketch, very emotional, about a drinker whose little daughter fetches him home from the pub.

Jan Toorop. Unfinished article about the painter Jan Toorop.

The music critic. Sharp characterization of the young Matthijs Vermeulen, later a famous Amsterdam reviewer, who catcalls and whistles a pianist at a gala concert. Interesting and well-written.

The secret (1913). Delightful, naïve story of a pastor who secretly visits a dying woman in her castle and persuades her to leave her possessions to the Church.

Margaretha. Fluently written personal reminiscence of a girl whom he met in his sixth and ninth years, and later re-encountered at the age of 19. Unfinished, but completed in the story 'A memory'.

Carlandy (July 1913). Wonderful romantic story about a Hungarian violinist who falls in love with a girl in the audience. Published in December 1914 in the highly-regarded magazine *Nederland.*

How they sang in the old days. Short, mocking sketch, not properly finished.

A memory. Beautiful and exciting story about a meeting with 'Margaretha' (see above). She has tuberculosis. Accomplished piece of writing, especially the beginning. The story has a remarkable fascination.

From a side-street. Unfinished story about a young boy who is forced by his father to earn money. The dialogue is striking.

Farewell. Brief impression of a farewell at a station. A boy says goodbye to his family.

Lilian. The story of a girl who loses her parents in a fire. She meets a young man, who points out to her that people who have suffered greatly perceive more in nature than others do.

An insignificant event. A young boy finds a penny in the street and is allowed to keep it.

Little sister. The writer discovers that he must change his opinion about a peasant girl in her favour. Interesting inner experience.

Memory. Hymn-like prose poem about a girl whom he loves and who does not return his love. A comparison with the Madonna.

Christmas Eve. Short description of a young émigré who wanders around miserably in a Dutch town on Christmas Eve, and remembers how he used to celebrate Christmas with his family in Holland.

Dear Fatherland. Three German sisters have emigrated to Holland and find it hard to put down roots there. They sit and watch the sunset and sing a song.

There must be something holy in her. To Miss Z.O. Description of a girl's Madonna experience. Celestial worship and earthly love are compared.

Little rascal. Particularly sad description of a beggar boy on a winter's day. Short and accomplished piece of writing. No hope at the end.

Modern painting (June 1914). Well-researched, longer article with detailed observations on the purpose of art and historical summary. Vincent van Gogh, Gauguin, Cézanne. Then discussions on modern movements: cubism, futurism and the Kandinsky school. A new style is apparent in this piece. Willem Zeylmans is now 21 years old.

The life story of Billy Jenkins. A Mexican tale. Lively story of a poor Mexican who unexpectedly finds gold.

The golden girl (October 1914). A longer, romantic-dramatic novella about a foreigner's tragic love for a girl, related from the girl's point of view, and that of her family and friends. The first attempt at a longer story. The novella was published in five parts in the Dutch student magazine *Minerva*.

The costume sewer (February 1917). Short description of a costume-maker at the Ballet theatre.

Ilena (July 1915) Drama in one act with prologue. Written in free verse. A 17-year-old princess is always serious and sad. A prince tells her that love will cheer her up. A surviving programme shows that Willem Zeylmans himself played Prince Harald, while Miss Droogleever Fortuyn played the part of the dancer.

Individuality (1916?). A society of dogs holds discussions. This rather ironical story is noticeable for the fact that, at the end, views on the difference between soul and spirit are discussed.

The sunken bell. (February 1916) A lecture on a play of the same name by Gerhard Hauptmann. The first piece in which he demonstrates a free and independent view. Composition and structure are interestingly handled. As well as praising the work, he criticizes Hauptmann for the fact that the 'spirits' in his play have half-human souls.

The dead speaks. A fairy-tale of light seriousness (March 1916). One of Willem Zeylmans' most successful literary works. An old pedlar, who has befriended trolls and elves, uses his life's wisdom to heal, one after another, a pair of young lovers, a poet, a monk, a widower and a professor. An interesting play, with religious and Goethean undertones.

Conversation (April 1916). Dialogue between a young man and a girl on whether morality exists. He describes his view of the world and life. She wishes to believe in good, but he interrupts to say: one should be honest—love is only egotism.

Directions (May 1916). A collection of fierce aphorisms on the one-sidedness of all persuasions and 'isms', the adherence to any of which leads to conventionalism. 'People who belong to a particular movement lack many spiritual limbs. They are therefore cripples.'—'Life without adherence to a movement requires permanent attention and awareness.'

Dialogue (June 1916). In a conversation between two students the power of imagination is defended. 'Imagination relates to reality as spirit to matter.'

The singing source (July 1916). Operetta in three acts. A minstrel has lost his soul in a spring after seeing a dancing nymph there. A devilish forest woman has stolen it from there. A wood nymph manages to get hold of his soul and return it to him.

The great light (July 1916). A fairy-tale in four parts: night, morning, midday, evening. The story of a prince who grows up in the dark. A little man shows him the dawn, light on an altar, the lights in a city. Then the prince wishes to see the most beautiful light in the world: with the greatest effort he ascends a steep mountain, sees the world of spirit—and stays there.

The poet and the eyes (July 1916). The terrifying story of 'eyes' which pursue a poet in a Hieronymus Bosch-type realm, and finally destroy him.

The mirror (August 1916). Dramatic summary and resolution of three previous pieces.

6 dreams (undated, probably before 1917). Description of 6 dreams on 3 pages, in various different handwriting styles.

The fairy-tale of the powers (September 1916). A longer fairy-tale about a boy under a spell who falls into other realms, together with the daughter of a female magician. First they come to a great, white town. The vision of a king on a white elephant is described; this section ends with the murder of the royal couple. Then the two come to a magic festival at the house of a count, with fireworks, processions and strange people. The count is also murdered by powers which end all earthly power. Finally they visit an old, wise man in a white domed building. This fairy-tale deals with profound issues of power and what it is.

Life values (September 1916). A short play in 3 dialogues, in which several young people exchange their views about life and the world.

The game of the dead (October 1916). Well-written short story, taking place in the realm of the dead.

The spiritual direction of the new painting—Jacoba van Heemskerck (January 1917). A longer article. Emotion, joy, rapture. Science as opposed to intuition. Then the author writes about impressionism, new directions in art and the 'Sturm' movement. The rest of the article deals with the painter Jacoba van Heemskerck and her cubist period, the colours in her works (each colour has a spiritual value: red, green, yellow, blue, crimson, orange, purple—the beginnings of colour psychology, as early as 1917!), her use of line and her motifs. Discussion of three paintings.

Laughter (January 1917). A prose piece describing a night in which the protagonist has three visions. The first and second are cynical and decadent, while the third vision is liberating. About how people laugh. How the protagonist finds his own laughter.

The wandering Jew (March 1917). The manuscript of a lecture about the book of the same name by August Vermeylen. A longer essay about the book, with detailed consideration of the purpose and nature of art in relation to the human soul. This has strong parallels with the piece on Jacoba van Heemskerck.

The drink of inspiration (May 1917). A play in three acts. About Odin.

The last night (July 1917). A very painterly monologue of an unhappy lover, with a Kafkaesque description of a monster or double. Description of one's own egotism, despair, emptiness.

Audience (July–October 1917). Collection of aphorisms.

Sketch for a play

The little dancing girl. Lovely fairy-tale written in dreamy and tragic mode, but with some distance and humour.

Little Ramsalin. Short, humorous stage-sketch.

The garden of youth. This is a typewritten manuscript and it is not clear whether the story is by Willem Zeylmans himself.

God-man (April 1918). A play. The scene opens on a moor, with satyrs and nymphs. A young man appears, who nearly drowns. Then a girl enters. First they find one another, then the young man goes to seek his death. Finally he frees himself from his self-destructive urges. Together they find their way out of the ghostly world. At the end stand the words: 'end of the prologue'.

Happiness (February 1919). Short tale about a clown who discovers how horribly repugnant and ugly people are when they laugh at his jokes. A magic girl, happiness, floats by and comforts him. Good psychological descriptions.

Three fairy-tales of Angelica (1919). Three symbolic fairy-tales. The last of Zeylmans' early works.

IV. Reminiscences and writings by other authors on F.W. Zeylmans van Emmichoven

The selection below refers only to those reminiscences available in English:

A.C. Harwood	'Dr. Zeylmans in England', in *Mededelingen van de Anthroposofische Vereniging in Nederland*, December 1961, page 449 (in English).
Ernst Katz	'In Memoriam Dr. F. W. Zeylmans van Emmichoven', in: *Newsletter Quarterly*, published by the Anthroposophical Society in America, New York, Winter 61/62.
Heinz Maurer	'Dr. F.W. Zeylmans van Emmichoven and the anthroposophical movement in Southern Africa', in *Newsletter of the Anthroposophical Society in Southern Africa*, Cape Town, December 1961.

Cora Over — 'Dr. F. W. Zeylmans van Emmichoven', in *Newsletter of the Anthroposophical Society in Southern Africa*, Cape Town, December 1961.

S.V. Petersen — 'Meditations on the Brink. Dedicated to the life and work of Willem Zeylmans van Emmichoven' (with 12 drawings by Adelbert Zeylmans). Zeist 1962.

Julian Schuurmans Stekhoven — 'The Youth Conference', in *Newsletter of the Anthroposophical Society in Southern Africa*, Cape Town, December 1961.

E. Wertheym Aymès — 'An impression of Dr. Zeylmans van Emmichoven' in *Newsletter of the Anthroposophical Society in Southern Africa*, Cape Town, December 1961.

Notes and References

The following is only a brief summary of some of the material quoted in this book. For detailed sources, please see the German edition.

Chapter 1: Material drawn from the Helmond regional archive and oral family sources.

Chapter 2: Archive research by A.L.M. Land.

Chapter 4: The autobiographical reminiscences published here for the first time are contained in the archives. All information on Jacoba van Heemskerck is drawn from research by A.H. Huussen, who wrote a monograph on this theme. The quote in this chapter from the essay 'Rudolf Steiner in Holland' is quoted with kind permission of the Verlag Freies Geistesleben, Stuttgart. Steiner quote from lecture on 23 December 1920: 'Search for the New Isis'.

Steiner quotes: from 'The history and conditions of the anthroposophical movement' (GA 258).

Schuré's text was later also translated into German by Robert Friedenthal.

In his essay 'Rudolf Steiner in Holland', Zeylmans gives the wrong date for Steiner's first visit to Holland, which took place in February 1921, and not in November of that year. The second visit is also wrongly dated: it should be Easter 1922, not Whitsun.

Chapter 5: Eye-witness report of 1 March 1921. See P. de Haan's reminiscences, which are extensively quoted in the following passages.

As regards the founding of the Dutch Anthroposophical Society on 18 November 1923, use has been made of earlier versions of W. Zeylmans' essay 'Rudolf Steiner in Holland', which are published here for the first time. Rudolf Steiner's comments on this day are taken from a shorthand report in the archives; and other discussions between Zeylmans and Dr Steiner are quoted from notebooks in the archives.

Chapter 6: Quotes on the 1923 Christmas Foundation Meeting from W. Zeylmans van Emmichoven *The Foundation Stone*.

Chapter 8: Material on Zeylmans' trip to Indonesia is drawn from brief diary notes and also Indian newspaper reviews.

Information on the Colour Psychology Society is due to the tireless research of A.L.M. Land, who rediscovered parts of the original archive owned by the Nederlandse Verenigung voor Kleurenstudie.

Chapter 10: For dates after 1947, Zeylmans' complete appointment diaries are available. He wrote letters to his wife about his trips to America, excerpts of which were then published. Zeylman's correspondence with his wife no longer exists.

I would like to thank Joanna Roche-Mazel, USA, for information on the Centre.

Chapter 11: The 1954 world trip was reconstructed from a few diary entries. A travel diary from South Africa onwards has been lost, and there are very few letters covering this period.

Additional Sources

The version of W. Zeylmans' 'From Bender Bole's Life Story' used in this edition (chapter 1–3) is partly taken from a German translation by Elisabeth Knottenbelt. The text of Rudolf Steiner's draft for the 'Appeal for founding a World School Association' (chapter 5) was kindly made available by Dr M. P. van Deventer (Arlesheim). On Zeylmans' descriptions of the first Goetheanum (chapter 5), see also Daniel van Bemmelen: *Rudolf Steiners farbige Gestaltung des Goetheanum*, Stuttgart 1973. On the origins of the first Dutch Waldorf school (chapter 5), interesting illustrated reminiscences by Daniel and Emmy van Bemmelen have since appeared in *Forum International* (The Hague), July–August 1979. The German translation of the poem *Mysteries* (chapter 9), by M.B.A. Laffrée (The Hague), was slightly reworked for this edition and put into prose for reasons of space. I have not been able to contact the author of the poem 'Conversation' (chapter 10), Herr Wolfgang Sydath, whom I would here like to thank in the hope that he has no objection to it being published. On the probable conclusion to Zeylmans' talk to the philosophical society of Pretoria University on 20 September 1961 (chapter 12), see: Stefan Leber: *Selbstverwirklichung—Mündigkeit—Sozialität. Eine Einführung in die Dreigliederung des sozialen Organismus*, Stuttgart 1978.

List of illustrations

Acknowledgements

A friend of mine, a Dutch researcher who was interested in this biography, wrote the following to me: 'Don't wait too long to publish your book—better to produce something incomplete soon than an exhaustive account which only appears ten years from now...' The (Swiss) publisher, too, Dr Andreas von Grunelius, to whose fatherly and friendly advice I owe the whole impetus for undertaking this work at all, also urged me to publish soon. So this biography, after some preparatory work, was written down in less than three months—too fast in my view. I would therefore like readers to regard the book as a *draft*. But I can understand that people want it to appear now . . . for time is pushing on. I am therefore sending this biography of my father out into the world, trusting that those who know more and better than I do will also add their knowledge to mine!

For many suggestions and much help I owe thanks to the following: Dr M.P. van Deventer (Arlesheim), Dr A.C. Henny (The Hague), Giel van Hoof (Helmond), A. H. Huussen (Haren), Dr Elisabeth Knottenbelt (The Hague), Addick L.M. Land (Doorn), Professor Dr G.W. Ovink (Amsterdam), Rosmarie Ris (Arlesheim), Frits Vonk (Bilthoven), Dr Frits Wilmar (Eckwälden) as well as a large number of friends of Dr Zeylmans van Emmichoven, who helped me either directly or indirectly. I would most especially like to thank Frau Gisela Schaich (Pfullingen) for her tireless work in preparing the manuscript, and Cordula Zeylmans van Emmichoven, my wife, who played a major part in writing and editing the text.

Reutlingen (Swabia)
5 August 1979

Afterword

I first encountered the Anthroposophical Society as a class teacher in São Paulo, Brazil, in the early '80s, when I also heard of the 1923–24 Christmas Foundation Meeting. At the time I felt, somehow, that I did not have the full picture. Not until 12 years later, in fact, when I came across Emanuel Zeylmans' three volumes on Ita Wegman, and met him myself, did I find the explanations I was looking for.

Ita Wegman had worked closely with Steiner in the last years of his life and was deeply connected with the 1923–24 re-founding of the Anthroposophical Society, also becoming the acknowledged leader of the anthroposophical medical movement. On my path of discovery I found that, following her and many others' dramatic expulsion from the General Anthroposophical Society in 1935, Wegman's esoteric work seemed to flow in a special way into the Dutch Anthroposophical Society instead, through an intense and fruitful exchange with Willem Zeylmans van Emmichoven, the subject of this biography, and other friends.

In further years of research, in interviews and long conversations in Europe and other places, I also found out about the 'Arlesheim group' that formed around 1947, not long after the Second World War and Ita Wegman's death. This was an esoteric circle that met annually at the Ita Wegman Klinik in Arlesheim, Switzerland. It included many important individuals in the anthroposophical movement, and kept alight on earth the flame that had been kindled at the Christmas Foundation Meeting, as well as the Foundation Stone Meditation Steiner gave in 1923–24. Subsequently this care passed slowly to the General Anthroposophical Society based in nearby Dornach. Willem Zeylmans van Emmichoven was one of those responsible for founding the Arlesheim group.

One of Willem Zeylmans' major achievements, besides his deep interest in the whole human race, his open-minded respect for free initiative, and profound research on the human soul, was his esoteric work on the Foundation Stone Meditation, as embodied in his book *The Foundation Stone*, now re-issued by Temple Lodge Publishing, to whom we are very grateful for their help and good will.

Through difficult times when these things could not be spoken of openly, Willem Zeylmans, among others, kept alight the torch lit at the re-founding of the Anthroposophical Society. It is due to Emanuel Zeylmans that this flame has now emerged into the light of day, contributing significantly to the efforts in progress to reform the Society, and the work based on it. I would therefore like to express my deep gratitude to an author whose detailed biographies of his father and Ita Wegman give us the historical background and basis for understanding the past, and for healing its wounds.

Josiana Arippol
Brazil/Netherlands